TO BRAD,

DARE TO DREAM
AND MAKE EVERY
SUNSET COUNT.

CHEERS TO LIFE,

BOBBY FRIED

Praise for
Igniting Your True Purpose and Passion

"A heart-felt roadmap to fulfill your true purpose and change the world for the better."

— **Guy Kawasaki,** Author of *Enchantment: The Art of Changing Hearts, Minds and Actions,* and former chief evangelist of Apple

"Igniting Your True Purpose And Passion is an uplifting, thought-provoking book. Read it and discover the secret to achieving true success."

— **Marci Shimoff,** NY Times best selling co-author of 6 *Chicken Soup For The Soul books,* co-star of *The Secret* video and best selling author of *Happy For No Reason* and *Love For No Reason*

"In a sports business where winning is innately linked to focus, purpose and true passion I view Fried's book as the ultimate *playbook* for anyone who strives to succeed in the challenging game of life."

— **Joseph B. McCormack,** Senior Vice President– Finance
Chief Financial Officer
The Los Angeles Lakers Inc.

"Take this exhilarating journey of self discovery to support yourself in actualizing your goals, dreams and aspirations."

— **Cynthia Kersey,** Best Selling Author of *Unstoppable* and *Unstoppable Women*

"This is a truly wonderful book from a master life and business strategist. Bobby Fried takes you through the ups and downs of life's challenges, showing you how to not only weather storms but enjoy the ride. Filled with enlightening personal stories that illustrate how to make meaning as well as money, this is one book you'll want to keep handy, write in the margins, and refer to often. A treasure."

— **Chellie Campbell,** Best-selling author of *Zero to Zillionaire* and *The Wealthy Spirit*

"Fried's practical minded book makes accessible what is often abstract and mysterious in our search for meaning and purpose."

— **Ron Croen,** Founder and former CEO of Nuance Communications and Silicon Valley entrepreneur

"An inspiring and insightful read that will prompt you to get outside your comfort zone and reinvent your unique brand for personal and business success."

— **John Barnickel,** Vice President, Pacific Northwest Cardiac and Vascular Group Medtronic, Inc.

Igniting Your True Purpose and Passion

A businesslike guide to
fulfill your professional goals
and personal dreams

ROBERT MICHAEL FRIED

Thirdwind
Publishing

Published by Thirdwind LLC
26355 Valley View Ave., Carmel, CA 93923, USA

This book is an original publication of Thirdwind Publishing.

Copyright © 2011 by Thirdwind L.L.C.

Book design by Candelaria Design

All rights reserved. No part of this publication may be reproduced, stored in a retrieval system, or transmitted, in any form or by any means, electronic, mechanical, photocopying, recording, or otherwise without the prior written permission of the publisher. Please do not participate in or encourage piracy of copyrighted materials in violation of the author's rights. Purchase only authorized editions. Printed in the United States of America.

Thirdwind trade paperback edition: November 2011

Library of Congress Control Number: 2011933591

ISBN 978-0-98379-770-8

Thirdwind books are available at special discounts for bulk purchases in the U.S. for corporations, institutions, colleges and universities, and other organizations. For more information, please contact Special Markets Department at Thirdwind LLC, 26355 Valley View Ave., Carmel, CA 93923 or email special.markets@thirdwind.com.

10 9 8 7 6 5 4 3 2 1

DEDICATION

This book is dedicated to my long-time friend and colleague Bob Zeichick, whose insightfulness and ability to stay focused in the moment I could only aspire to emulate. And to everyone who has the courage to leave the shoreline to discover new oceans.

ACKNOWLEDGEMENTS

This book is the result of embarking on a seven-year journey of self-discovery. When the dust cleared, I learned that it was the journey itself that really mattered in the end. I'd like to fully acknowledge those who helped make my journey and personal transformation possible.

To my insightful long-time friend and business partner Bob Zeichick who came up with the idea to write a sequel to my first book and who guided the whole project to fruition. A debt of gratitude goes out to Giselle Shapiro, Founder of Literary Launch, who poured her heart and soul into researching and producing the manuscript. To Ernesto Altamarino who tackled the business side of the research with great zeal and accomplishment. Many thanks to my accomplished proofreader Judy Huddleston, whose keen eye for details kept me on track.

I am especially thankful to my brilliant and supportive friend Marilyn Bellock who helped frame the overall tone and direction of the book. My deep gratitude goes out to my good friends and accomplished business colleagues Bert Davey and Mike Downey for their never-ending support.

Special thanks to Michelle Howry who skillfully edited my first book at Penguin and who continues to be a superb source of information and encouragement.

Kudos to Andy Candelaria, whose creativity and wonderful graphic design made this book really come alive.

I'd also like to acknowledge those of you who helped me launch my first book. Without your help there wouldn't be this sequel.

I'd like to recognize my brother Dennis for his continued support and my sister Karen who continues to be the true backbone and matriarch of our family. Her work providing dignity and comfort to terminally ill patients is a source of inspiration to all of us.

Lastly, I'd like to commend all my readers who had the courage and fortitude to take the right risk and find their true purpose in life. I hope your journey of self-discovery leads you on the path to true success.

CONTENTS

Preface		2
Introduction		7
Chapter 1	Define the Business You Should Be In	13
	Figuring Out Who You Are and Who You Want to Become	18
Chapter 2	Assess the Market	31
	Capitalizing On Your Strengths	34
Chapter 3	Identify the Target Customer	47
	Discovering the Authentic You	53
Chapter 4	Launch Your Strategy	65
	Finding Your Niche – and Daring to Risk	70
Chapter 5	Weather the Product Cycles	81
	Reinventing Yourself At Every Stage	86
Chapter 6	Build Your Business Brand	99
	Building Your Personal Brand	104
Chapter 7	Expand Your Reach	113
	Creating a Living Legacy	121
Chapter 8	Build a High-Impact Advertising Campaign	131
	Reawakening the Creativity Within You	137
Chapter 9	Plan Your Distribution	151
	Investing Your Time and Energy Wisely	155
Chapter 10	Achieve Your Sales Goals	167
	Reaching Out to Make Your Personal Goals a Reality	173
Chapter 11	Analyze Profit and Loss	183
	Tallying Your Personal Balance Sheet	191
Chapter 12	Establish Targets of Opportunity	203
	Making Your Dreams Come True	207
Epilogue		220
Personal Exercises		225
Subject Index		246
Business Index		248
Name Index		250
Photo Credits		253

PREFACE

Much has happened since I wrote my first book, *A Marketing Plan For Life*. A great financial tsunami has swept over our world. The economic meltdown was the catalyst that caused us to re-assess our core values and take a step back to re-visit our definition of "true" success. During the financial crisis, a litany of bank and real estate failures triggered double-digit unemployment rates. Once venerable institutions seemed to be built on unstable foundations of quicksand. Highly admired CEOs came under sharp attacks while celebrity chefs became new rockstars.

The very fabric of the American Dream appeared to be coming apart at its seams. But the American Dream was not dead… it was we who had gone amok by straying from the core values that made this country great. Our Declaration of Independence reinforces the values of life, liberty and the pursuit of happiness. There's nothing written in the document about four chickens in every pot, using your home as a cash cow account or driving all alone in a gas guzzling SUV.

The valuable lessons we learned from the economic meltdown will provide the jumpstart we need to re-visit the American Dream: a dream that focuses on self worth as much as net worth, a dream that exemplifies what author Nelson Henderson meant when he spoke to his son on graduation day, "The true meaning of life is to plant trees under whose shade you do not expect to sit."

In many ways, the turbulent times we've been through in the last (or should I say "lost" decade) will likely be transformative. It may very well be the silver lining we need to ignite our personal renaissance, enabling us to become entrepreneurs of our own existence. It may help us understand more fully that true success is all about giving back.

Numerous surveys and Gallop polls indicate that we are increasingly getting back to our core values and honing in on what really matters most. There is less emphasis on showing off bling and more focus heeding our true calling in life. We are putting a lid on indiscriminate spending. We are beginning to understand the notion that our valuables are not nearly as important as the people and causes we value.

In *A Marketing Plan For Life*, I made the point that the same principles inherent in a good marketing plan could be reapplied in ways that could lead to a more balanced, fulfilling, and meaningful life. The fact is that many corporations and financial institutions took short cuts and departed from the sound business principles and corporate values that helped them become highly valued entities in the first place. Other companies like Apple, Google, Southwest Airlines and Amazon continued to thrive even in chaotic times by sticking to their core values.

In business, a marketing plan needs to be continuously re-examined and modified as market conditions change. This needs to be done on a personal level as well. As our personal situation changes or unexpected events alter our lives, we need to continuously re-examine our core values and goals for shifts in our reality. However, we should be careful not to over-plan because life inevitably throws us some curveballs along the way. John Lennon once famously observed, "Life is what happens when you're busy making other plans."

In the last few years, I have been on a journey of self-discovery. I tried to make meaning as well as money by volunteering my marketing acumen toward causes higher than myself. I had to apply some of my own lessons to my life and learn that the best things in life are not actual "things" and that true success always involves others. During turbulent economic times, my journey of self-discovery proved to be one great balancing act. Sometimes I felt I was about to fall off the high wire. Somehow I knew that if I lost my balance a bit along the way, there would be a safety net to catch me. The words of Abraham Lincoln keep echoing in my ear, "In the end it's not the years in your life that count, it's the life in your years." It was the striving towards a life of depth that helped my self-esteem to soar, even as my net worth tried to keep pace with the charitable causes that now counted on me for support.

Although the road has been winding and at times strewn with potholes and boulders, I would gladly take the same path of self-discovery again because it led to igniting my life's true purpose and passion. Remember as you embark on your own path of discovery the insightful words of noted author Ursula K. Le Guin, "It is good to have an end to journey towards, but it is the journey that matters in the end."

For those of you who read my previous best-selling book, *A Marketing Plan For Life*, this new book, *Igniting Your True Purpose and Passion*, is built upon the same work/life planning process. However, it offers the following updated, greatly expanded, value-added content:

- The book has been totally updated to reflect today's socio-economic and changing times.
- There are seven jumpstarting steps for each chapter that allow the reader to take action and focus on reaching their full personal growth potential.
- The book offers significantly updated content. It is chock full of new anecdotes, business and life stories, and notable quotes that make the book come alive for the reader.

▶ Finally, the "exercises" section at the end of the book offers the flexibility to address your pertinent life questions in any of these three ways:

1 Answer the exercise questions at the end of the book on your own notepad and keep them in a drawer or file cabinet for future review. I'm suggesting you don't write your answers in the book so that you can share the questions with your friends and family without influencing their answers.

2 Sign-up at www.ignitingyourtruepurpose.com/exercises and we'll email you a form to fill in your answers. Or if you want to go old school we'll mail you two sets of pre-printed questionnaires. Store the finished questionnaires where they are easily retrievable for future review. Remember, this life planning process is a living, always changing thing. You'll want to revisit these questions from year-to-year.

3 Log on to www.ignitingyourtruepurpose.com. Create a personal profile and you can answer the questions right there. We'll securely store your answers for your future review. That way you'll never misplace your work and have the opportunity to apprise your plan every six months or update whenever inevitable life-altering events suggest that you take another look at your plan going forward. Once you've registered at www.ignitingyourtruepurpose.com, you'll have the option of joining our online community of others who are on the path to Jumpstart their lives to greater heights.

I'm so glad you've taken the time to join me on this journey. You can reach me via email at bobby@ignitingyourtruepurpose.com.

INTRODUCTION

"Success"

*To laugh often and much;
to win the respect of intelligent people
and the affection of children;
to earn the appreciation of honest critics
and endure the betrayal of a false friendship;
to appreciate beauty, to find the best in others,
to leave the world a bit better, whether by
a healthy child or garden patch or
a redeemed social condition;
to know even one life has breathed easier
because you have lived.
This is to have succeeded.*

—Ralph Waldo Emerson

End of Act 1

I sat anxiously in my office. Hopefully, this would be the phone call I've worked for all my life. Finally, it rang. It was my Chief Financial Officer, calling to confirm that the company I helped launch had just gone public. I had tons of stock and was now officially wealthy (at least on paper). My years of hard work and keeping my nose to the grindstone had finally paid off. But I felt something deep inside me was missing. If I was so successful how come I wasn't happier?

I drove the short distance from work to home knowing I was totally lost. Then it hit me like a lightening bolt. My definition of success up to that point was centered on self. It was all about the proverbial "me".

I had always thought that Ralph Waldo Emerson had a meaningful handle "on success", especially for the turbulent times we find ourselves. His riveting quote on true success drove a stake through my newfound heart. I had to learn that true success always involves reaching out to people beyond ourselves. The true meaning of success is more than the fancy home we live in, the luxury car we drive, or for that matter, a fatter paycheck.

Until a couple of years ago, I was as guilty of this type of this narrow definition of success as most Americans. I was a so-called "successful" global marketing executive. I drove a BMW convertible. I lived in a lovely oceanfront home. But I knew something was missing. By Emerson's standard of success, I wasn't very successful. I was a guy who made my fair share of money but not a lot of meaning. I was a person who clearly confused having a good career with having a good life. In short, I was all about the scoreboard… how much… and how soon? I had yet to learn that true success was not just getting what you want, but wanting what you get.

Linda Ellis, the author of *Dash*, tells us that on our tombstone there will be two dates: our date of birth and the date we died. The time in between is how we lived our life and the impact we made while on this planet. After taking a step back and realizing a broader, more meaningful concept of success… I had a personal epiphany. I decided it wasn't enough to have etched on my tombstone, "Here lies Bobby Fried; he sold a lot of stuff." I needed to make it my business to improve my life/work balance. I knew I needed to make my life my best venture yet. Knowing this, I set out to become an entrepreneur of my own existence.

But how do we learn to achieve the full measure of success, as articulated by Emerson? While pondering this question, I began to realize that the same marketing discipline I had successfully used on a wide range of Fortune 500 and start-up companies could be applied back to our personal lives as well. In short, the basic principles inherent in any good marketing plan could be reapplied in ways that could lead to a more balanced, fulfilling, and meaningful life. The same business road map that helped steer companies in the right direction could steer us as well. Too many of us save our best selves for work and never think about applying our well-developed skills to personal advantage. Accordingly, I believe we should consider developing our personal life plan as if it were a marketing plan for our business. I call this life/work process a Marketing Plan for Life.

In life as well as business, we need to take an inventory every now and then. It has always amazed me that we routinely take our cars in for a six-month checkup or hire a floral service to water our office plants on a regular basis, but many of us let our personal lives go without maintenance. Equally astounding is that couples plan their wedding ceremony and reception for a year, but spend almost no time planning the rest of their lives that they intend to share together. Is it any wonder that our divorce rate is so high?

The premise of this book is profoundly simple: if we take the same amount of time, energy, and focus in planning our personal lives as we do in planning our professional lives, we can live a more balanced, purposeful, and meaningful life. All of this sounds simple. However, making it happen is no easy task. It's not an overnight thing—it's a process. But if you stick with it, our life/work planning process will help you ignite your true purpose and passion.

Defining Ourselves by Our Careers

Success and monetary achievement has always been an integral part of the American Way of Life. But now more than ever, we need to take a step back and wonder if we haven't been defining success far too narrowly, for far too long. I had to learn, even in business circles today, it's not just about making a profit; it's about standing up for authentic values. Let's face it, throughout the years, many of us cut our teeth in business. It has typically been the way to achieve the American Dream. Our education and well-honed skills were acquired to get ahead and succeed—sometimes at all costs. As we happily leaped through every professional hoop presented to us, is it any wonder that many of us come to define our success and ourselves solely by our careers?

Your career identifies what you do, but not necessarily who you are. Who are you at your very core, at your very essence? When you strip away the veneer, are you just a financial planner, a working mother, a clinical psychologist, a teacher, a firefighter, a writer, a marketing executive? Many of us like to believe and live out career labels. But here's one stumbling block: When you live only by your career label, you immediately set up boundaries that limit the ways you can become truly successful. Having an impressive career presents only one criteria of success.

The business section of the marketing-plan process originates in part from the Harvard Business School, my former mentor at Motorola, and my own personal school of hard knocks as to what works and doesn't work in the real world. This process has been successfully applied to companies like Motorola, Quasar Electronics, Marantz, Laura Ashley, Eddie Bauer Eyewear, Revlon, bebe eyewear, Nicole Miller and Nautilus, as well as Silicon Valley startups.

The same systemic process that helped build the brands of these companies can help you build your personal brand as well. The following outline gives an executive summary of how this life/work planning processes works. Subsequent chapters will go through each point separately.

TWELVE-POINT BUSINESS AND LIFE-PLANNING OUTLINE

MARKETING STATEMENT

I. Define the Business You're In

II. Assess the Market

III. Identify the Target Customer

IV. Launch Your Strategy

V. Weather the Product Cycles

VI. Brand Building

VII. Expand Your Reach

VIII. Build a High-Impact Advertising Campaign

IX. Plan Your Distribution

X. Achieve Your Sales Goals

XI. Analyze the Profit and Loss

XII. Establish Targets of Opportunity

PERSONAL RESTATEMENT

I. Figure Out Who You Are and Who You Want to Become

II. Capitalize on Your Strengths

III. Discover the Authentic You

IV. Find Your Niche –Take the Right Risk

V. Reinvent Yourself at Every Stage

VI. Build Your Personal Brand

VII. Create a Living Legacy

VIII. Reawaken the Creativity Within You

IX. Invest Your Time and Energy Wisely

IX. Reach Out to Make Your Personal Goals a Reality

XI. Tally Your Personal Balance Sheet

XII. Make Your Dreams Come True

Be not afraid of going slowly.
Be afraid of standing still.

—Chinese proverb

Benefits of a Life/Work Plan

Now it's time to take ourselves on an exciting journey: a courageous journey, a journey of self-discovery. I'm not just coming along for the ride—I'm taking the entire journey with you. We don't need to have all the answers. The quest or the journey itself is an integral part of the answer.

By the time we finish this book together, you'll be well on your way to developing and jumpstarting your own life plan. A word of caution, however: this plan is a living, breathing document, not something that gathers dust on the bookshelf in your den or idly resides somewhere deep in the memory of your smart phone. Similar to a marketing plan for a business, it needs to be reviewed at least every six months. Just as market conditions constantly change, our personal lives are in a constant state of flux. Revisit your plan at least every six months. Make sure it remains in alignment with your true purpose or special calling in life.

Nobody said life is easy. Sometimes it's a struggle. But often in the struggle we find meaning. When asked what it was like to be a living legend, longtime Rolling Stones lead guitarist Keith Richards answered, "The legend part is easy. It's the living part that's hard."

CHAPTER 1

Define the Business You Should Be In

Figuring Out Who You Are and Who You Want To Become

The purpose of life is a life of purpose.
—Robert Byrne

The importance of finding your true purpose or proper calling can not be overlooked in life or business.

The first step in the overall marketing-plan process is to define the business you should be in. Answering this question forces a company to articulate exactly what it does, as well as its raison d'être, or reason for being. It's the beginning of the solid foundation upon which the entire company will be built.

It's important not to underestimate the importance of this seemingly simple question. For example, if the Pennsylvania Railroad understood that they were in the overall transportation business rather than just the railroad business, perhaps they would be in business today. Pity the poor guy in the early 1900s who clung to the notion that he was in the buggy-whip business when the first Model Ts came onto the scene. Stop and think about it: what business is Calvin Klein in? He said it himself: "I don't design clothes, I design dreams." McDonald's is not really in the hamburger business—it's primarily in the real estate business.

Many stock analysts raised their eyebrows when Disney acquired ESPN. They should have understood that the Disney acquisition was a natural extension of the business they were already in – namely, the family entertainment business. What is more family friendly and entertaining than sports? As you know, ESPN doesn't just give the scores; they describe the action on the field in a fun and entertaining way. Other companies have clearly defined or redefined themselves. Google is no longer just the gold standard of the search business; it's in the media business. Apple has naturally evolved into the consumer electronics business. IBM is in the information technology business. I think you get the picture.

Early in my career, while working with the highly respected Marantz stereo company, I was challenged with a classic case of defining the business for a company. This was an integral part of our turnaround marketing plan to restore the company to its former glory and profitability. After several weeks of research and analysis, I defined the business we should be in as "the good sound business." Simply put, I proclaimed that if our product did not have good sound, we ought not to make the product. When I presented my findings to my brilliant-yet-crusty, seventy-year-old CEO, he was less than impressed. "You mean it took you four weeks to write what I already knew?" he asked impatiently. While he readily agreed that "good sound" was indeed the business we should be in, he thought my contribution was basic and unimaginative, especially considering that he was paying me the big bucks to refurbish his once great brand.

As the spirit of youth would have it, I countered with an explanation. "Well, how's this for imagination? We have four separate divisions in our company, yet only one division has anything to do with good sound." I strongly suggested that the company sell the other three divisions that had absolutely nothing to do with the good sound business and apply the proceeds back to the core good sound division. My boss beamed and gave me a youthful smile while acknowledging the point. The other divisions were sold, and we succeeded in returning the company back to its former greatness.

Later in my career, I was chief marketing officer for a small, but fledging company that distributed eyewear frames to eye doctors throughout the country. When I first arrived, I asked the single question, "What business should we be in?" The answers startled me. Management at this small company thought it was in the business of dispensing medical implements to hold corrective lenses. Remember, they were selling eyewear frames. Dismissing the medical jargon, we redefined the company from the medical implements business to the fashion accessory business. At the time, all frames tended to look alike. They were either preppie or unisex. Once we defined that we were really in the fashion accessory business, we gave each eyewear frame a distinctive personality to secure several marketing niches. We licensed the Laura Ashley brand to own the feminine niche. Our Eddie Bauer license captured the spirit of the great outdoors. The bebe license offered the promise of confident sensuality and Nicole Miller gave us a New York fashion designer brand. By redefining the business, company sales soared and set the tone for the optical industry to view itself as fashion-driven, versus medically driven.

Constant Redefinition

Motivational speaker Zig Ziglar tells the story of a Cadillac car sales representative from Little Rock, Arkansas, who sold a record number of cars because he defined the business he was in quite differently from the rest of his sales colleagues. "Cadillac Jack," as he was nicknamed, viewed himself as not just a car salesman, but as a "transportation specialist." Accordingly, he offered his customers a variety of services that fit with the way he defined his business. Just a few of the transportation specialist services he offered his customers included the following:

- He picked up the customers' cars at their home or place of business whenever the car needed repair.
- He offered the customer free towing service.
- If a customer locked themselves out or lost their keys, he provided a new set of keys.
- He'd jump-start a customer's dead battery free of charge.
- He renewed the customer's auto registration.

Cadillac Jack's record sales came from not only repeat customers, but from a positive whispering campaign that gained him numerous sales leads and referrals. Now there's a guy who truly knows what business he should be in.

Even United Parcel Service (UPS), the venerable package delivery service, has redefined its business. The company repositioned itself from satisfying the customer's small package domestic needs to synchronizing global commerce. In essence, UPS is now in the time-definite worldwide delivery business.

In redefining its business, the company has grown from doing business in twenty-seven states several years ago to doing business in two hundred countries worldwide today. As of this writing, the company's sales have mushroomed from $1 billion to $30 billion and are growing. "Globalization," said UPS CEO Eskew, "is a whole new exciting business for us. We're challenged every day to do things we haven't done in the past: fly to new places, deal with different governments, and open new trade between countries."

You don't have to be a big company or a hotshot salesperson to redefine your business. My friend Dimitri was a world-class chef and a gregarious restaurant owner. When his restaurant business slowed down, he redefined his business more broadly. Dimitri went from the restaurant-only business to the overall hospitality business. He partnered with a luxury senior citizen's home—offering guests wonderful, nourishing cuisine, warm and comfortable room environments, and imaginative leisure time and travel activities. In doing this, Dimitri not only broadened his business, he heightened his purpose in life. "I love to see the smiles on my guests' faces when I do the little things that really matter for them," he said. "It could be something as simple as giving them a glass of apple juice and a home-made cookie, long after the kitchen is closed."

Remember, although Dimitri broadened the definition of his business—he still stayed within his core competency. He stayed within the wheelhouse of what he does best—serving excellent food and offering good hospitality.

Figuring Out Who You Are and Who You Want To Become

The greater thing in this world is not so much where we stand, as in what direction we are moving.

—Oliver Wendell Holmes

As we would with a business, it's important that we personally define or redefine who we are—and more importantly, who we'd really like to be. Oftentimes, we have to recognize the disparity or gap between who we are and who we dream of becoming. There may be some accountants out there who dream of becoming world-class chefs. There are a lot of waiters and waitresses who want to be Broadway theater stars. There are lawyers who no longer want to practice law. There are administrative assistants who want to write a screenplay. We have to recognize not only who we are but also who we want to become.

Defining Who You Are

We all need to define or redefine our true purpose or "true north" in life. What if Mohandas Gandhi had remained a lawyer and never liberated India? What if Winston Churchill had decided to become a full-time artist, rather than saving Europe from Hitler's tyranny? What if Elvis Presley had decided to remain a truck driver instead of becoming the King of Rock 'n' Roll? What if Abraham Lincoln, a five-time political election loser, gave up on his desire to serve and decided not to run for president of the United States? What if Rev. Dr. Martin Luther King, Jr. didn't have a dream? What if President Barack Obama didn't believe in change?

All of these people had a purpose. Once they defined their purpose, they took positive action to fulfill it. We all need to know what our true purpose really is. In her thought-provoking book *I Will Not Die an Unlived Life*, author Dawna Markova explores purpose. "Purpose is the drive to close that circle, finish that song, scratch that itch, bridge that gap; it's the natural energy in each of us—urging growth." Markova urges us to ask ourselves these key questions in exploring our life's purpose:

- ▶ What's unfinished for me to experience?
- ▶ What's unfinished for me to give?

- What's unfinished for me to learn?
- What's unfinished for me to heal?

Here are some additional questions I think we should ask ourselves:

- Am I now following a path that leads me to my true purpose in life?
- Am I doing what I really want to do?
- Do I even know what I'd really like to do? (That's the kicker question.)

Don't expect these answers to come in a flash. Exploring your life's purpose is a process. This book will start you on that journey of discovery.

Living a Life of Purpose

Just as a company has to have its mission or purpose, we as individuals need to find our reason for being. We need to find our true purpose in life. Purpose produces meaning. It helps us discover what truly matters most to us. Purpose provides the answer to the questions, "Why am I here? What is my mission or true calling in life? What is my song? Why was I put on this planet in the first place?"

Rick Warren, in his best-selling book *The Purpose-Driven Life*, explores purpose a bit further: "Without a purpose, life is a motion without a meaning, activity without direction, and events without reason. Without a purpose, life is trivial, petty, and pointless. The greatest tragedy is not death, but a life without purpose."

Sometimes when I struggle with the words I'm writing now, I go back to the very purpose for writing the book: to motivate and encourage people to take action on what matters most to them. I've convinced myself that I'm not just writing a book: I'm helping people to focus on attaining their goals, dreams, and aspirations. In doing so, maybe, just maybe, I'll help myself as well in my own life's journey. For sure, I have a need to go beyond just selling more stuff. I'm finally beginning to understand that true success goes way beyond me. I'm beginning to clarify my true purpose. It feels good to have that clarity in my gut and in my heart.

Robert Byrne put it succinctly when he said, "The purpose of life is a life of purpose."

But how do we discover our life's purpose? How do we live a life of meaning? These are courageous conversations we need to have with ourselves on the road to discovering what matters most.

Po Bronson, author of the best-selling book *What Should I Do With My Life?*, states that we all have a true purpose; we just need to work hard to find it because it doesn't always come wrapped as an epiphany. "Purpose doesn't arrive neatly packaged as a destiny," he writes. "We only get but a whisper. A blank, nonspecific urge. This is how it starts."

The moment you begin to wonder about finding your true purpose, you're well on your way to discovering it. To be sure, purpose resides somewhere deep within our souls. Coaxing it to come out is no easy task. It takes hard work.

According to author Julie Jordan Scott, one way to know how to define your purpose is to clarify what it is not. "Purpose," writes Scott, "is not living on automatic pilot; it is not hiding behind the veil of shoulds, woulds, or oughts. Living on purpose is living with laser-like focus. It is responding from an authentic place, deep within the heart. It is aligning with your highest calling, taking a stand for your own truth."

When you live with purpose, you are in essence defining the authentic you—the you you've always wanted to become. Having a purpose allows you to focus like a laser beam on those things that are most important to you. You become very selective as to those things you choose to do and those things you choose not to do.

It's very difficult to have direction in our lives if we cannot define our true purpose or true calling. However, once we do find it, we have a sense of where we are going and why.

There's an inspiring scene in the movie *The Rookie*, starring Dennis Quaid, which was based on a true story. Quaid's character is a forty-year-old baseball pitcher who still has dreams of making it to the major leagues, even though he failed in an attempt twenty years earlier. In order to try out again to become a major league pitcher, he has to give up his teaching position—putting a significant strain on his family's finances. Looking for guidance, he goes to his father who tells him, "It's OK to do what you have to do until you figure out what you are meant to do." The rookie made it to the big leagues at age forty.

> *The purpose of life is to be true to yourself.*
> —Po Bronson

It's obvious that defining your true purpose is not an overnight process; as mentioned earlier, it takes a lot of hard work. Most of us don't have a clue why we were placed on this planet. In fact, in a research study, psychologist William Morton asked three thousand respondents the question "what do I have to live for?" A whopping ninety-four percent responded by saying they had no definite purpose in their lives. If that's the case, I'll tell you what unhappiness is: unhappiness is not knowing what you want and killing yourself to get it! Remember, if you don't know where you're going, any road you take is OK. Carl Sandburg once wrote, "I'm an idealist—I don't know where I'm going but I'm on the way."

But how do you figure out what you are meant to do? Here's an exercise I wrote that was inspired by Cynthia Kersey in her stimulating book *Unstoppable* that might help you define your true purpose in life. The chart won't give you all the answers, but it will be useful in stimulating your thinking about your purpose in life.

To jumpstart you a bit, I've included my answers here:

Defining My Purpose (Robert Fried's Answers)

WHAT IGNITES MY PASSION?	WHAT CAN I DO BEST TO SERVE OTHERS?	WHAT IS MY TRUE PURPOSE IN LIFE?	WHAT ACTION DO I NEED TO TAKE TO REALIZE MY TRUE PURPOSE?
Empowering others to realize their full potential.	Encourage and motivate people and organizations to realize both their personal and professional goals.	Develop a company that offers uplifting books, seminars, products and services that help people realize their goals, dreams and aspirations.	Start a new company called Thirdwind that will offer books, online courses, seminars, products, and services dedicated to helping people discover and take action to realize their professional goals and personal dreams.

Now it's time to explore your own true calling or reason for being. It starts by defining your own true purpose. Don't panic if it doesn't come to you straight away. It's more of a process than an exercise. By the time you finish the book, your purpose will come into clearer focus. However, I'd like you to start to think about it now. Later you can circle back and crystalize the reasons you are on this planet.

Defining Your Purpose (Your Answers)

WHAT IGNITES MY PASSION?

WHAT CAN I DO BEST TO SERVE OTHERS?

WHAT IS MY TRUE PURPOSE IN LIFE?

WHAT ACTION DO I NEED TO TAKE TO REALIZE MY TRUE PURPOSE?

What I especially like about this exercise is that it prevents you from wasting time on activities that are not aligned with your true calling. We're only on this earth for a short while. So pursue things that are in harmony with what matters most to you. Duke University's head basketball coach Mike Krzyzewski is the epitome of a man who knows what really matters most. He decided against pursuing a lucrative head-coaching job with the storied Los Angeles Lakers franchise, to stay at Duke to teach basketball, life, and leadership at the collegiate level. When Coach "K" turned down one of the best jobs in sports, he chose purpose and happiness over money and glamour. "Sometimes in order to be happy," said Krzyzewski, "you have to follow your heart and lead with it." In short, Coach "K" lives what he teaches.

Author Po Bronson puts it into perspective: "The purpose of life is to be true to yourself. To be the authentic you, don't turn your back on your higher purpose."

Igniting Your Passion

While purpose rallies our indomitable spirit and steers us in the right direction, it is passion that provides the fire in our belly to constantly keep us going toward our true calling. Passion is the pilot light that, once ignited, can help us overcome the potholes and boulders that are strewn along life's highway. Passion is what gets us up in the morning to set the world on fire. Dante once proclaimed, "a mighty flame followeth a tiny spark."

Passion moves the heart. In his classic book *The Little Prince*, author Antoine de Saint-Exupéry tells us, "One sees clearly only with the heart." Honoré de Balzac sums up passion with these words: "Passion is the universal humanity. Without it, religion, history, romance, and art would be useless."

Guy Kawasaki in his thought-provoking book, *Enchantment*, urges us to pursue and project our passions to the outside world. He contends that our passion should be front and center - not on the back burner. "Tell the world," extols Kawasaki, "that you love cooking, hockey, NASCAR, or knitting – whatever it is – because pursuing your passion makes you more interesting, and interesting people are enchanting."

When you're truly passionate about what you do, time seems to fly by quickly. You're not constantly watching the clock. You don't mind working extra hours because your passion provides you with sustainable energy. When you are passionate about something, there's often a blur between work and play.

Winemaker extraordinaire, Gary Pisoni is the epitome of someone who achieves that passionate balance between work and play. Gary, known by many enthusiasts as "the King of Pinot Noir," is the founder of the famed Pisoni Vineyards that virtually put the Santa Lucia Highlands region (located on California's Central Coast) on the wine-making map. Gary has an effervescent personality that bubbles over, larger than life. Some people call him eccentric, but nobody challenges his passion for making some of the best Pinot Noir on the planet. Gary does not fill us with sophisticated platitudes about how to enjoy wine. His simple maxim goes something like this: "If you like it… continue to drink it. If not, don't. The best glass of wine should always be the one in your hand."

Gary is not only passionate about what he does, but he has loads of fun doing it. But make no mistake about it; he takes his winemaking (with his two sons, Mark and Jeff) very seriously. He likes to say that, "Wine is made by God in the vineyard… I am merely the attentive custodian of the land."

Pisoni is so passionate about his dream to make great Pinot Noir that he persisted for nine years before he finally found enough water (with the help of a Native American dowser) on his family's cattle grazing land to grow great grapes. After visiting the Pisoni Vineyards, journalist Mark C. Anderson captured the passion of Pisoni. He writes about Gary, "He evangelizes his love of good wine with a preacher's passion and while Jesus may have turned water into wine, Pisoni turned no water into wine."

Pisoni's passion for Pinot Noir has no limits. He believes that wine often transports us back to that special place, during that extraordinary time. Good wine conjures up memorable experiences with loved ones, that someone special, family and friends. It would be wonderful if we could all bottle Gary's boundless energy and enthusiasm.

> *Let the beauty of what you love, be what you do.*
> —Rumi

Michael Singer, in his thought-provoking book, *The Untethered Soul*, also extols the virtues of passion: "What actually gives life meaning is the willingness to live it fully. It isn't one particular event; it's the willingness to experience life's events." Sometimes it's not just what you're doing – it's how much you are passionately involved in doing it.

I'd like to point out that just because you're naturally good at something doesn't mean you have a passion for it. I know a young parish priest who happens to be an excellent rock-and-roll singer, but that doesn't mean he should give up his true calling to run off and join a rock band.

There's a significant difference between being passionate about something versus being obsessed with something. Passion offers controllable, positive energy, while an obsession is negative and generally uncontrollable. I may love lasagna but that doesn't mean I need to eat it five times a week. I may love good wine but that doesn't mean I need to become an alcoholic. And with respect to my professional life, while I certainly love my work, I try to maintain a sensible work/life balance.

In summary, defining your true calling and real purpose in life is no easy task. In fact, it's hard work. The struggling, however, is a vital sign that you are on a productive journey toward discovering your true purpose.

We only become truly successful by aligning ourselves with our true purpose and passion in life. When it comes to your true purpose and passion, heed the call. Discover what really matters most to you. Go to your sweet spot and your energy and productivity will soar to heights you've never imagined. When you listen to your true calling, you'll also be a lot happier. Remember, success is not the key to happiness. It's happiness that unlocks the door to success. If you are passionate about life and love what you are doing, you will find that "true success" Emerson extols.

Here are some thought starters you can utilize to help discover and ignite your passion.

- **Know what you do best.** You need to be candid with yourself here. You might even need to brag a bit. What is it that you do as well or better than most? It could range from baking an apple pie, to dancing up a storm, to making a compelling business presentation, to serving your community, to caring for others, to being a passionate lover. As Bruce Lee once so perfectly suggested, "Love is like a friendship caught on fire!"

- **Remember the joy.** Think about the times in your life that you were filled with unbridled joy. What was the circumstance? What was the setting? What special event resonated with your being? Was it the birth of a baby? When you got that long-deserved promotion? When you aced that test in school? When your favorite sports team finally won a championship? (Think Boston Red Sox in 2004 after 86 years of waiting to win a World Series Championship.). When you were in the garden tending to your roses?

- **Recognize when time flies by.** Define what you are normally doing when you lose total track of time. Are you watching a great movie or reading a wonderful book? Are you writing? Are you painting? Are you working on a meaningful project at work? Are you making Eggplant Parmesan? Are you playing with your kids, or helping them with their homework? Remember when you don't watch the clock, you are likely to be passionately engrossed in what you are doing.

- **Get in touch with your childhood dreams.** Remember when you were a kid and filled with childlike wonderment? What did you dream about? Did you dream about becoming a dancer? A novelist? A gourmet chef? A great parent? An inventor? Entrepreneur? Sometimes it helps to go back so you can move forward and reignite the passion within you.

- **Narrow-cast your passion list.** Make a list of your passions and hone in on one or two things that ignite your fire and add fuel to your positive energy. You might use a rating system: one being the highest, five being the lowest. Remember, passion doesn't sit well on the back burner. Make quality time to pursue your passion.

America's Passion with Sports

One of my personal passions, like many people, is my love affair with sports. I'm totally into sports because in many ways, sports mirror life itself. Think about it; it's north against south, east against west, the home team versus the visiting team, and often David (the underdog) against Goliath (the favorite). Unlike a scripted movie, Shakespearean play, or book we might have read before, with sports, we never know the ending in advance. Team sports in particular, offer a riveting form of drama. In his insightful book *The Meaning of Sports*, Michael Mandelbaum asserts that "sports resemble the oldest of literary forms – the epic. Like, the greatest of them, *The Odyssey*, the protagonist – in the case of sports, the *team* – encounters a series of challenges that it must meet to achieve its ultimate goal." Sports are literally obsessed with goal keeping statistics that can compare one player or team over time with that of another – often causing the great debate as to which team or player is best.

The word "sport" means to divert ones-self. Sports are a welcome diversion from the turbulent times in which we live and help us look up to heroes that we so badly need, especially in this chaotic day and age.

Personally, although I am far from a couch potato, the games I watch today transport me back to the carefree times of my youth, when I was an athlete. Playing, or even watching sports, helps me to stay competitive in my mind, body and spirit. In short, sports fuel my passion.

Towards the end of each chapter in this book, I will provide seven Jumpstarts (or thought starters) to help you take action on the key elements or pertinent points inherent in the chapter. My goal is to focus you directly on the essence of each chapter.

SEVEN JUMPSTARTS TO FIND YOUR TRUE PURPOSE

1. **Define what really matters most.** Make a list of people, causes, activities, business interests, and dreams that will give you a better reason to get up in the morning filled with anticipation and excitement to conquer yet another day.

2. **Define your vision for a better world.** Write down the causes or meaningful activities that will allow you to best serve others; perhaps it's to protect and preserve our environment. You might have a political interest, or maybe you are concerned about childhood obesity, or the plight of homeless people in our society. Maybe you care about child abuse or the cure for cancer. It could be something as important as improving special education, or just making people laugh. It's your vision, get in touch with it.

3. **See clearly with your heart.** Get in touch with those things, causes, or activities that ignite and fuel your passion. Hone in on those things you know you do best. The things that give you unbridled joy. The things you do when time just seems to fly by.

4. **Work backwards.** Sometimes, it's easier to work backwards and eliminate those distractions that are clearly not aligned with your purpose and passion. Many of us get stuck doing things that are not in concert with our true calling or passion. We get stuck in a corner office and wonder, "How did I end up here?" Know what you don't want to be, and move forward on the reason you were placed on this planet.

5. **Create your "most admired" list.** Jot down those famous, or not so famous, people, and the reasons you admire them. You might admire Oprah Winfrey for the way she uplifts and motivates others, or Robert Redford for his work in encouraging creativity with his Sundance Foundation. You might admire your parents, or a family member who inspired you as a youth and instilled the core values you exemplify today. When you get in touch with what you admire about others, it can lead directly to your own path of purpose.

6 **Heed the call.** List the short and long-range actions you need to take to realize your true calling. You might want to rethink your present job. You might want to start up or join a company that is more aligned with your true purpose and passion. The point is to take action and heed your true calling.

7 **Make meaning as well as money.** One of the biggest challenges in life is to make meaning as well as money. It's one great balancing act, but well worth the effort to align your purpose with your purse strings.

Executive Summary

The first step in the overall marketing planning process is to define the business you should be in. Answering this question forces a company to articulate exactly what it does as well as its reason for being. This is the initial step in establishing the strategic direction for a company.

Similar to what a business would do, we as individuals need to define our reason for being. We have to recognize and close the gap between who we are and who we dream of becoming. In short, we need to explore our true calling or purpose in life. Finding our true purpose is no easy task—it's a process. We need to have some courageous conversations with ourselves: Why am I here? What would give my life more meaning?

Defining your purpose focuses you on those things that really matter most to you. Having a purpose tends to ignite our passion. Passion provides the fire in our belly that heads us toward our true calling. Remember the words of Robert Byrne: "the purpose of life is a life of purpose."

Time to Reflect

Am I currently on a path that will lead me to my true purpose in life?

Note:

There is a workbook-type exercise section at the end of the book linked to each chapter. You'll find challenging but highly fruitful questions that relate to both jumpstarting your business and your life. Answering these questions will be a lot easier if you read the entire book first. Remember, your answers are not cast in concrete. Certainly on the personal side, they probably will change with triggering events that you'll face in your life (e.g. getting married, having children, changing jobs, moving to another area, getting a divorce, and the loss of a parent or family member.) Accordingly, you should revisit your answers every six months to make sure they are still aligned with your true purpose and passion.

Finally the "exercises" section at the end of the book offers the flexibility to address your pertinent life questions in any of these three ways:

1 Answer the exercise questions at the end of the book on your own notepad and keep them in a drawer or file cabinet for future review. I'm suggesting you don't write your answers in the book so that you can share the questions with your friends and family without influencing their answers.

2 Sign-up at www.ignitingyourtruepurpose.com/exercises and we'll email you a form to fill in your answers. Or if you want to go old school we'll mail you two sets of pre-printed questionnaires. Store the finished questionnaires where they are easily retrievable for future review. Remember, this life planning process is a living, always changing thing. You'll want to revisit these questions from year-to-year.

3 Log on to www.ignitingyourtruepurpose.com. Create a personal profile and you can answer the questions right there. We'll securely store your answers for your future review. That way you'll never misplace your work and have the opportunity to apprise your plan every six months or update whenever inevitable life-altering events suggest that you take another look at your plan going forward.

Once you've registered at www.ignitingyourtruepurpose.com, you'll have the option of joining our online community of others who are on the path to achieving their professional goals and personal dreams

CHAPTER 2

Assess The Market

Capitalizing On Your Strengths

*Do the things at which you are great,
not what you were never made for.*
—Ralph Waldo Emerson

In life, the market section of our personal plan is about honing in on your strengths and managing your weaknesses. In business, the market section deals with evaluating your company's strengths and weaknesses as well as understanding the strengths and weaknesses of your competition.

This section will help you to take a snapshot of the market (your life) and also allow you to begin the process of finding your company's marketing niche (your personal strengths and advantages). Successful companies use this section of the plan to identify the competition, research the various channels of trade, and measure the vitality of their industry.

Here's an example: In 1995, Levi Strauss came out with a research study claiming that by the year 2000, eighty percent of American white-collar workers would have the option to dress casual every day. Levi's Dockers brand of clothing capitalized on the casual trend—it built upon Levi's strengths (casual wear, denim) and applied them to create office-appropriate casual wear (those ubiquitous khaki pants). Dockers met the surging demand for casual office attire, and Dockers soon became the casual uniform for the everyday man.

Jeans, however, remain Levi's core strength. At first, the Levi brand had attributes that other jean brands could never possess – namely its heritage and patented denim-reinforcing copper rivets. While Levi's have been around since 1873, in recent years the company's jean business began to fade. The company specialized in selling off-the-rack jeans – primarily at the mid-price level. But the jean market was changing. Jeans that were selling best were the custom fit, higher-end of the market, with newer brands like True Religion, Lucky and Seven. Levi's had been selling jeans as a commodity, but jeans were becoming a true fashion statement. Seemingly caught with its pants down, Levi's decided to throw its women's line of jeans some curves. The company studied 60,000 body scans of women around the world. The research resulted in a new curvaceous line of women's jeans. The company now offers custom fit jeans for all women in various shapes and sizes. By understanding the ever-changing trends of the market, the proud heritage of Levi's will continue to remain an American icon brand.

Building on Your Key Strengths

Another example of surveying the marketplace and exploiting your strengths against the weaknesses of the competition is Budweiser beer. Budweiser is a mammoth brewer with twelve breweries in the United States alone. Bud also has an extensive wholesaler network that uses temperature-controlled warehouses, strict quality-control standards, and the lowest inventory of the nation's fastest-selling brands. In the 1990s, Budweiser was facing a competitive marketplace getting even more crowded with a tidal wave of smaller, independent microbrew beer makers. The microbreweries boasted handcrafted production techniques and exceptional taste with regional influences. Budweiser's parent company, Anheuser-Busch, had brewery locations all over the world, with a vast distribution system to boot. As the very antithesis of a microbrewery, it was arguable that Budweiser could ever compete with microbrews and other beer brands strictly on taste. But Budweiser could go up against anyone on freshness. Budweiser leveraged its key strengths—multiple brewing locations and a sophisticated distribution network—to create its "born-on date" feature. Many beers had pull dates on their product, but this only indicates when the beer is no longer fresh. Budweiser's born-on date, stamped on every bottle, was proof positive of the product's freshness. Freshness really matters for beer and Budweiser communicated this to their customers. Beer drinkers responded. Bud Light became the country's top-selling beer.

There are a litany of other companies that have prospered by recognizing their core competencies and focusing on their strengths. Apple is noted for easy to use, innovative designs that create a loyal customer experience. Amazon's strength is its one-stop online shopping. Southwest offers a no frills airline that gets you to multiple destinations on time. Nordstrom is noted for its legendary customer service. The strength of FedEx is on time delivery and easy tracking. Audi exhibits its strength by both performance and design. DirecTV flaunts its strength via its plethora of channel choices that you direct. By accentuating their strengths, these companies have emerged as among the most admired companies in the world.

He who knows others is wise;
He who knows himself is enlightened.

— Lao Tzu

Capitalizing on Your Strengths

Defining Strength

On a personal level, as well as business, we need to focus on our individual strengths and attributes.

What is a strength? Webster's Universal College Dictionary defines "strength" as "a strong or valuable attribute." But if you make just one meal well, that doesn't necessarily make you a great cook. If you hit one great backhand down the line but can't do it consistently, you're not a great tennis player. So let's try that definition of strength again. A strength is only a strength when you can display your strong attributes on a consistent, day-in, day-out basis. A strength is doing things well, repeatedly, with a sense of passion and joy.

Based on this expanded definition of strength, what is it you're consistently good at? What brings you unadulterated passion and joy? What are your strong and valuable assets? What attributes do you consistently display to others? As we'll see in this chapter, when you can identify your strengths and apply them to your work, your chances for success—and your enjoyment of your life—increase dramatically.

My friend Andrew has always harbored a love for the great outdoors. He is an avid fisherman, joyful backpacker and loves to trek the foothills of the world's most majestic mountain ranges. He has always had a passionate concern for protecting the environment. Andrew recognized this was also a concern for all humanity. Harnessing his concern for the environment, Andrew started an eco-backpacking tour company.

His tours not only showcased the beauty of the great outdoors, but also focused on protecting the environment. Andrew capitalized not only on what he loved, but also on his strengths. By doing so, he filled a market niche that could make a difference for future generations.

Simply put, a strength is any activity that makes you feel alive and strong. A well-defined strength renders you the emotional power to come alive and accomplish great things in the wheelhouse of your core competencies. When you really "know your strengths" and utilize them fully, it gives you the distinct feeling that you were put on a life stage for a reason higher than yourself. Please note that a strength is not necessarily what you do well. I might have been a good high school wrestler, but that doesn't mean I want to be a pro wrestler and get cauliflower ears. I might enjoy cooking at home for friends on weekends, but that doesn't mean

I want to quit my day job, open up a restaurant and spend 16 hours a day prepping and cooking.

Along these same lines, how can you tell when a strength is genuine versus something you might just be good at? Tom Rath, best-selling author and strength-finder expert offers us these vital S.I.G.N.S. that will help us identify our true strengths:

▶ **Successful** – You feel totally confident that nobody can do it better than you.

▶ **Instinctive** – You feel thoroughly engaged and feel you're headed in the right direction.

▶ **Growing** – You love what you're doing so much you have an unquenchable thirst for even more knowledge, so you can do it even better.

▶ **Needs** – Your emotional and recognition needs are being met; people that matter most to you are happy that you seem to be going to your true strengths.

These signs have a lot to do with the feelings you get when you're on a roll, utilizing your talents, and doing what you do best. It's not so much what you do, but rather how you feel when you're doing it that matters most. Personally, I've always felt comfortable and strongest when I'm at the podium or writing a book that helps motivate others to realize their fullest potential. One time when I was nearing the end of the question-and-answer session of a prominent college lecture, I was stopped in my tracks by a question from the audience. The question came from a graduate student of short stature. She asked, "Given my physical limitations, what do you think my subject matter should be if I were to become a motivational speaker?"

I paused, for what seemed to be an interminable amount of time, before answering: "I think you should motivate others to think big!" I got a huge round of applause from the audience for thinking adroitly on my feet. But to me, the only response that mattered was what my questioner thought of my answer. When she smiled and said, "Sweet," I felt a keen sense of relief and not a small sense of accomplishment. Last I heard, the former graduate student was doing very well on the lecture circuit. The subject of her talks was "thinking big!"

> *The unexamined life is not worth living.*
>
> —Socrates

Taking a Personal Snapshot

Applying the concept of going to our strengths requires an honest self-analysis. In essence, we need to take a personal snapshot of ourselves.

We need to initiate a personal "situation review." As Chinese philosopher Lao Tzu said, "He who knows himself is wise." In essence, what we're talking about here is cross-examining and taking personal stock of ourselves. What are your true strengths? What are your weaknesses? Are your strengths aligned with your true passion and goals in life? Remember, it's a strength to know your weaknesses. But it's an even bigger strength to know your strengths. Later, in the workbook section, you'll have an opportunity to hone in on your specific personal strengths and how to capitalize on them.

Harvard University Professor Larry Smith sums up the introspective process nicely: "I think there's a sweet spot that everyone has," he says. "It's the kind of work you want to perform, the kind of work that makes us proud. But finding that sweet spot is self knowledge: I think of this process as developmental self-interrogation. You're working on a mental model of yourself always."

Many of us spend too much time worrying about our weaknesses and not enough time taking advantage of our strengths. We succeed most in life by going to our strengths—not patchwork quilting our weaknesses. In short, we should be accenting the positive, not the negative. We should be less fixated on our faults and more centered on discovering, refining, and honing our strengths. Unfortunately, sometimes we take jobs that do not showcase our strengths. In fact, according to Marcus Buckingham and Donald Clifton, in their marvelous book *Now, Discover Your Strengths*, most companies remain startlingly inefficient in capitalizing on the strengths of their people. Utilizing a Gallup database, when asked if they had the opportunity to do what they did best only 20 percent of those polled (out of 1.7 million employees) said yes. But that's not all. Buckingham and Clifton also noted that the longer an employee stays at a company and the higher they go up the corporate ladder—the less likely they are to utilize their true strengths.

> *The person born with talent they are meant to use will find their greatest happiness in using it.*
>
> —Johann Wolfgang von Goethe

We can't ignore our weaknesses, but we should manage them so we have the time to continue to do what we do best. Legendary football coach Vince Lombardi successfully employed the "go to your strengths" approach with his world-champion Green Bay Packers. Lombardi's players totally bought into his "lead from your strengths" strategy that went something like this: "Men, I want you to know that if we block, we tackle, and we execute the basic fundamentals of our game plan, no team can stop us—even if they know our plays in advance." Under Coach Lombardi's tutelage, his highly motivated team went on to win five NFL championships and the first two Super Bowls.

Remember, when listing your strengths and weaknesses, it's important to go beyond your job or profession. For instance, if you're a good mother or father, write it down as a strength. If you're a good golfer or tennis player, jot that down. To jumpstart you a bit, if a loved one or somebody you respected and admired saw you doing what you do best—what would you be doing? Giving a great marketing presentation? Being a great teacher? Cooking a great meal? Conversely, if they saw you at your worst—what would you be doing? Perhaps crunching numbers, or trying to cook a great meal! Unfortunately, many of us get stuck doing what we're not passionate about. Go to your strengths—go to your passion. Heed your true calling. Follow your true north. Go to the sound of the bugles!

In his book *Work To Live*, author Joe Robinson suggests we create a new calling card that goes beyond our job, profession, or business title. He urges us to carry an ID card that relates more to how we view our strengths. For instance, Joe Smith: Renaissance Man, Jane Doe: Galloping Gourmet, Ken White: Storyteller Extraordinaire. How would your new calling card read?

Complementary Capabilities

Each of us possesses unique talents and strengths. Our greatest room for personal growth is in cultivating these strengths—not in trying to fix our weaknesses. For instance, in my case, my strength is setting or repositioning the strategic tone and direction for a company. I'm good at steering companies in the right direction. I'm weaker in the area of executing the specific details of the plan. I have a partner, however, who is excellent in executing all aspects of the plan. My partner and I possess "complementary capabilities." All good companies and all good relationships seem to have that needed balance of complementary skills. One person's weakness is covered by another person's strength.

Indeed, in many relationships opposites attract. A shy person who is a good listener may actually feel more comfortable in the company of an outgoing, more extroverted person. The outgoing person may feel more comfortable in the midst of a crowd than a one-on-one situation. These different personality traits are often viewed as positive and complementary, although it's clearly important to have similar core values.

When I was a second lieutenant in the U.S. Army, I was almost fanatical about the need for my platoon to be in the best physical shape possible. I was so hard on my men when it came to fitness, that I required each soldier to attempt at least three pull-ups prior to joining the mess hall. I was very young at the time and didn't understand that the same person that couldn't do three pull-ups might be the very same person that could read the map to enable the rest of the platoon to capture the hill or other key strategic terrain. The Army taught me about the need to have complimentary capabilities in order to have a winning team.

It Takes Two To Tango

For me, the importance of having complementary capabilities would be greatly reinforced several years later during a job interview. Let me share my story. When I was a young pink-faced junior executive at Motorola, I was flattered to be asked to interview for the top marketing position at a growing telecommunication company. I really didn't think I wanted the job, but I wanted to see how I would stack up against my competition in a highly competitive interview process.

After my interview, I was told I was the clear front-runner for the job. All that remained was to take the company's standardized tests. The first part of the test was verbal comprehension that counted for 90% of the total test score. I was told I passed with flying colors.

The last part of the test counted for the remaining 10% of the test score. It was a standard manual dexterity exercise for all prospective employees. My first thought led me to visualize those linemen who had to climb telephone poles and do other various high-wire tasks. Not exactly my moxie. My instructor dutifully spread 25 pieces of a puzzle on his desk, but before he asked me to assemble them, I surveyed the scattered pieces and told him that the puzzle, when completed, would depict a lady proudly pushing a baby carriage down the tree-lined streets of the Champs-Élysées in Paris. The interviewer was so amazed that he piled 25 pieces of a different puzzle on his desk and asked me to repeat my visionary Houdini act. I scanned the randomly thrown blocks and proclaimed that "the puzzle, when completed, will show a football player catching a touchdown pass in the far corner of the end zone with fans cheering wildly in the stands.

The instructor decided to invite several of his colleagues in to witness my ability to see the end result before the pieces of the puzzle were assembled. That proved to be my undoing. One of my instructor's colleagues asked me to manually assemble the pieces of the puzzle that I had so adroitly envisioned. I couldn't. In fact, I could not even come close to assembling the blocks – even though I could clearly see the end result. The moral? Simple. It takes two to tango. The person who has the vision often needs the complementary skill sets of others to help them put the pieces of the puzzle together to realize their goals. To succeed it often takes teamwork and complimentary capabilities. By the way, the telecom company offered me the job anyway, claiming it would be highly unlikely that I would be climbing telephone poles anytime soon. Not taking any high wire chances, I decided to stay grounded at Motorola.

The other thing to keep in mind in an interview like that… always make sure you quickly search for the cover of the puzzle boxes when you first enter the room!

Real Strengths

If you want to take full advantage of your strengths, it's important that your strengths are real. You must possess underlying talent to serve as the pillar and foundation of your strengths. For example, you might fancy yourself as a great financier, but you need the skill set and financial aptitude or you're just kidding yourself and others. Superstar Dwight Howard has many talents on the basketball court. Unfortunately, free-throw shooting is not one of them. His career average is just above 50 percent of foul shots made per attempts. He can practice all he wants, but until he has the proper skill and techniques down pat, foul shooting will never be Dwight's forte.

So don't kid yourself, make sure you go to your real strengths—not strengths that serve as false monuments to your good intentions.

> *A man should not deny his manifest abilities,*
> *for that is to evade his obligations.*
> —William Feather

Don't Avoid Your Strengths

Believe it or not, some people actually do not utilize their gifts or talents. Sometimes we don't recognize our strengths or attributes for what they are. Sometimes we're afraid to see how our strengths stack up with the competition around us.

My college roommate, Paul, was a shy but brilliant premed student. He was accepted to some of the nation's finest medical schools, including Harvard, Cornell, Yale, and Stanford. His "safety-net school," Vermont, also accepted Paul on the very same day. I took Paul out to the local campus pub to celebrate his scholastic achievement. Over a glass of beer, I toasted Paul and said, "Well, here's to Harvard!" But my roommate flabbergasted me by saying he had already decided to go to Vermont. A good school for sure, but certainly not as highly acclaimed as the other schools that had accepted him. I asked Paul why he decided to take the safe route. He responded: "Look, I'm comfortable with the surroundings in Vermont. Besides, I don't need the competitive culture that exists in Ivy League schools."

I literally grabbed him in a mock chokehold and said, "You're going to Harvard. Harvard needs people like you! If you don't like it, then become an instrument of change." To my delight, Paul reconsidered and went to Harvard. Paul has gone on to become an outstanding pediatrician. Vermont's loss was Harvard's gain.

Benjamin Franklin counsels us: "Hide not your talents. They for use were made. What's a sundial in the shade?"

Managing Your Weaknesses

Let's talk about our weaknesses for a moment. As mentioned earlier, many of us become fixated on our weaknesses—but we still need to manage them. First of all, let's try to define weakness. According to Webster's Universal College Dictionary, "weakness" can be defined as "an inadequate, defective quality or trait."

As a boy, I was always very weak in math. Try as I might, I just couldn't seem to grasp anything that had to do with numbers—let alone algebra, formulas, and geometry. Through my sheer ability to memorize (a strength) I somehow pulled through in math. But it didn't mask the fact that I had a real weakness that needed to be addressed. Enter Donald, my mentor. He let me know straight away that I probably wouldn't make it as an accountant or vice president of finance. But he felt strongly that I needed to have a better understanding of how money worked—especially since I was about to enter the business world. Accordingly, Donald took me to a series of investment seminars that got me interested in the mechanics of how money worked and how to invest my money wisely at an early age. He taught me about bonds and the stock market and how to make money by investing over time. In short, Donald taught me how to make money so I could afford to pay somebody else to help me count it!

There are several ways to deal with your weaknesses:

1. Educate yourself about your weaknesses—take a class, read a book, consult with an expert—take training. Don't let a lack of knowledge make you weak.

2. Find a partner with complementary capabilities who can cover your weaknesses. Often the best partners cover each other—if I'm strong in marketing but weak in finances, an ideal partner is somebody who can count!

3. Ignore your weaknesses and continue to work on your strengths. Why kill yourself trying to do something you don't have the aptitude, skill, or talent for?

Your Strength Can Be Your Weakness

Sometimes your strength can also be a weakness. For instance, I have worked with some pretty competitive people, and by and large I consider that a strength. But being too competitive can sometimes become a weakness.

During our company's annual picnic we had a softball game. Each team was made up of employees of all ages. In fact, the catcher on our team was a sixty-four-year-old grandmother of five. Later, in what most of us thought was just a fun pickup game our grandma was literally bowled over by a young, highly competitive twenty-five-year-old man who claimed the granny was blocking the plate. He scored. She was sent to the hospital in an ambulance. This guy's competitive nature was clearly out of control. His biggest strength (being competitive) was also his biggest weakness.

If you're not careful, you can even get competitive over something as wonderful as Christmas. In this regard, I would like to share a personal story. While on a business trip to Italy, I was invited to a Christmas party at a stunningly beautiful villa perched on a hilltop overlooking Turin. After arriving at the party, I saw an exquisite miniature replica of a 16th century Italian village replete with a life-like nativity scene. I was fascinated by what appeared to be an authentic electric train type village, but a lot older and obviously without the trains. The village was called a "presepio." It featured tiny terra cotta figurines going about their 16th century daily life of tending sheep, baking bread, churning butter, encasing sausages, and pounding horseshoes. The figurines were hand-crafted along Italy's famed Amalfi Coast and were only sold on the street corners and shops between December 8th and Christmas Eve.

Among Italian families, the presepio was a wonderful Christmas tradition, handed down from generation to generation; in many families, far more important than a Christmas tree. I was told it took many years to complete the authentic 16th century village. Noticing my keen interest in this fantastic Christmas display was a willowy Italian lady guest who was already half inebriated. In her thick Italian accent, she sarcastically reminded me that the presepio was a unique Italian experience – something that no American could ever authentically replicate. The lady exclaimed in an excruciating tone, "This is not like making plastic tortellini." I've always loved the childlike wonderment of Christmas, but this lady was beginning to get on my nerves.

I told the lady, "Listen, I don't want to get competitive about Christmas, but I'll build my own authentic presepio by next Christmas." She retorted by betting that I could not complete this task and said she would be in California the following Christmas on a pre-planned vacation trip to collect on her bet. Fast-forward to October of the following year when I decided to take on the challenge to build my presepio. Unfortunately, the only artisan I knew was a lovely lady that happened to make African masks. I wanted to send her to Italy, in the interest time, but she was too busy to go. Accordingly, we had to resort to books, photos from the library, and my own vivid recollections. This was just before the advent of Google and Wikipedia, when you still had to research things on your own, or actually go to the library. After several false starts, my mask lady created a village that was incredible – certainly as authentic as any presepio I had previously seen in Italy. But now all I had was a beautiful, but empty, 16th century village. I had totally forgotten about the terra cotta figurines that were only sold on the streets of Italy during Christmas season. I decided to call a business associate in Italy who came to my rescue by FedExing me 24 terra cotta figurines to my home.

As promised, my dubious Italian provocateur showed up in L.A. several days before Christmas to collect on her bet. Let's just say my lady mask designer and I were looking forward to her holiday visit. When she arrived, the Italian lady took one look at our authentically made in America presepio and loudly proclaimed, "All bets are off; you obviously paid an Italian artisan a king's ransom to create this presepio." Then I proudly introduced her to my mask-making turned presepio-creator friend, who had never been to Italy. The look on the Italian lady's face was incredulous. But, if I lived to be a hundred, I'll never forget the look of pride and accomplishment on the face of my American born artisan.

During subsequent business trips, I have added over 300 terra cotta figurines to my quaint Italian village. The presepio is now part of our family tradition and my way of welcoming in the true, albeit, in this case, somewhat competitive spirit of Christmas.

Finding Strength in Weakness

Sometimes it works the other way around. Your apparent weakness can become a strength.

A boy who decided to study judo, despite the fact he had lost his left arm in a horrific car accident, began taking judo lessons with an old Japanese master. However, after three months of training the master had only taught the boy one judo move. "Shouldn't I be learning more moves?" the boy asked his master.

"This is the only move you'll know—but it's the only move you need to know," the sensei replied.

Several months later, the sensei took the boy to his first judo tournament. Amazingly, the boy won his first three matches quite easily on his way to the tournament final. However, in the championship match, he would face an opponent who was bigger, stronger, and faster. In fact, the boy appeared to be overmatched. Concerned the boy might get hurt, the referee was about to stop the match. "No," the sensei insisted, "let him continue." As the match resumed, the boy's opponent made a critical mistake—he dropped his guard. Instantly, the boy used the one move that he was taught and pinned his opponent. The one-armed boy was the champion of the judo tournament.

On the way home from the match, the boy asked his sensei how he was able to win the tournament with only one move. "You won for two reasons," the sensei responded. "First, you've almost mastered one of the most difficult throws in all of judo, and second, the only known defense for that move is for your opponent to grab your left arm."

In this case, the boy's very weakness turned out to be a strength because he didn't dwell on the loss of his left arm. He let his supposed vulnerability work in his favor. Similarly, we know that Helen Keller was blind but she had the ability to "see" many things more clearly than most of us. Ludwig van Beethoven was deaf but he could "hear" things that other people couldn't and went on to compose some of the greatest classical music of all time.

Communicating Your Strengths

Our turbulent economy and high unemployment levels forced many people out of the job market for the first time in years. Identifying and clearly communicating your personal strengths is one of the key ingredients in acing that all important job interview. When you clearly communicate your personal attributes and strengths, you put yourself over the top in the job selection process. One of the most common queries raised by interviewers or search firms is: "tell me about your strengths." According to Don Parker, Senior Partner at the search firm Nosal Partners, the strengths that most interviewers look for are as follows:

- **Confidence** – The ability to express concepts, products and strategies in a highly confident, clear and concise manner.
- **Leadership** – The ability to motivate others towards a desired goal.
- **Integrity** – Your word is your bond. You actually do what you say you are going to do.
- **Great Communication Skills** – Ability to communicate clearly, both verbally and in writing.
- **Problem-Solving Expertise** – Your ability to handle challenges and crisis situations.
- **Demonstrate Growth** – Show how you've transformed a weakness into a strength in the past.

Don't Let Anyone Talk You Out of What You Do Best

Don't let other people, especially family members, divert you from going to your strengths and doing what you do best. Whenever I can, I mentor people to hone in on their strengths so they can realize their personal goals, dreams, and aspirations.

One day, John, a very prominent lawyer, asked me to visit his younger brother, Scott. Scott was a classically-trained pianist and a graduate from the famous Julliard School of Music. Although Scott was a great musician, he had trouble making his financial ends meet. Playing the piano in a swanky Beverly Hills hotel didn't pay enough to support his new and growing family. In fact, Scott's older brother urged me to convince him that he should give up his music and go to law school—just like he did. When I talked to Scott, we talked about his strengths, including his joy and great passion for music. It turns out he had another strength—he had excellent organizational skills.

I urged Scott to take his joy for music and combine it with his organizational skills to develop community music festivals to heighten peoples' awareness and appreciation for classical music. Today he is happy and passionate about organizing classical music festivals and makes excellent money doing what he does best— doing what he loves to do. The point: Don't let other people, especially family members talk you out of your passion. Remember to heed the call. Go to your strengths—go to the sound of the bugles! If you do, your chances of being truly happy will greatly increase.

The task of life is to determine what your gifts are and then decide how to use them.

—Rachelle Disbennett-Lee

Go for Greatness

One of the best ways to realize your goals, dreams, and aspirations is to cease dwelling on your weaknesses and to hone in on your positive strengths, attributes, and achievements. You only limit your potential by dwelling on your weaknesses or what you don't do well. We all have greatness within us just waiting to be unleashed on the world.

One of life's glorious things is to understand and value our gifts and attributes, and then reapply them positively to others. As personal coach Rachelle Disbennett-Lee says, "We may want to turn our gifts into a profession, or use our gifts in our volunteer work or a hobby. We don't have to make money with our gifts to have them be of value. Using them to make our lives and others' richer is priceless." I repeat, go to your strengths—go to the sound of the bugles!

SEVEN JUMPSTARTS TO FOCUS ON YOUR STRENGTHS

1. **Make a list, check it twice.** Clearly define your strengths. Remember, strengths require doing things well repeatedly with a sense of passion and joy.

2. **Take personal stock.** Look inside yourself to make sure your strengths are aligned with your work, passion, and true purpose in life.

3. **Accent the positive.** Go to your strengths rather than patchwork quilting your weaknesses. You only limit your potential obsessing over things you don't do well.

4. **Search for the zone.** Hone in on those strong moments when you were at your absolute peak performance. Remember what you were doing and how it felt. Make it real. Just because you're good at something doesn't necessarily mean you should be doing it for a living.

5. **Use it or lose it.** Make sure you fully utilize your talents and skills. Don't be afraid to measure yourself against others with similar strengths.

6 **Don't get sucked in.** Far too many people squander their life stuck in the wrong job or position. Put yourself in position to go for greatness by utilizing your strengths and skill-sets.

7 **Go forward by looking back.** Sometimes, to go forward we have to look back. Identifying your strengths can often be found in your childhood. What did you love doing as a kid? Did you draw finger paintings on the fridge? Did you sing songs or tell stories? What did you get straight A's in at school?

Executive Summary

In business, the market section of the planning process recognizes market trends and takes action steps to address them in order to begin the first phase of finding the company's true niche. On the business front, the market section also examines the strengths and weaknesses of the competition.

Just like the market section of the plan, we as individuals need to do some self-analysis and take an overall snapshot of ourselves. We should initiate a personal-situation review. It is very important that we define our personal strengths and weaknesses. However, our major focus should be to capitalize on our strengths and manage our weaknesses. We excel in life by maximizing our strengths, not by trying to make a patchwork quilt to camouflage our weaknesses. So, know and respect your strengths. "Go to the sound of the bugles."

Time to Reflect

Think about how you can best capitalize on your strengths and manage your weaknesses.

CHAPTER 3

Identify the Target Customer

Discovering the Authentic You

It's never too late to be what you might have been.
— George Eliot

In life, this section is all about discovering the authentic you... the you at your very core.

In the business world, truly authentic companies define their target audience and hone in on whom they are trying to reach, so they can eventually deliver the products and services that their customers really want and need.

Many companies define the target audience based on traditional demographics —gender, age, income, and education. This research helps to narrow down the focus to the most lucrative segment of the market for a company's product or service.

But truly effective target-customer profiles also include psychographics—the psyche beyond the numbers. For example, a person can be thirty-five years old but think like they are fifty. A family can make $50,000 per year but spend like they make $150,000. Think about men's cologne. The product is clearly designed for men, but the end customer (purchaser) is frequently a woman, buying the product for the man in her life. When crafting a marketing strategy, men's cologne manufacturers consider targeting not only the end user (probably a man) but also the purchaser (frequently a woman).

One of the best examples of looking beyond traditional demographic data was the introduction of the Ford Mustang. When it first came out in 1964, Ford's Lee Iacocca positioned the Mustang as a sporty, affordable graduation gift for young adults. But what happened in reality was that the dad flipped the keys of his station wagon to his kid and drove off in the sporty Mustang, thinking and feeling twenty-five years younger! Much like the example of men's cologne, Ford marketing executives discovered—after the fact—that their target customer was indeed multi-faceted. When identifying a target customer, companies must search deeper, delve into the customer's psyche, and look for the true meaning beyond the numbers.

The combined use of traditional demographics and psychographics is the best way to construct an authentic profile of a target audience. It also provides direction to product development, communications, advertising, sales, and the rest of the elements of a good marketing plan. Without a clear target-customer profile, a company may waste effort and resources developing products and creating communications to reach people outside the profile. Companies must take care not to stray too far from their core target audience in an effort to extend the reach of their brand. A wide focus targets more people, but speaks to no one in particular, and customers of all kinds will question the authenticity of the watered-down message. A company must take great care in defining its true customer base and know when enough is enough when attempting to extend their brand beyond the initial target focus.

Authenticity Is Key

In today's fast-paced digital media world, consumers are rapidly moving towards brands that are perceived to be authentic. Purveying goods and services is no longer enough. Today's consumer is drawn to real, purpose-driven goods like green products, organic foods and functional outdoor clothing that can actually withstand the rigorous elements of the great outdoors. David Lewis and David Bridges in their book *The Soul of the Consumer* argue that developed countries are moving from "scarcity to abundance – from abundance to authenticity." Indeed, I believe that authenticity ranks right up there with quality as the most important marketing criteria.

Bill Green, in his authentic branding article in *Fast Company* magazine underscores the four major elements needed for a brand to be truly authentic. I will briefly summarize here.

- ▶ **Sense of Place** – The champagne region of France gives bubbly like Dom Perignon a special cachet. That's one of the reasons authentic French champagne is far more expensive that other white sparkling wines. Similarly, Samuel Adams beer was born in Boston, which gives it an almost patriotic revolutionary appeal.

- ▶ **Pure Passion** – CEOs like Apple's late Steve Jobs, Jeff Bezos of Amazon, and Richard Branson of Virgin have a total passion for what they do every day. They lead with their hearts as well as their heads. Their passion for their products and services overflows to their customers who feel engaged and connected to these leaders and therefore to their brands.

▶ **Purpose** – Today's consumers have to believe that the company has a purpose beyond just making money. They seek out genuine companies that are also trying to make meaning. Companies like Nature's Path, Caribou Coffee, Whole Foods, LL Bean, Tom's of Maine, and Ben and Jerry's resonate with their customers because they have a mission of purpose beyond making profits.

▶ **Integrity** – Car companies like Hyundai are now giving what amounts to lifetime warranties. Nordstrom's will take every purchase back for a refund without question or argument. These are companies that back up their word, and do what they say they are going to do – no questions asked.

Sometimes however, it is tough to determine what is real and what is disingenuous. Is there any wonder why people are still a bit skeptical of McDonald's new healthy menu after serving us a lifetime of fatty burgers and fries? When Clorox entered the green market with its Green Works brand, backed by the Sierra Club, it raised a few eyebrows. Are they willing to admit that all their other Clorox products beyond Green Works are unhealthy for our environment?

However, as Tim Manners points out in his *Fast Company* article on "Patagonia Values," there are some exceptions to the laws of authenticity. As Manners observes, "It is indeed possible for some brands under some conditions to embrace values that are at odds with their established images and make a success of it." Manners, cites Patagonia as an exception to the authenticity rule. Patagonia has moved away from its long established roots in mountain sports and is shifting half of its production into water sports. Skeptics raised their eyebrows, but Patagonia's success is based on the authentic thinking of this seemingly contrarian move. Patagonia's founder, Yvon Chouinard declared, "We are getting into the surf market because it's never going to snow again and the waves are going to get bigger and bigger." In essence, Patagonia has repositioned its marketing strategy based on the assumption that our planet is melting. Patagonia's premise is remarkably authentic because it comes from the genuine environmentalist roots of its founder. Chouinard has rolled the company dice on what he truly believes. You can't get more genuine and believable than that.

Eddie Bauer has long made outdoor-inspired apparel for the casual lifestyle. People familiar with the brand make the distinction between Eddie Bauer and more gear-oriented brands like The North Face with the quip, "If you can die doing it, it's probably not Eddie Bauer." Though designed for less extreme use than some competitors, the brand built its success by proving itself to be an authentic outdoor-apparel brand name with its legitimate link to the outdoor lifestyle. In fact, the company's founder and namesake started an outdoor sporting goods store in Seattle in 1920. An avid outdoorsman, Bauer nearly froze to death while on expedition and the experience inspired him to design a unique goose-down quilted jacket, which he later patented.

Years later, the company maintains a link to this outdoor heritage and has usually paid the consequences when it strayed too far from the brand's authentic roots. In the late 1990s, Eddie Bauer de-emphasized the more rugged outdoor roots of the brand and positioned itself against successful casual and office-attire retailers Banana Republic and J. Crew. As Eddie Bauer sales slumped, the fast-fading retailer filed for bankruptcy and was eventually acquired by Golden Gate Capital who rapidly returned the company to its authentic mountaineering roots. In short, the company is focusing less on its multiple colored t-shirts and is aiming to recapture its frozen tundra origins. Further adding to its great outdoor legitimacy, the company hired a dream team of famous mountain climbers to design the chain's First Accent line of pants, backpacks and products designed to withstand the rigors of the wilderness. The company's new collection underscores its legacy of making products that offer both function and performance. Clearly, Eddie Bauer's loyal customers were delighted that the company returned to its authentic roots.

Porsche is another company deeply rooted in authenticity. In the early days of the company, founder Ferdinand Porsche couldn't find the car of his dreams, so he built one himself with integrity of design and high performance in mind. Knowing what the car is capable of doing is an integral part of Porsche owner's mystique. Most Porsche customers know they will never really push the car to its full performance and speed limits. But for Porsche drivers that contributes greatly to their joy of driving. It's amazing to note that the company estimates that 70% of all Porsches built are still on the road today.

Good companies also understand the importance of authenticity in product and marketing messages when it comes to reaching their target customer. One company actually names their product to reflect its authenticity. Majestic Athletic, a licensed supplier of replica jerseys and merchandise to Major League Baseball and the National Basketball Association, launched a new product line called the MLB Authentic Collection. The Authentic Collection is a line of apparel identical to what is worn on the field by all thirty Major League Baseball clubs, including jackets, jerseys, uniforms, batting jerseys, outerwear, turtlenecks, T-shirts, and fleece. For longtime baseball fans that have endured cheap and substandard facsimile caps and jerseys, Majestic's Authentic Collection is a welcome change. Majestic clearly understands the desire of baseball fans to wear the exact same jerseys and hats that their favorite players wear on the field. The fact that they name the collection Authentic is a powerful gesture of this commitment to their customers. The net result is the company's Authentic Collection has achieved record sales and growth.

Sweet Simplicity

Coca-Cola is one of the world's most recognized brand names. But as early as the 1950s, rival Pepsi started to make inroads on the perennial soda beverage king. Pepsi used lower prices and youthful advertising campaigns, but nothing was as effective as the taste issue. In blind tests run by both Pepsi and Coke, consumers consistently preferred the taste of Pepsi basically because Pepsi is much sweeter. At first try, people would get a smoother taste with Pepsi on a sip-by-sip basis. Coke, meanwhile, had never changed its formula in over ninety years of existence. But market research made Coke consider the unthinkable: change the taste. They did taste tests and ran focus groups, and the findings seemed to support changing the taste. In retrospect they asked their customers every question in the book except the only one they really needed to ask: "If we took away Coca-Cola and gave you New Coke, would you accept it?"

Well, the answer can be found in most marketing textbooks. Consumers made it clear—both vocally and in their actions—that they wanted the original formula, and seventy-seven days later they brought Classic Coke back. Acknowledging the consumers' power in the marketplace, Coke learned that its customers' love of the classic formula went beyond taste—they clearly loved the authenticity of the brand as well. And as soon as the company tinkered with the formula in an effort to expand the appeal, the core target customers rejected the new product immediately. However, by returning to the simpler, original formula, Coke once again became "the real thing." Today, Coke capitalizes on the simplicity, heritage, and "classic" nature of its brand. It learned the hard way that less is often more.

> *We all wear masks and the time comes when we cannot remove them without removing some of our own skin.*
>
> — Andre Berthiaume

Discovering the Authentic You

It's not the mountain we conquer—but ourselves.

—Sir Edmund Hillary

Be True To Yourself

On a personal level, the target customer you're trying to identify is the real you—the authentic you. The you at your very core. The you that's left when you strip away the veneer. The you that resonates when you listen to your inner voice. The you that emerges from the pit of your stomach saying, "Hey, this just doesn't feel right—this is not the real me. This is not what I want to be."

But how do you find yourself? How do you set out to discover the real you? How do you capture the true essence of your being? An authentic life is best built from the inside out—by taking a personal inventory. To discover our authenticity we need to ask ourselves these courageous questions: What matters most to me? Who do I need to be to give my life more meaning or purpose? You find your authenticity when you carve out a life that is in harmony with what matters most. When you accomplish this, you are well on the road to unmasking yourself and becoming the authentic person you were always meant to be.

Be who you are and say what you feel, because those who mind don't matter, and those who matter don't mind.

—Dr. Seuss

When you live authentically you're being true to yourself because you're living a life that is aligned and in sync with your purpose. Being authentic means you reflect your value system, your true essence—your core beliefs. When you live an authentic life, there is no need to keep up with the next-door neighbor. There's only the need to stay true to yourself and honor your true essence.

Authenticity is staying connected to the truth of who you are—not what others perceive you to be. When I was about to choose a graduate school, my dad wanted me to be a lawyer. I almost went to law school out of sheer respect for my father. But deep down I knew I could only be a good lawyer—never a great one. I thought I'd be great arguing my case in front of a jury but merely OK at doing the nitty-gritty research and paying attention to the details that are required of a great lawyer.

I passed on being a lawyer because it just wasn't me.

To discover the real you, you need to be like an archaeologist. You need to dig deep and delve into your own psyche to discover who you are, and importantly, who you are not. According to author Dr. Dwight "Ike" Reighard, in his book *Discovering Your North Star*, "We experience significant stress pretending to be someone we're not. It's like trying to hold balloons under water. We may be able to wrestle one or two beneath the surface, but sooner or later one pops up... usually with intensity."

> *The ability to simplify means to eliminate the unnecessary so the necessary may speak.*
> —Hans Hoffman

Less Is More

In order to connect with our authenticity, we might also do well to simplify our lives, not make them more complicated. Remember, a sculptor creates a beautiful statue by chipping away at those parts of the marble stone that are not needed. Maybe we should manage less stuff, not more. Create fewer options—not so many that we fail to exercise any of them. It might do us all well to concentrate less on the things we'd like to acquire and more on who we'd like to become.

Shortly after his wife died, the late comedian and satirist George Carlin wrote eloquently on the concept of enough-ness and the paradox of our time:

- ▶ "The paradox of our time in history is that we have taller buildings, but shorter tempers; wider freeways, but narrower viewpoints; we spend more, but have less; we buy more, but enjoy it less."
- ▶ "We have bigger houses and smaller families; more conveniences, but less time; we have more degrees, but less sense; more knowledge, but less judgment; more experts, but more problems; more medicine, but less wellness."
- ▶ "We drink too much, smoke too much, spend too recklessly, laugh too little, drive too fast, get angry too quickly, stay up too late, get up too tired, read too seldom, watch TV too much, and pray too seldom."
- ▶ "We have multiplied our possessions, but reduced our values. We talk too much, love too seldom, and hate too often. We've learned how to make a living, but not a life; we've added years to life, not life to years."

One of the keys to living a fulfilled life—a life centered on purpose—is realizing when enough is enough. In life as well as business, we once again see that less sometimes is more. William Blake once wrote, "You never know what is enough, until you know what is more than enough." Even in relationships, sometimes more ends up being less. Although I can't remember the singer for the life of me, there's this song that goes something like this, "I wanted more from you and now I'm less."

> *We all wear masks and the time comes when we cannot remove them, without removing some of our own skin.*
>
> —André Berthiaume

Masking the Real You

Let's face it: most of us are less than honest when it comes to letting people know who we really are. In fact, some of us wear masks pretending to be somebody we're not. In Ancient Greek and Roman theater, men wore masks to play different roles, including that of a woman. In fact, the word "hypocrite" comes from the Greek word hypocrites, which means actor, one who plays a role, pretends, or wears a mask. Of course, one definition of mask is a device that wholly or partially conceals the face. It is interesting to note that even the word "person" is derived from the Greek word meaning mask or role played by an actor. OK, so where am I taking you with all this? Simple: All of us wear masks at one time or another—pretending to be somebody we're not. Shakespeare said, "God has given you one face and you make yourself another."

When I was a very young man, I was once told that I sometimes wore a comical mask to hide my true intensity. Some bullies wear tough-guy masks to hide their innate sensitivity. Others wear a frightful mask to hide the fact that they are frightened to death. Some people wear the mask of a warrior when in reality they lack the courage to fight for themselves and stand up for what they truly believe. When we mask ourselves we are pretending to be someone we're not. When we wear a mask, we're living a lie—a life of pretense. A life in which the mask you wear hides your true face to the world. Nathaniel Hawthorne wrote in his famous novel *The Scarlet Letter*, "No man for any considerable period can wear one face to himself and another to the multitude without finally getting bewildered as to which may be true."

According to Bill Treasurer, author of the *Right Risk*, there are real benefits in living an authentic life: "The benefit of being our authentic selves is that instead of wasting time pretending to be someone we're not, we have more impassioned energy to get on with the business of living. Living a life of authenticity represents the end to an exhausting game of make-believe." What real benefit is there in playing hide-and-seek? We only waste our energy trying to be somebody we're not.

> *It is better to be hated for who you are than to be liked for something you are not.*
> — André Gide

This "peek-a-boo, I see you" mask thing just doesn't cut it. We need to take off our mask and reveal our authentic self to the outside world. To find our true meaning in life we must do more than put on a good face—we must become who we were meant to be. Using a biblical metaphor, it's not so much "I am who I am" but rather, "I am the me I'm meant to be." Gene Mage, president of Soaring Oaks Consulting, puts it into perspective: "Tragically, too many people wake up one day, look in the mirror, and no longer recognize the person looking back. If you have to give up who you really are to get somewhere, perhaps it's somewhere you ought not to go." The point is simple: you don't have to give up who you really are to get where you want to go. As Steve Jobs of Apple and Pixar fame asked in his historic Stanford University commencement speech, "What good is it if we are wired for success, but short circuit our souls in the process?" Being the real you will get you there sooner because the real you is more aligned with your true purpose in life.

> *Man's main task in life is to give birth to himself to become what he potentially is.*
> — Erich Fromm

Rediscovering Your Authentic Self

As a baby, we are born without masks; we are as authentic and genuine as a breath of fresh air. We even smell pure and clean without the aid of foo-foo perfumed scents. Dr. Phil tells us, "Your authentic self is the you at your absolute core. It goes beyond what you do for a living. It's comprised of all those things that make you unique."

Authenticity is all about integrity of being. Bill Treasurer reminds us that "throughout history, a well known prescription for personal well-being is: 'Be who you must be.'"

> *To be what we are and to become*
> *capable of becoming is the only end in life.*
>
> —Robert Louis Stevenson

What are some of the traits that characterize a truly authentic person?

1. **Staying in the moment.** You are authentic when you listen first and hear another person's point of view before interpreting them with your own thoughts and proclamations.

2. **Echo a consistent voice.** You don't say things to one person that you wouldn't say to another. Don't be the type of person who proclaims, "Do what I say, not what I do."

3. **Show humility.** I found that when I give lectures on my book, people resonate with the fact that I am on the same journey as the reader – human warts and all.

4. **Integrity.** Simply put, authentic people do what they say they are going to do. They try to do the right thing even if it's hard and they might lose face.

There are certain celebrity types that would make up my "all genuine" team, beyond the obvious authentically all-star stalwarts such as Oprah Winfrey, Tom Hanks, and Robert Redford. Former Monday Night Football commentator, John Madden is admired by all for explaining the game in a genuine way that all of us can readily understand. Rachel Ray shows us how to make great meals that won't break our piggy bank. Actor Michael J. Fox comes to mind as an activist for Parkinson's disease that he himself contracted years earlier. Jon Stewart, the ever popular host of the "Daily Show" believes that most network news shows on traditional media outlets have become a mere parody of themselves. Although a staunch Democrat, Stewart has become an equal opportunity offender. He does not hesitate to call out a Democratic president when he doesn't live up to our expectations and core values. Stewart's ability to tell it like it is in a satirical way makes him one of America's most influential and authentic people. All this genuineness comes from a person who started out hosting a comedy fake news show. Who makes your all-genuine team? Most of us don't have to look outside our own family. My mother, bless her soul, was widely admired because she told it like it is, sprinkled with an authentic sense of empathy and caring.

It doesn't take long to get booted off the all-genuine team. Before his late

November crash of 2009, the world was seemingly Tiger Wood's oyster. He was truly a marketer's dream: a champion golfer and well-grounded family man off the course. Corporate sponsors like Nike, Accenture, Gillette, and AT&T happily jumped to invest millions in Wood's so-called "squeaky clean, totally under control image." When it was revealed that Tiger was cavorting with a harem of mistresses outside of his marriage – his world seemed to crumble at his feet. His wife divorced him. Some corporate sponsors dropped Tiger like a hot potato. Those that didn't drop him lessened his exposure. His disingenuous mask was revealed for the entire world to see. When he returned to golf a humbled man, he no longer seemed unbeatable. In fact, he lost his status as the world's number one ranked golfer. The good thing about Tiger is that he no longer has to live a lie. He can take off his mask. Stay tuned, Tiger's story is far from over. The world loves comebacks, both on and off the course – especially, if the story is authentic.

> *Success is not the key to happiness.*
> *Happiness is the key to success.*
> — Herman Cain

Happiness and Personal Enrichment

An integral part of being the real you is being satisfied with what you have. Harriet Rubin, in an article in *Fast Company* magazine, refers to the U.S.A. as the "United States of Anxiety." We're among the best-paid people in the world, the best fed, and among the highest educated. Yet our divorce rates continue to soar, our suicide rates are rising, and experts tell us there's no real correlation between having money and being happy. In fact, research consistently indicates that although the United States ranks among the world's wealthiest nations, we are not among the leaders when it comes to overall happiness of our population. In fact, a *Forbes* magazine survey taken in 2010 ranks the United States 12th in its poll of the world's most happy countries – just slightly ahead of Turkmenistan! Scandinavian countries like Denmark, Finland, Norway, and Sweden are ranked on the top of the happiness charts. The likely reason is that these countries have their basic needs largely taken care of by their socially conscious governments. But daily happiness also has a lot to do with how a person's social and psychological needs are being met. How else could one explain that a relatively poor country like Costa Rica, currently ranks 6th among the world's most happy countries?

In Costa Rica, there is a high premium placed on social interaction and community engagement. Individuals tend to be happy, regardless of how much money they have stashed away. Happiness experts seem to agree that once your basic needs are met, additional income does little to raise your sense of happiness. In fact, happiness scholar Dr. Martin Seligman in his classic book *Authentic Happiness* cites there are three major components to achieve a happy life. The first is pleasure (think joy and healthy relationships). The second is engagement (think depth of interaction with family and friends). The third is purpose (think creating a mission and meaning, higher than yourself). Among the three components, Seligman believes that engagement and purpose are by far the most important to achieving happiness and a personally enriched life.

A less scholarly formula for happiness, but no less wiser is offered by Scottish writer Alexander Chalmers who offered this sage advice: "The three essentials to happiness are something to do, someone to love, and something to hope for!" It all boils down to this: If you have to ask: "Am I happy?" you're probably not.

So, happiness is not about accumulating or consuming more stuff—it's enjoying what we have. It's about living fuller lives. It's not about becoming rich—it's about living a life of personal enrichment.

How do you really know when enough is really enough? Consider the story of Alexander the Great, who visited his good friend and mentor Diogenes after a major victory on the battlefield. When asked what his future plans were, Alexander claimed that after he conquered Greece he would go on to conquer Asia Minor and then the entire world. Diogenes then queried, "And then what?" Alexander said that after all the conquering was accomplished, he planned to relax and enjoy himself. To which Diogenes responded, "Why not save yourself a lot of trouble by relaxing and enjoying yourself now?" Obviously, Alexander never really quite got the point. He died two years later at the age of thirty-two—supposedly from malaria caught on the battlefield.

I always thought that once I made a certain amount of money, I would be free to let the authentic me out in the open. But I learned, like others before me, the more money you make, the more you need to make—it's a never-ending cycle. Even if you become a multimillionaire, you're reminded, "money doesn't buy what it used to." In fact, TNS Financial Services reported as of mid-2011 there were nearly 10,500,000 households in America with a net worth of at least $1 million or more. How many of them thought they had enough money?

Many of us are on a monetary treadmill… and when it comes to money, we don't know when to get off. The more we have, the more we want. And having more isn't enough—unless someone else has less. University of Southern California economic historian Richard Easterlin describes this dilemma as the "Easterlin Paradox"—according to him, because we judge ourselves in relation to others, any real jump in income makes little difference in how we feel about ourselves. So sometimes, the more we get, the less happy we become.

Dr. Dan Baker talks about the concept of enough-ness in his book *What Happy People Know*. "At Canyon Ranch, I often hear people talk about hunting—for diamonds, planes, houses, paintings, and boats—but what I really hear beneath the surface of their conversation are people talking about hunting down the big prize that will finally free them from two basic survivalist fears that have haunted people from the Stone Age: the fears of not having enough and of not being enough."

> *Success is getting what you want.*
> *Happiness is wanting what you get.*
> —Dave Gardner

However, when it comes to defining true or authentic wealth, things may be changing for the better. Authors Ed Keller and Jon Berry provide a glimpse of hope when they talk about an emerging, powerful new leadership class of target consumers called the "Influentials." The Influentials are comprised of twenty-one million people whose thoughts, behavior, and lifestyle patterns influence the rest of our country. They are profiled as college-educated, married homeowners with solid jobs. They read a lot, exercise, and tend to be volunteers. The subculture of this influential group is explored by Keller and Berry in their book, *The Influentials: One American in Ten Tells the Other Nine, How to Vote, Where to Eat, and What to Buy*. In their book, some of the most important issues facing these Influentials are: "What matters most?" and "Am I being true to myself?" At the bottom of the list were four issues: impressing others, status, wealth, and power. The Influentials are not obsessed with keeping up with the Joneses. "When it comes to acquiring stuff," said Barry, "the key criteria is what is going to be engaging and interesting, rather than accumulating badges and status symbols."

Author Margaret Young feels that a lot of us live our lives backward. We try to acquire more money to buy more things so that we'll be happy—when in reality, the process works in reverse. According to Young, "We must first be who we really are in order to have what we want." Antoine de St. Exupéry said, "Perfection is achieved not when there's nothing else to add but when there's nothing left to take away." Our true essence is only revealed when we strip away the veneer and get down to our basic foundation—our true values.

> It's better to be on the lower rung of a ladder you want to be on than to be midway up a ladder you don't.
> —*The Office* TV Show

It's Never Too Late to Be Authentic

Think about it: have you been putting your own dreams on hold to make someone else's dream a reality? Do you use your pending mortgage payments as a reason not to move on the things that matter most to you? Do you use the emotional security of your kids as an excuse not to become who you were meant to be? Do you wear a mask and pretend to be someone you're not? Don't put the real you on the back burner. You come alive when you let the real you shine through.

Jungian analyst Nathan Schwartz-Salant said, "Some people feel they might have been a different person, a better person, if they had gone another route." Harriet Rubin adds this insight from her article in *Fast Company* magazine, "You feel the need to justify the choices you've made—so you end up wanting to destroy not who you are but who you never became."

Being authentic is clearly a matter of choice. Once again, Bill Treasurer hits the nail on the head: "The Bible tells us that 'many are called but few are chosen.' I see it differently. I think that all are called, but few choose." When you choose to be authentic, you are well on your way to becoming the person you were always meant to be.

In act one, scene three of Shakespeare's *Hamlet*, Lord Polonius uttered his now-famous words "This above all, to thine own self be true." Don't put the real you eternally on hold. Be who you are. Be authentic to your very core and the world will rally around you. When you live an authentic life, you can look at yourself in the mirror and say, "Now here's a person worthy of my own respect."

> The greatest way to live with honor in this world is to be what we pretend to be
> —Socrates

Being truly authentic essentially comes down to this. The more honest you can be with yourself and others as to who you really are, the more likely you are to create a fulfilling and meaningful life—a life that is in synchronicity and harmony with your true purpose. Author Suzanne Zoglio urges us not to deny our inner truth. "Denying inner truth is like trying to keep the lid on a pressure cooker that has built up too much steam. Try as you will, you can't contain it." If we want to live authentically, we cannot mask who we are deep down inside our souls.

SEVEN JUMPSTARTS TO GET IN TOUCH WITH YOUR AUTHENTIC SELF

1. **Don't try to mask yourself.** Don't deny who you are. Don't wear a mask pretending to be someone you're not. Stand up for who you really are.

2. **Don't put your trust in "a broken compass".** Don't send yourself false information – hone in on the real you. As Dr. Phil asserts, "Relying on information from your fictional self means you're putting your trust in a broken compass."

3. **Be true to yourself.** Don't try to be somebody that others want you to be. You don't want to be someone you're not just to fit in with the crowd and please others.

4. **Listen to your gut.** Your inner voice, more often than not, will lead you to the trough of authenticity. When something just doesn't feel right – it probably isn't right for you.

5. **Align yourself with your core values.** Align yourself with what really matters most and get in sync with your core values. Follow your own path, not the path that other people chose for you.

6. **Less is more.** Concentrate less on things you'd like to acquire and more on who you'd like to become. Strip away the veneer and peel all the way down to the real you.

7. **It's never too late.** Authenticity is clearly a matter of choice. It's never too late to become the person you were destined to be. Let the real you shine through and your life will flourish.

Executive Summary

In business circles the target customer section hones in on who the company is trying to reach with its product or service. This customer profile deals not only with demographics but also psychographics—namely, the true meaning or authenticity behind the numbers. A company must take great care in defining its true customer and needs to know when "enough is enough" in attempting to extend their brand beyond the initial core-customer focus.

On a personal level, the target consumer you're trying to reach is the real you—the authentic you. Not the you behind the mask, but the you that is aligned with your true calling and purpose. We need to be like archaeologists and dig deep into our psyche to discover who we are and what would give our life more meaning. In order to know who we are, it is important to know who we are not and what we need less of in our life. Our lifestyle is chock-full of stuff, but more stuff doesn't seem to make us happier. True happiness is not getting what you want… it's wanting what you get. You can't put the real you on the back burner. Shakespeare said it best in his play *Hamlet*: "This above all, to thine own self be true." When we look in the mirror we want to be able to say, "Now here's a person worthy of my own respect."

Time to Reflect

Are you currently the person you were meant to be?

CHAPTER 4

Launch Your Strategy

Finding Your Niche–and Daring to Risk

*It's not enough to stare up the steps.
We must step up the stairs.*
—Vance Havner

Implementing an active strategy is a vitally important element in both business and life. It's the part that sets the overall tone and direction. Strategy dictates those action steps that a company needs to take going forward. You can come up with all the bright ideas and exciting dreams you want, but without a strategy to implement them and courage to take the first step, your goals in business or life simply won't be accomplished.

There are literally hundreds of books written about corporate strategy. Suffice it to say, a good strategy should focus on the following five major points. All of these points can easily be mirrored in our personal lives as well.

1 **Keep it simple.** Everybody in your company should understand the direction in which the company is headed and sing off the same sheet of music. For example, all McDonald's employees are aware that the company is now headed in a healthy menu direction.

2 **Carve out your own rightful niche.** Companies like Seventh Generation, Method, and Planet have carved out a niche in the environmentally safe green household cleaning sector.

3 **Offer a unique competence.** Apple, Google, Harley Davidson, and Facebook offer a unique competence and aura that allows them to be heard above the competitive noise.

4 **Offer a clarion call to action.** A good strategy should evoke a clarion call to action. Nike's advertising tagline "Just Do it" urges you to get off your butt and get going.

5 Take the right risk. The best strategy in the world is useless unless you are willing to take the right risk and put your plan into action. Google, for instance, took the right risk by repositioning themselves from just a search company to one of the biggest media and advertising companies in the world.

A good example of a strong strategy is found with the rental car company Avis, whose "We try harder" approach was understood by everyone in the company—from the person who cleaned the car to the person who sold the rental agreement. The Avis strategy would never have worked unless all facets of the company reached out to actually serve customers better than its number-one competitor—Hertz. Avis had the fortitude to stay the course and proudly proclaim its number-two status in sales while taking over the number-one spot in customer service.

Unique Competence: Where's the Beef?

The Wendy's hamburger chain developed a strategy in the late 1970s that put it on the map at a time when arguably there was no need for yet another fast-food burger franchise. With the hamburger landscape dominated by McDonald's and Burger King, Wendy's did its market research and found that of the billions of burgers being served by their mammoth competitors, none offered a large beef patty familiar to anyone who was old enough to have enjoyed an oversized delicacy at the corner drugstore counter. Recognizing this, Wendy's strategic initiative was to publicize the company's oversize burger that, in fact, exceeded the size of the bun. Wendy's executed this strategy with an advertising campaign that saw an elderly woman—confounded by what is obviously a competitor's diminutive burger—exclaim, "Where's the beef?"

In a nod to the generation that actually consumed large-size burgers at the corner drugstore, the campaign amplified what Wendy's saw so clearly in their market survey (billions of small burgers served) and at the same time promoted their ample-size offering. Wendy's took its unique competence into consideration as it found an open niche for that competence in the crowded burger landscape. But the firm did take a risk in terms of timing. In the late 1970's there was a fitness boom under way, and people were rediscovering chicken as the price of beef rose. Despite the far-from-perfect timing, Wendy's went into action anyway and successfully executed their strategy. The company took the right risk and it paid off handsomely with increased sales and profits.

Build It and They Will Come

Build-a-Bear Workshop's strategy was to build a close-up and unique relationship with kids of all ages – from the kids themselves, to their parents and grandparents. The company provided a "make your own stuffed animal" retailing experience second to none. Build-a-Bear Workshop guests got to stuff, fluff, dress, accessorize, and appoint names to their Teddy Bears and other stuffed animals. The company's strategy tapped into experienced based retailing that capitalizes on the fun and wide appeal of stuffed animals. The company also launched an online venture called Build-a-Bearville, which uses a virtual world to engage kids in programs and games that feature its upcoming stuffed product offerings. Build-a-Bear took all the right strategy risks. So much so, its competition had to just grin and bear it.

The Right Risk in Changing Strategies

The United States Army had the courage to shift from its famous strategy of "Be All You Can Be" to "An Army of One" to "Army Strong." The strategic thinking here was that the "Be All You Can Be" strategy focused mostly on physical aspects of being in the Army. While the "Army of One" eventually lacked the teamwork element so important to our armed forces, "Army Strong" signified a shift to a triad combination of mental, physical and teamwork strength. In short, the Army now wants to promote the complete soldier. Sound in mind, body and spirit.

The TED Conference is another prime example of taking the right risk and shifting strategic priorities. The company has shifted from promoting ideas only at its very expensive annual live event to spreading thought-provoking concepts online via its famous 18-minute video presentations. What started as a live event only has become what *Fast Company* magazine describes as potentially the "New Global Classroom of the 21st Century." The most highly regarded TED speakers have their 18-minute talks posted online and on YouTube, many of which have clocked more than five million viewers globally. The TED Conference not only represents a Harvard case study in strategic repositioning – higher institutions across the country might learn a thing or two about online education.

Strategy and Risk Keep Nike on Track

A good strategic statement keeps a company on track and keeps it from straying from its stated purpose. Just a few well chosen, inspiring words can galvanize an entire company to all pull the same oar in the right direction. Athletic shoe manufacturer Nike had a simple brand strategy that was clearly understood by everyone in the company: "Authentic Athletic Performance." It guided the integrity and purity of everything the company executed; nothing was to be contrived. This strategy reached all the way to the models Nike used in their product catalogs: if they were modeling running shoes, their models had better be accomplished track athletes. All products and services associated with Nike were to be athletic, not for leisure use. This strategic directive prevented possibly ill-fated ventures into casual and "sports-inspired" dress shoes. Finally, every Nike product had to exude world-class performance and meet the demands of accomplished athletes. This strategy was often expensive and complex to execute and implement. But it did serve to guide the company and kept it from deviating from its stated niche positioning.

Perhaps the best articulation of this simple strategy was in the Nike advertising slogan, "Just Do It." These three simple words captured the state of mind of a world-class athlete, who wins not only under the bright lights of competition but on dark foggy mornings when the alarm goes off for the day's first workout. "Just Do It" captured the hearts, minds, and souls of the accomplished athlete—and the weekend jogger. It was a call to action in executing the company's overall strategic initiative. Nike recognizes that unless a company is willing to take the right risk with its brand, it risks not being the brand of choice in the future. So, Nike just did it.

The most important element in launching an effective strategy is the implementation. Clearly, nothing gets done without a clarion call to action. But more often than not, action requires a degree of risk. The commonsense point to make here is that prior to formulating a strategic plan to take action, a good measure of due diligence is recommended. This separates recklessness from taking a calculated risk that may spell the difference between business failure and success. However, when a company does its due diligence—surveys the marketplace, measures risk—it must pull the ripcord! The emphasis on taking action cannot be overstated. At some point, every company realizes that the absolute perfect time to do something will probably never present itself. Somebody has to do something, not just try to do something.

Successful companies are not afraid to take risks, but good companies take calculated or right risks—risks that play to their strengths. They take risks that are well within the wheelhouse of their core competency. Great companies understand that the right risk can reap profitable rewards. General George Patton barked; "A good plan vigorously executed right now is far better than a perfect plan executed next week."

> It is not enough to stare up the steps.
> We must step up the stairs.
>
> — Vance Havner

Finding Your Niche–and Daring to Risk

Your Personal Mission Statement

In life as well as business, we need to take our unique competence—namely our strengths—and utilize them to find our personal niche or true purpose in life. As we discussed in chapter one, discovering your personal niche allows you to answer some of life's key questions. Why am I here? What is my mission in life? What drives me? What really matters most?

In a sense, your life strategy is your personal mission statement of where you want to take your life and what action you need to take to get there.

In chapter two, you identified your unique competencies. And in chapter three you worked to identify your proper niche—where you want to spend more time and effort, and where you don't want to waste your time. This chapter, then, will help you begin to identify a plan (a strategy) to get you from where you are to where you want to be.

> *The smallest of actions is always better than the noblest of intentions.*
>
> —Robin Sharma

A Clear Call to Action: There Is No Try

It's not enough just to know where you want to go in life. You have to have the courage to act so you can actually get there. It's not good enough just to have a mission in life—you need to be actively engaged. You need to be on a mission. You need to be in motion. Writing personal strategy statements that only gather dust in some dark filing cabinet of our den or on your hard drive is not going to cut it here. A strategy is only as good as the implementation. It must be accompanied by action. Eventually, we need to take the leap and have faith that there's a safety net below to catch us.

Implementing your personal strategy requires a clear call to action. You can't just try to do something. Remember the famous scene in *The Empire Strikes Back*? Luke Skywalker crashes his spacecraft in a swamp. He laments to Yoda, the old Jedi warrior, that he'll never get it out. Yoda suggests to Skywalker that he *will* get the spaceship out, by "feeling the Force." To which Skywalker says, "I'll try." To which Yoda counters with his now-classic lines: "Try not. Do. Or do not. There is no try." It's a fact of life that to get at our true purpose and fulfill our personal niche, we need to pull the ripcord. We need to act. Nothing will happen without action. Bodhidharma, a sixth-century Zen Master, said, "All know the way, but few actually walk it." Former British prime minister Benjamin Disraeli said, "Action may not always bring happiness, but there is no happiness without action."

> *We judge ourselves by what we feel capable of doing, while others judge us by what we have already done.*
>
> —Henry Wadsworth Longfellow

How many of us have stayed too long at a job we hated because we didn't have the courage to act? The next thing you know, you've frittered away ten good years of your life—just because you didn't have the guts to make a change. American industrialist Andrew Carnegie said, "As I grow older, I pay less attention to what men say. I just watch what they do."

The truth is we're a society plagued with inaction. How many times have you or someone you know felt stuck in a relationship that was going nowhere, but found it more comfortable not to do anything about it? How many times have we said to ourselves; If only I had done this, or if only I had done that? The godfather of computer entertainment, Nolan Bushnell, said, "The critical ingredient in life is getting off our butt and actually doing something. It's as simple as that. A lot of people have ideas, but there are few who decide to do something about them now. Not tomorrow. Not next week. But today. We can't just contemplate doing things. Our achievement in life is in the actual doing. It's what we actually do in life that makes us who we are."

There's an old Italian proverb that puts it quite succinctly, "It's not enough to aim, you must shoot."

> *To know and not to do is not yet to know.*
>
> —Zen saying

Action Speaks Louder Than Words

We've all heard the expression "Action speaks louder than words" or "He's all talk and no action." It's what we actually do that counts in real life. Be a person of action. Put your wheels in motion. After all, what good is a life plan if you're not going to implement it? The things that separate us from the daydreamers are the things we actually do.

Charles de Gaulle once said, "Deliberation is the work of many people. Action of one alone." You may dream of writing a screenplay or becoming a published author. But are you really willing to do the work and take the action steps necessary to get there? Are you willing to pound the keyboard and actually do the writing? People who achieve their goals are not afraid to act.

I have a doctor friend who absolutely has the Midas touch when it comes to investing in real estate. He has a simple real-estate investing strategy—buy the worst house in the most desired wooded or oceanfront area. He's not afraid to pay the going price for his property, and never got involved with risky sub-prime mortgage loans. When asked how he amassed his real-estate fortune, the doctor's answer was profoundly simple: "When I see the right property, I act. While others are still standing on the sidelines, I sign on the dotted line. It's my ability to take action that has allowed me to amass my fortune in real estate."

A large number of major league baseball players have emerged recently from the beautiful, but poverty-stricken country of Dominican Republic. Dominican players have a saying; "You can't walk off the island!" They know they have to take aggressive action at the plate and hit the ball hard to make it all the way to the big leagues.

Even a clock that does not work is right twice a day.
—Polish Proverb

Sometimes Taking No Action Is Action

The Tao philosophy teaches us a lot about action. It suggests that we observe the heron standing in the water. The bird only moves when it must; it does not move when stillness is more appropriate. Accordingly, there are times when taking no action is an action in and of itself. When billionaire investor Warren Buffett decided not to buy tech stocks during the tech-buying frenzy of the late 1990s, his very non-action turned out to be a positive action (especially when tech stocks took a nosedive by March of 2000). His action was planned non-action.

Heartfelt kudos go out to those who refrained from buying that second home prior to the prime lending mortgage crisis of 2008-2009. Not selling your home in a down real estate market would be another good example of active non-action.

> *You need chaos in your soul*
> *to give birth to a dancing star.*
>
> —Friedrich Nietzsche

Discomfort Leads to Action

Hall of Fame tennis great Billy Jean King used to say, "When you're going for greatness pressure is a privilege."

Sometimes we need to be taken out of our comfort zone in order to finally act. Since I started writing this book, a series of events have taken place that have catapulted me into action on things I've always wanted to do (but always found a way to put on the back burner). First, my father died, an in-my-face reminder of my own mortality. Then, shortly afterward, I realized that my lucrative marketing position was no longer aligned with my true purpose in life. I was suddenly uncomfortable going to work and living a lie. The pit of my stomach was giving me signals that it was time to move on. I now realize that my discomfort caused me to act. My story is still unfolding, but I can see the epilogue clearly in my mind. I no longer have that pit in the middle of my stomach. I am acting on my true purpose and discovering my true self. Every day is an attempt to heed and harness my own advice.

When it comes to taking action, a lot of us are like dazed deer caught in the headlights. We fear making the wrong choice. We fear taking the risk, so we take no action at all. Bandleader Les Brown once said, "You don't have to be great to get started, but you have to get started to be great." Don't wait to get started on the life you've always envisioned for yourself.

> *Yesterday is the past and tomorrow's the future.*
> *Today is a gift – which is why they call it the present.*
>
> —Bill Keane

The Perfect Time Is Now

Eckhart Tolle in his runaway bestselling book entitled *The Power of Now* urges us to stay in the moment. He believes most of us have an endless preoccupation with the past and future, coupled with an unwillingness to honor and engage in the present moment. Tolle believes that the more we focus on the past and future, the more we miss the most precious thing of all: the now. Tolle extols us to "realize deeply that the present moment is all you'll ever have. Make the 'now' the primary focus in your life. Always say yes to the present moment." A Zen embodiment of

Tolle's philosophy would be simply stated: if not now, when? Tolle ardently believes that accessing the power of now and staying in the present moment is the secret sauce to living a truly successful and purposeful life.

For years, I've admired my good friend and business partner Bob Zeichick for his ability to stay engrossed in the present moment. He's learned that silence is a most potent carrier of his presence. Zeichick, in any type of meeting, has the ability to listen carefully to what's being said between the lines. He hears more than just words. He understands that the secret to good communication is to listen to not only what's being said, but to the full range of emotions behind the words. People feel connected to him. That's why when he does speak, people tend to listen to him with high antennas. I'm proud to call him my partner. I'll be even prouder if I can someday emulate his example of staying the moment.

> *You cannot discover new oceans unless you have the courage to lose sight of the shore.*
> —Daniel Abraham

Don't Wait for That Perfect Time

One of life's real tragedies is our fear of committing to action. How many times have you been on the cusp of a decision and found yourself frozen, waiting for the absolutely perfect time to act. The perfect time never seems to arrive. Authors Ron Rubin and Stuart Avery Gold in their book, *Tiger Heart, Tiger Mind*, address the issue of perfect timing. "We tend to put off action, waiting for just the right time and just the right place to act, while the very act of waiting actually pushes desired events away from us. A self-inflicted analysis paralysis."

Sometimes trying to time everything just right can cost us our dreams. Let me share a perfect timing issue I faced a few years ago. Ever since I visited Big Sur in California as a twenty-year-old, I have wanted to live there. Located just twenty-six miles south of Carmel, Big Sur is acknowledged as one of the most beautiful spots on earth. It has a rugged coastline beauty that rivals the best of Scotland, with far better weather. Big Sur offers breathtaking ocean views, especially along the famed U.S. Highway 1. It is not uncommon to have the ocean spray kick high off the rocks and throw a light mist over your shoulder. I still had not been able to fulfill my dream, partly because I'd always waited for the perfect time. At that particular time of my life, there was always a built-in excuse not to live in the land of my dreams.

When interest rates were low, prices seemed too high. When prices were lower, interest rates soared higher. Later, I'll swing back and tell you the rest of the story.

> *The greatest risk in life is to risk nothing.*
> —William Arthur Ward

Taking the Leap

As a college administrator at Texas Wesleyan, William Arthur Ward had a unique perspective on the greatest risks of life when he offered the following advice: "To laugh is to risk appearing the fool. To weep is to risk being called sentimental. To reach out to another is to risk involvement. To expose feelings is to risk showing your true self. To place your ideas and your dreams before the crowd is to risk being naïve. To love is to risk not being loved in return. To live is to risk dying. To hope is to risk despair. To try is to risk failure. But risks must be taken, because the greatest risk in life is to risk nothing."

When I was younger, my attitude was always "take the leap." As we get older, however, we tend to lose some of our youthful exuberance. We tend to look at things more cautiously as we age. It's more like "look before you leap." There's an incident that happened to me several years ago that reinforces this very point. When I was just a kid, I loved diving off the fifteen-meter high-dive platform. It never crossed my mind that I could get hurt. I didn't care much about style points. A perfect swan dive or belly whopper was all the same to me. I dove for the pure joy of it. A strange thing happens, however, when we get older. We lose some of those kid-like, positive qualities that allow us to take risks for the pure exhilaration of it.

One day, I was relaxing at an Olympic-size swimming pool when I heard a young mother screaming in distress. Her five-year-old boy had somehow climbed halfway up a fifteen-meter diving platform and was too frightened to come down. For whatever reason, there was no lifeguard in sight, so I gallantly climbed up the platform and retrieved the boy, taking him to his mother. Almost without thinking, I decided to relive my youth and re-climb the steps to the very top of the diving platform. I wanted to take just one more leap off the high dive—just for the fun of it. However, as I was climbing up the last rungs of the ladder, my mind wandered in ways that never happened when I was a kid full of youth, vim, and vigor. What if I slip and fall off the ladder? It's been so long since I did this—what if I broke my neck? Does my life insurance cover this? How much money do I have in my 401k? All these things entered my mind. When I finally got to the top of the platform, my knees were shaking because the platform seemed twice as high as when I was a kid. Putting all these negative adult thoughts aside, I decided to take the leap. Notice I said leap. I decided at the last second not to dive off the platform but to hold my nose as I jumped feet first into the water. As I emerged safely from the pool, the young mother and others congratulated me for helping her child. Somehow I didn't feel like much of a hero inside. Instead, I wondered whatever happened to my youthful exuberance. Why did a simple dive I took so many times as a kid feel like such a big risk?

We can't turn back the clock. We're clearly not the same people we were as kids. Wouldn't it be great to regain some of the spirit of our youth? When we risk, we regain a bit of that fearless, bold, youthful spirit. But when is a risk brave, and when is it simply foolish?

The Right Risk for You

Like it or not, risk taking will always be an inescapable part of our lives. Whether you are changing jobs, beginning a new relationship, making an investment, or choosing the right school to attend, you will ultimately be confronted with risk. You really have to look at risk through a two-sided mirror. There's a risk of action, and the maybe even bigger risk, that of no action at all. By not acting on our passion, we could lose out on some golden opportunities.

It's often been said there are three types of people in the world. Those that make things happen. Those that watch things happen. And of course, those that wonder what just happened. To reach your fullest potential, you need to be in the first group that acts to make things happen.

Here's a key question concerning risk: how do you know when taking a certain risk is right for you? Bill Treasurer, in his insightful book *Right Risk*, tells us that risk is right when it's aligned with our true purpose, values, and passions in life. He suggests that successful people take risks because it completes them in some way. It is directed toward a specific destination. According to Treasurer, "right risks are deliberate, focused, and rich with meaning. Unlike ego-based risks, they transcend the bipolar fields of gain and loss and are instead anchored to a higher purpose. Rather than feed one's ego, right risks strengthen one's character. They are fulfilling not because they are fun and exciting (although they often are), and not because they are materially rewarding (although they can be), but because they transport us from where we are to where we ought to be." Taking a right risk will help you close the gap between who you are and who you dream of becoming.

*It's not because things are difficult, we do not dare.
It is because we do not dare that things are difficult.*

—Seneca

A Classic "What If" Story

In a place where risk-taking and innovation are a normal part of life, Ron Wayne became Silicon Valley's famed "What if, heartbreak kid story." Wayne was an original Apple co-founder with Steve Jobs and Steve Wozniak. He designed the company's initial logo and drafted its first technical manual for the Apple I computer. He later drafted Apple's original partnership agreement that gave him a 10% ownership stake in Apple, which would have been valued at $22 billion today had he held on to it. But he didn't. He was afraid that his partners' wild spending habits would ultimately lead to Apple's failure. So he decided to sell his shares back to Jobs and Wozniak for... ready for this? Eight hundred dollars! This is a classic case of pessimism and lacking the courage to take the leap. Sir Winston Churchill tells us "An optimist sees an opportunity in every calamity; a pessimist sees a calamity in every opportunity."

Make no mistake about it—it takes courage to take a risk. When we risk, we often act in spite of our fear. If we set out to start a new business, we risk failure. If we reach out to love someone, we take the risk of not having that love returned. When we give a party, we take the risk that our invited guests might not show up. When we expose our true feelings, we risk being exposed. Anyway, you get the picture.

Life is full of risks, but the greatest rewards go to those who take them. One of life's great tragedies is to risk nothing and gain nothing. We've all heard the expression, "Nothing ventured, nothing gained." Years from now, you don't want to look back on an unfulfilled life and say, "If only I would have taken more risks." As Bill Treasurer says, "Many a bar stool has been warmed by the seat of a man whose taunting recollections are the risks he didn't take." Even though it takes a lot of courage and guts, the great humorist Will Rogers urges us to take the risks in life: "Why not go out on the limb—that's where the fruit is." If we don't take risks we lessen the risk of getting hurt, but we never live life to the fullest either. When it comes to risk taking, it's the historic Scottish patriot William Wallace's voice that firmly echoes in our ear: "Every man dies, but not every man lives."

SEVEN JUMPSTARTS TO TAKE YOUR RIGHT RISK

1 **Listen to your heart.** Follow your heart, not just your reason. You seldom go wrong when you listen to your own inner voice.

2 **Get out of your comfort zone.** Golden opportunities often lie just outside our comfort zone. Have the courage and fortitude to grab that brass ring.

3 **Avoid analysis paralysis.** Do your homework, but ultimately you need to take action. Somehow the biggest risk is not to risk at all. Don't wait for your ship to come in... row out and meet it.

4 **Don't wait for the perfect time.** There will never be a truly perfect time to act. In life, you generally learn more by doing than waiting. The perfect time to act is now!

5 **Face your fears.** Feel the fear and do it anyway. Have the courage to work through your fear and use it to propel your spirit and rekindle your focus.

6 **Live in the present.** Make the present the primary focus in your life, not the past or the future. Remember, life is a gift; that's why they call it a present. The present moment is all you'll ever have in your life.

7 **Take the leap.** Aristotle once said, "Courage is the first of all human qualities because it is the one that guarantees all others." Have the courage to take the leap and close the gap between your dreams and reality.

Executive Summary

In business, a successful strategy offers a clarion call to action. But an action strategy often requires a certain degree of risk. Once a company completes its market research with due diligence, it's time to pull the ripcord.

In a sense, our own life strategy is a mission statement. But it's not good enough to just have a mission. We need to act. Any strategy is only as good as the implementation. We need to take the action steps necessary to make things happen. Often, our action strategy requires that we take risks. The key is to take the right risk for us—the risks that transport us to where we ought to be. It often takes courage to take the right risk. If we don't take risks, we lessen our chances of getting hurt, but we never really live life to the fullest. If we don't act on life, life has its own way of acting on us.

As my grandfather use to say, "You can't fall off the floor."

Time to Reflect

When was the last time you risked failure for something you passionately believed in?

CHAPTER 5

Weather the Product Cycles

Reinventing Yourself at Every Stage

*We live life going forward,
but we understand it looking backward.*
—Søren Kierkegaard

We all need to constantly re-invent ourselves as we go through the cycles of life. Likewise in business there are product cycles.

By and large, investors do not want to invest in a "one-hit wonder." They'd like to know that a company has several layers of product in development that could be profitable for many years to come, and that the firm is nimble enough to change and reinvent itself to keep up with the current trends. Drug companies are good examples of reinvention. A pharmaceutical company like Merck needs to continually develop new prescription drug offerings, because even their most successful proprietary products will eventually become generic products. Companies need to continually re-imagine and reinvent their products to keep their vitality ongoing for years to come.

Companies Reinvent Themselves

In the early stages of Hewlett-Packard, the company knew virtually nothing about computers, but a lot about the test and measurement business. HP decided to reinvent itself. It spun off its test and measurement business to Agilent while the remaining Hewlett-Packard brand refocused its efforts on personal computers and printers. Today HP is the largest personal computer company in the world with sales over $120 billion. Likewise, IBM reinvented itself by getting out of the hard goods computer business and focusing mainly on service and providing business solutions in the rapidly growing e-commerce market sector. Today IBM reigns as the largest information technology company in the world.

As the personal computer business matured, Apple wisely decided to change its name from Apple Computers to simply Apple. The company wanted to reflect the fact that by layering-on the introduction of iPod, iTunes, iPad and the like, it was reinventing itself primarily from a personal computer company to a consumer electronics company. The product layering-on chart of Apple (as of this writing) shows the natural evolution of the company from computers to consumer electronics.

APPLE PRODUCT LAYERING-ON CHART

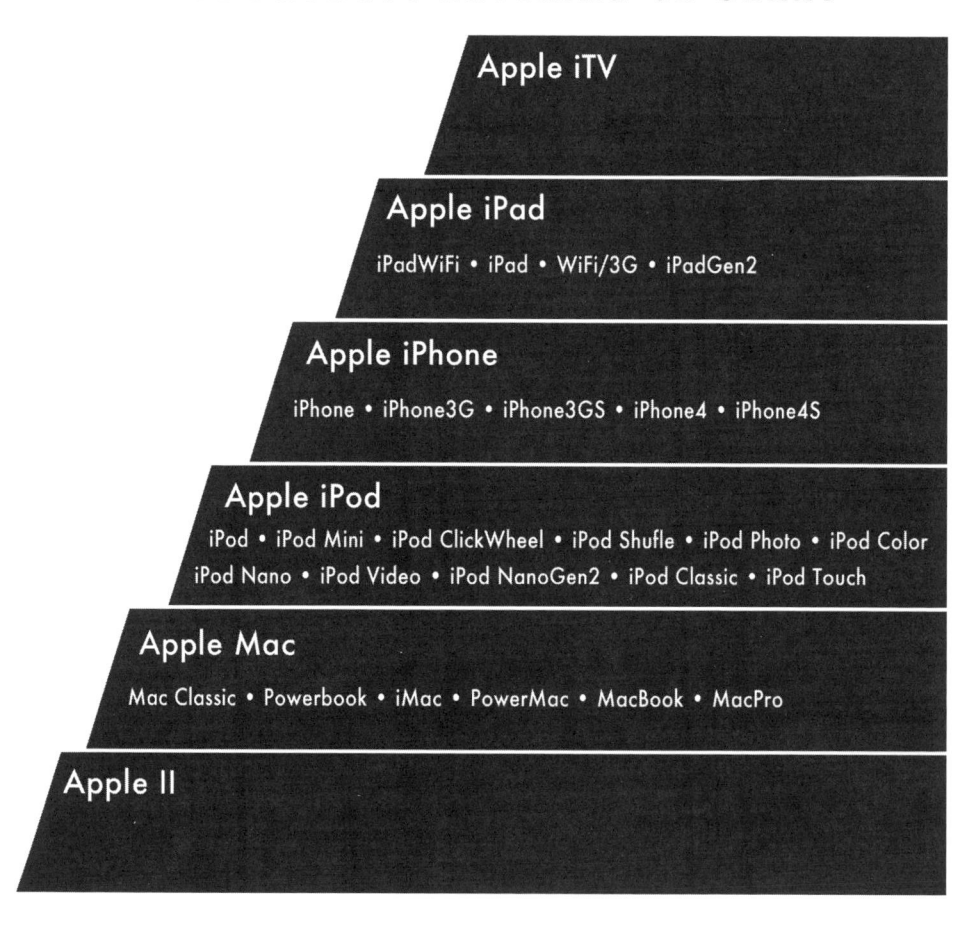

Apple iTV

Apple iPad
iPadWiFi • iPad • WiFi/3G • iPadGen2

Apple iPhone
iPhone • iPhone3G • iPhone3GS • iPhone4 • iPhone4S

Apple iPod
iPod • iPod Mini • iPod ClickWheel • iPod Shufle • iPod Photo • iPod Color
iPod Nano • iPod Video • iPod NanoGen2 • iPod Classic • iPod Touch

Apple Mac
Mac Classic • Powerbook • iMac • PowerMac • MacBook • MacPro

Apple II

Even Domino's Pizza got into the reinvention act. The company's sales literally soared after making a gut-wrenching business decision to reinvent its pizza recipe after marketing research indicated that many people thought their dough tasted like cardboard.

Consider also the second act of cable TV channel MSNBC. The company reinvented itself from a beleaguered low-rated, no point-of-difference station, to a highly rated political forum channel.

A luxury brand like Coach needed to re-boot itself to tune into turbulent economic times. Founded in 1941, the brand has always been renowned for high quality and the durability of its leather products. The Coach branded ladies handbags mostly sold in the range of $300. Then came the 2008 financial meltdown and with the recession, Coach had to adapt to a more cost conscious consumer. Accordingly, the company designed an affordable luxury line of purses and accessories that could be priced to suit tough times without tarnishing or cheapening the Coach brand image. The company worked diligently with leather and fabric suppliers to create the less pricey Poppy line and reappraised its product mix to lower the average handbag price to under $300. The Coach brand clearly had to change with the climate of the times. "It required a mind-shift," says Coach CEO Lew Frankfort. We took the view that the world will be forever different and we needed to acclimate ourselves."

Even cities reinvent themselves. The city of Las Vegas is in a constant state of reinventing itself in reaction to competitors and changing consumer demands. Las Vegas began as a gambling oasis in the middle of the Nevada desert. Soon after the 1940s, the city continued to offer gambling with an increasing number of headline acts and bargain accommodations to lure people to the desert. Still later, the city positioned itself as a family destination offering something for everyone in the family: gambling for mom and dad, and plenty of diversions for the kids (think Circus Circus and Treasure Island). Facing eastern competition and increased migration westward, a true building boom and renovation commenced in the 1990s. The new Las Vegas offered huge sprawling hotels, faithfully built around bigger-than-life themes like New York City, Paris, Venice, and the Egyptian pyramids. Once renowned for bargain room rates subsidized by casinos, Las Vegas now offers luxury accommodations, gourmet dining, fine shopping around the clock, and top entertainment. In a natural extension of its move to luxury and spectacle—and partly fueled by nostalgia for the excesses of the Rat Pack era—Las Vegas today appeals to the inherent need to make a spectacle of one's self. Stylish nightclubs and plenty of adult entertainment compete with the casinos and other attractions for attention and tourist dollars. Now more than ever, the house rule in Las Vegas is that as long as you don't bother the other customers, you can do just about anything you want and be whoever you want to be.

At every point in its evolution, Las Vegas has skillfully reinvented itself, altering its strategy and product offerings in reaction to market forces and consumer trends. So, whether it's the boom of amusement parks, casinos in Atlantic

City, casinos on Native American lands, a boom economy, a bust economy, or nostalgia for a bygone era, Las Vegas remains light on its feet and somehow always succeeds in giving customers what they want. The city wants its customers to believe that Las Vegas can be the ultimate escape from the mundane, a place where everyone can let their hair down and let it all hang out. The City's 24/7 motto therefore proudly proclaims: "What happens in Vegas, stays in Vegas."

Companies need to layer on new products and occasionally reinvent themselves to stay in front of their customers. But it is important for these companies to remain within their core competencies affirmed in the "define the business you're in" section, which is step one of the planning process. This constant movement is also a survival technique, since the marketplace is in a constant state of change year in and year out.

> *No man steps in the same river twice, for it's not the same river and he's not the same man.*
>
> — Heraclitus

Reinventing Yourself at Every Stage

*Each age is a dream that is dying,
or one that is coming to birth.*
—Arthur O'Shaughnessy

Lifecycles

Similar to the product layering-on process, each of us is constantly reinventing ourselves. Just as a company has to have definitive "product cycles," we as individuals have "life cycles." We have to constantly redefine or reinvent ourselves as we go through life's passages. This transformation takes place in several ways. We could be changing our career path. We could be altering our lifestyles. In some cases, we might even be changing the way people perceive us. People, like companies, are in a constant state of evolution. The very fact that you picked up this book indicates that you feel an urge for change in your life. The road to rediscovery is an ongoing process. Part of this process is the need to redefine or reinvent ourselves—not just once, but as many times as needed as we go through the cycles of life.

If nothing changed, there would be no butterflies.
—Unknown

Reinventing Yourself

A striking example of personal reinvention can be illustrated by following the captivating story of Mark Wahlberg, who has literally carved out a fascinating career by re-booting himself, again and again.

Mark grew up the youngest of nine children in the poor and scrappy section of Dorchester, Massachusetts, just outside of Boston. He stole, fought and roamed the streets, dropping out of school by age 13. At 16, he maliciously attacked a man with a wooden stick and was sent to prison, serving 45 days for assault. In prison, with the guidance of his parish priest, Mark realized he had to turn his life around if he wanted to fulfill his dreams. Wahlberg first came to fame by being part of a boy's band called New Kids On The Block, with his brother Donny. Later on as Marky Mark and the Funky Bunch he recorded a number one song with New Vibrations.

After appearing in a provocative music video, Wahlberg's well-toned physique was prominently displayed in a series of suggestive underwear ads for Calvin Klein. Now highly recognized (and awed by the massive female movie-going audience), Mark made his movie debut with Danny DeVito in *Renaissance Man*. He continued to gain acclaim for his roles in hit movies like *The Basketball Diaries*, *Boogie Nights*, *The Perfect Storm*, and *Invincible*. In 2006, Wahlberg played a trench-mouthed state police officer in Martin Scorsese's critically acclaimed thriller, *The Departed*. His convincing role earned him an Academy Award Nomination for Best Supporting Actor.

Later Wahlberg transformed himself again, this time on the other side of the camera by executive producing the HBO hit series *Entourage*, which was loosely based on his own Hollywood experiences. He later produced the highly acclaimed HBO mini-series *Boardwalk Empire*. In 2010 he returned to his working-class neighborhood roots by producing and starring in *The Fighter*. The film garnered seven Academy Award Nominations including Best Picture. *The Fighter* went on to win Oscars for Best Supporting Actor (Christian Bale) and Best Actress (Melissa Leo). After a turbulent life, Mark Wahlberg has seemingly reinvented himself brick-by-brick to become "one of the most powerful people in Hollywood". One has to wonder what's next for Mark? I guess we'll all have to wait for his next act of transformation.

Eight-time major tennis champion Andre Agassi, though a high school dropout, reinvented himself by creating the Andre Agassi Preparatory Academy, an acclaimed K-12 charter school for underprivileged kids, located in his hometown of Las Vegas. Although infamous at one time for his refusal to don traditional white tennis attire at Wimbledon, Agassi strictly enforces the dress code at his school. He doesn't want to have the poorest kids look any different than those that have the money to buy nice clothes.

Time is a dressmaker specializing in alterations.
—Faith Baldwin

Here are just a few recognizable people who reinvented themselves by altering their careers, lifestyles, and in some cases, their values over time.

Sean Diddy Combs – went from rapper, to music producer, to budding actor, to acclaimed men's fashion designer to Hollywood power broker. Even his name has evolved from Puff Daddy, to P. Diddy, to simply Diddy.

Hillary Clinton – went from the beleaguered wife of a president to Senator of New York to a prime candidate for president in her own right and on to U.S. Secretary of State, arguably the most powerful diplomat in the world.

George Foreman – evolved from surly heavyweight champion boxer, to a minister, to a beloved 45-year-old who recaptured the heavyweight championship to a highly successful pitchman for the George Foremen Grilling Machine, to a purveyor of natural green cleaning products.

Martha Stewart – went from being a successful stockbroker, to founding her Martha Stewart lifestyle media empire, to jail for conspiracy, obstruction, and making false statements to federal investigators relating to her stock transactions, then back to her highly successful media empire without skipping a beat. She also launched an environmentally friendly household product cleaning line.

Al Franken – reinvented himself from prominent writer and performer on Saturday Night Live, to author, to radio host, to senator of the state of Minnesota.

Mickey Rourke – went from an amateur boxer, to a supporting role actor in TV and small films, to blockbuster success as a high grossing actor, to a failure at the box office, to an Academy Award nomination for his portrayal as a washed-up wrestler.

Bill Gates – went from the CEO of Microsoft and his lofty perch as the world's richest man, to the world's most generous philanthropist by creating the Bill and Melinda Gates Foundation and the creator of The Giving Pledge, where the super wealthy commit at least half of their fortunes to charity under a philanthropic campaign.

Jesse Ventura – a former Navy Seal and professional wrestler, Ventura went on to become Governor of Minnesota and later taught a study group at Harvard.

John Grisham – his background as a lawyer and Mississippi state representative served him well for his second career as a bestselling fiction writer. His bestselling novel *A Time to Kill* came to him when he was engrossed in a Mississippi court case.

Curtis Jackson AKA 50 Cent – went from rapper, to actor, to highly successful business entrepreneur. He made over $100 million by working with the Glaceau Company to develop a vitamin water that was eventually sold to Coca-Cola Company.

Paula Abdul – the former Laker Girl, turned famed choreographer, went on to record a number one album and became part of the judging panel for the highly rated American Idol Show. She is definitely television's X-Factor.

Earvin "Magic" Johnson – The Hall of Fame basketball player became the most recognized spokesperson for HIV and remade himself. He evolved into a business savvy entrepreneur, holding sizable stakes in varied inner city business enterprises.

Tyra Banks – the former super model quit modeling to start up her own production company called Bankable Productions which produces the Tyra Banks Show. She is also an advocate for plus size women.

Madonna – literally transforms her look and trendsetting music/video performances every couple of years. Her children's book *The English Roses* hit the New York Times best-seller list. Madonna is the epitome of a superstar who understands the importance of reinventing herself to stay on top.

Ronald Reagan – went from making B movies to become President of the United States.

Tony Bennett – with the aid of his son, who managed his career, transformed himself from aging superstar singer to hip Grammy Award winner, whose popularity extended to young people in their twenties and thirties.

John Glenn – evolved from one of our earliest astronauts to senator of Ohio, and back again as the oldest astronaut to travel in space.

Dwight D. Eisenhower – went from the commander of our allied forces in World War II to president of prestigious Columbia University to President of the United States.

Kevin Costner – evolved from a sexy film star to a determined and talented Academy Award–winning director for his movie *Dances with Wolves* to the owner of an oil spill cleanup company that furthers his interest in environmental enhancement.

Stella McCartney – the daughter of famed Beatle Paul McCartney, could have followed in her father's musical footsteps. Instead she chose the path less traveled and became a highly acclaimed fashion designer focusing on earth-friendly high fashion.

My dear friend Walter is the epitome of a person who has totally reinvented himself. At one time, Walter was one of the top personal-injury lawyers in town. Then one morning the police arrived at his home, handcuffed him, and drove him away in a squad car. Walter was booked and charged with insurance fraud and filing false income-tax returns. He was forced to resign from the California bar and slapped with a five-year prison sentence.

While in prison, Walter started to study psychology through a correspondence course. During his confinement, he learned that his young grandson had been diagnosed with autism, a serious lifelong developmental disorder. Walter became interested in securing special educational programs and rights for disabled children, and once he was out on parole, his interest in helping disabled children with their special educational needs began to escalate. He formed a new nonprofit corporation called Professional Advocates for Special Students, or P.A.S.S. The company is dedicated to helping disabled children receive their special educational needs.

Over the past couple of years, Walter has received literally hundreds of letters from thankful parents of specially challenged children whom he has helped. Today, Walter is a widely recognized expert in the field of special education, often assisting others without compensation.

Recognizing that he reinvented himself toward a higher purpose, the state of California has reinstated Walter to the bar. My Irish mother had an expression for people like Walter: "Never judge a sailor on a calm sea." Walter has survived the choppy waters of life. He has redefined himself. The world of special education is now in a safer harbor because of his unselfish work.

> *Because things are the way they are,*
> *things will not stay the way they are.*
>
> —Bertolt Brecht

Winds of Life

All of us go through various stages or passages in life. These passages could easily be represented in metaphor by the Three Winds of Life:

First Wind: Dedication and Adventure

This is the dedication and adventure stage. You'll do anything it takes to get ahead. You'll even accept the assignment to go for coffee and doughnuts if you have to! If you're like me, you might move five times in this period and never think twice about it. You're not averse to taking the right risks. Life is an exciting adventure.

Second Wind: Making Your Mark

Here you've reached a certain level of success and begin to make your mark. But attached to success comes a cost. Under the guise of convincing yourself that you're sacrificing for the overall good of the family, you begin to miss those little things in life that in retrospect aren't so little after all. You miss your son's little league game, your daughter's soccer match, and put off the epic family vacation that you promised your spouse you'd take. You've been promoted at work. Now you have more money but far less time to enjoy it. You begin to wonder, "If I'm so successful, how come I'm not happier?" Sound familiar?

Third Wind: Discovery

You begin to recognize that what you do is not necessarily who you are. By this time, you might have experienced a failed marriage, an unfulfilled career, or the sadness and realization of your own mortality from the loss of a parent. You begin to seriously question your own legacy or purpose in life. Having a life of meaning becomes a priority. You're beginning to discover what matters most to you. And when you do, the wind will be at your back.

The Three Winds of Life are not necessarily linked to age. You can experience defining moments in your life that thrust you into a different wind beyond your age. Take former tennis champion Jennifer Capriati for instance. At age fifteen, she was the number-two ranked women's tennis player in the world. Two years later, after arrests for shoplifting and drug possession, her game evaporated and she fell to a ranking of 220 in the world.

Jennifer then made an incredible comeback. After her second dramatic win in the Australian Open, an enterprising reporter asked her about getting a second wind—to which she responded, "Heck, no, I got my third wind" (and we all know she wasn't just talking about tennis!).

I am part of all I have met.
—Alfred Lord Tennyson

Defining Moments

Each of life's stages or winds are accompanied by defining moments in time that often become turning points in our lives. A good way to understand the changes you go through is to examine the defining moments of your life by each decade of your existence. This isn't an easy task. However, when done thoroughly, it will help you clarify your goals, dreams, and aspirations going forward. You'll be able to see turning points and key moments that will have a significant impact on the way you choose to live your life. The way you respond to these events will shape how you feel about yourself, who you are, and who you want to become. Ike Reighard in his book *Discovering Your North Star* said, "Our lives are like tapestries, we can look at the back and see a mess of dangling strings, but when we look at the front we see a wonderful design that God is weaving."

You don't connect the dots of your life going forward; you connect them looking backward to link the threads of commonality. Alfred Lord Tennyson puts things in perspective when he pronounced, "I am part of all that I have met."

To jumpstart you a bit, here's the decade's exercise that I completed on my own life. For the next several pages, I'll be unveiling myself in front of you in a way I've never done before.

Remember, each choice we make creates a ripple effect in our lives. When things happen to us, good or bad, it's how we react to them that can make a difference between our glass being half empty or half full.

Decade One (1–10 Years Old)

▶ Hit by a car. I was never supposed to walk again.

▶ Private tutor schooling. I get all the attention; (I still crave it).

▶ My dad's landmark restaurant is booming (good news).
  He spends a lot of time at the restaurant (bad news).

Decade Two (11–20 Years Old)

▶ Major hip surgery allows me to walk again (albeit with a limp).

▶ Get game winning hit in little league all-star game. My doctor is very proud.

- Begin high school.
- Discover girls.
- Accepted to college in New England. I make dean's list, but recognize that there are much smarter people in the world than me.

> *Out of difficult times grow miracles.*
> —Jean De La Bruyere

Perspective: Decades One and Two

Looking back on my own life, decades one and two had a lot to do with perseverance and not giving in to the likely prospect of never walking again. A few defining moments clearly pop into my head:

When I was nine years old, I was hit by a car. I had a mangled left hip and was told I would never walk again. My mother and father took me to some of the finest orthopedic surgeons, but all of them refused to operate, claiming the situation was hopeless. Then one day we visited the head of orthopedic surgery for the New York Knicks basketball team. His name was Dr. Yanagisawa. The doctor told me I had a fifty-fifty chance of walking again if he operated on me. I told him I'd like to take that chance. It was clearly the right thing for me. My mom and dad agreed. After a successful operation, I was walking again (albeit with a severe limp which I was told I'd probably have to live with for the rest of my life).

A year later, I made the Little League all-star team, which made my doctor extremely proud. And then it happened—playing against the previous year's Little League state champions, I drove in the winning run in the last inning with a base-clearing double. I was mobbed by my fellow teammates. I knew I had done something great because our coaches took us later for a celebratory pizza with all the toppings (a clear sign of achievement if ever there was one).

The game was well covered by local press. I couldn't wait to read the story of our victory and my game-winning hit. I got up really early the next day and read the headline coverage of the game, which read: "Limping Boy's Hit Wins Ballgame!" I defiantly strode into the local press office and demanded to see the sports editor. I threw the sports section in his embarrassed face, vowing never to limp again. From that day forward, my limp almost miraculously disappeared. Now, when people around me tell me they can't do something, I always think of that game-winning hit and the limp that was literally willed away.

Decade Three (21–30 Years Old)

- ▶ Receive master's degree. Write thesis titled "Host City Marketing for the Olympic Games."
- ▶ Stint as second lieutenant in U.S. Army.
- ▶ Start my marketing career at Motorola. Meet my marketing mentor who teaches me the Twelve-Point Marketing Plan Discipline.
- ▶ Meet my life mentor, Donald.
- ▶ Visit Carmel/Big Sur, California, area for the first time; vow to live there someday.

Perspective: Decade Three

Looking back on decade three, a key turning point in my life came at Motorola when I wasn't afraid to take the right risk. Let me explain.

One day Ed, my Harvard-Business-School-educated boss, called me into his office with an open invitation. He wanted me to come to his beautiful farm in the rolling hills of Barrington, Illinois, to see if I could master his famous Twelve-Point Marketing Plan discipline. That's right, it's the same discipline that provides the foundation of this book. There was only one catch to my boss's invitation. If he felt that I couldn't grasp or have the aptitude for his marketing-plan process, he was going to "fire me on the spot." I remember asking Ed if I was his first invitee. He informed me that there had been four other "marketing impostors" who had preceded me—none of whom made the cut. None of whom were still with the firm.

As it happened, it was a magical weekend. I was enthralled with Ed's marketing-plan process, and according to my boss, I showed a strong aptitude for capturing the essence of his process. After several months, Ed was so delighted with my progress that he sent me to Motorola Canada in Toronto to implement the plan in our international division. Once in a while, you're in the right place at the right time. Our sales at Motorola Canada tripled and my career and salary skyrocketed.

Decade Four (31–40 Years Old)

- ▶ Work for corporate conglomerate in Indiana. Learn to appreciate Midwest values.
- ▶ Move to Los Angeles for bigger bucks to work for a consumer electronics company. My core values are severely tested.
- ▶ Meet my eventual business partner and long time friend, Bob Zeichick.

- ▶ Turn around another California consumer electronics firm. Named one of top marketing executives under forty by an industry business magazine.
- ▶ My partner and I start up our own marketing consulting firm that becomes very successful (if you define success only as making money—which is what this book challenges).
- ▶ We begin to explore the idea to start Thirdwind, a company that would help people discover and take action on that which really matters most to them.
- ▶ Instead, we put Thirdwind on hold and take over the management reins of a major fitness-equipment company. Once again, we sell out for the big bucks (I'm beginning to see a disturbing pattern here).

> *When we are no longer able to change a situation, we are challenged to change ourselves.*
> —Victor Frankl

Perspective: Decade Four

As I look back on decade four, I detect a disturbing pattern—a pattern that manifests itself with many people in their early forties. We lose perspective—our work becomes our life—while often, more important things are shifted to the back burner. As we move up the ladder of "success," we make money, but not necessarily meaning. In my own case, I always wanted to have kids, but time just seemed to slip by. I begin to reassess things. I begin to revisit the dreams of my youth. I know that the greatest opportunity for self-discovery still awaits me.

Decade Five (41–50 Years Old)

- ▶ I launch several successful companies.
- ▶ I love kids—but I still don't have any of my own.
- ▶ Stock market booms, then busts (lessons learned).
- ▶ My parents die. I feel lost without them and need to reexamine my own life and how I want to live it beyond work.
- ▶ We begin to move our ideas for Thirdwind forward, with seminars, radio interviews, etc.
- ▶ Penguin, one of the world's leading book publishers, makes decision to publish my first book entitled *A Marketing Plan for Life*.

▶ I am still yearning to move to Carmel/Big Sur. Perhaps my own book will propel me there sooner than later.

Perspective: Decade Five

The turning point in decade five was the loss of both of my parents. Your perspective on life changes when your parents are gone. You begin to realize that life on this planet is short and you won't be here forever. You come in touch with your own mortality. You reassess things. You wonder if you are on course to realize the goals, dreams, and aspirations of your youth. You ask yourself, has my life made a difference to others? If I died tomorrow, what would be my legacy? And it's here that many of us begin a wonderful journey to discover and take action on what really matters most.

> *It's not the events in your life that determine who you are, it's how you choose to respond to them.*
>
> —Victor Frankl

Looking Back/Going Forward

As I look back on my own personal decades' experiences, I take solace in the perspective offered by that Victor Frankl quote.

A story can be told about two brothers. A man asked the oldest brother why he smoked. He answered, "I smoke because when I was young my mother smoked." The youngest brother was asked the reverse question, "Why don't you smoke?" His answer: "I don't smoke because when I was young my mother smoked."

Frankl was right: it's not what happens to us—it's how we choose to respond to what happens to us that shapes us and determines who we really are. Frankl counsels us to roll with the punches. "When we are no longer able to change a situation, we are challenged to change ourselves."

Life is not always fair. It is often strewn with potholes and boulders along the way. Author Virginia Satir adds, "Life is not always the way it's supposed to be. It is the way it is. The way you cope with it is what makes the difference."

> *Nothing is written in stone—*
> *not even what has already happened.*
>
> —Dr. Dan Baker

Our Story Is Still Unfolding

Life throws us some knuckleballs. We really don't know if an event or defining moment is good or bad until we look back in retrospect. How did it shape us? Did it make us a better person? Did we crumble under its weight or did it only give us more determination?

In an article in *Psychology Today*, Maryanne Garry and Devon Polaschek talk about the importance of our past in gaining perspective on our future: "The autobiographical memories that tell a story of our lives are always undergoing revision—precisely because our sense of self is too. We are continually extracting new information from old experiences and filling gaps in ways that serve some current demand." Consciously or unconsciously, we use information from the past to reinvent our present or future.

Personal reinvention is the action that occurs when we adapt to life's changes, turning points, defining moments, or just process new information that affects our lives. Philosopher Søren Kierkegaard adds this sound perspective: "We live life going forward, but we understand it looking backward." By drawing from the past, we can better understand our future. Remember, as long as we have life, our life story is still unfolding.

SEVEN JUMPSTARTS TO REINVENT YOURSELF

1. **Reboot yourself.** We all have the power to reinvent or reboot ourselves. We regularly upgrade things like our cars, computers and our stereo systems. Reboot your life and layer on the next exciting adventure.

2. **Keep an open mind.** Life is filled with an abundance of possibilities. Align your dreams, goals and aspirations with the pulse of your passion. If you can dream it you can make it happen.

3. **Be the change you want.** Make your own personal makeover list. Be daring. Is there always something you wanted to do, but lack the nerve and courage to follow up? Go for it. Reach for the brass ring and be the change you envisioned for yourself.

4. **Go back to move forward.** Chart your life map by decades and connect the dots by looking backwards then moving forward. You'll be able to identify with turning points in your life that will have significant impact on how you reinvent yourself in the future.

5. **By the light of the silvery moon.** Try moonlighting before you make a significant leap. Get your feet wet in your new endeavor before you dive in head first. For instance, if you want to be a jazz singer, sing first at some weekend clubs and get a feel for how you'll perform in front of a live audience.

6. **Take control of your destiny.** Don't use a recession or bad job market as an excuse to avoid reinventing yourself. You alone have the power to change and create your new reality. So take full control over your own destiny by acting now. Remember, there's never a perfect time to act.

7. **Script yourself for success.** See yourself succeeding. Use creative visualization to put yourself in the proper mindset to reinvent yourself. People who succeed take mental rehearsals. They script themselves for success, often visualizing the change long before it happens.

Executive Summary

This chapter introduces the product "layering-on" process and the need for all good companies to consistently redefine or reinvent their products and services. It is underscored by the fact that on a personal level, each of us goes through various stages or winds in our ever-changing lives. Just as a company has product cycles, we have life cycles. We have to constantly redefine or reinvent ourselves as we go through life's passages. The defining moments in our life deeply affect our ability to realize our goals, dreams, and aspirations. By drawing from the past, we can better understand our future. As long as we have life, our life story is still unfolding.

Time to Reflect

When was the last time you reinvented yourself to better realize your goals, dreams, and aspirations?

CHAPTER 6

Build Your Business Brand

Building Your Personal Brand

> *In the whole of recorded history,*
> *there will never be another such as you.*
> *Each of us is a miracle in uniqueness.*
>
> —Pablo Casals

Heart of Branding

The sixth section of the Twelve-Point Marketing Plan process discusses the need to build a corporate brand. Later on in the chapter we'll talk about the need to build and take charge of your own personal brand.

Brand building is far more than just another corporate buzzword. Creating an authentic brand stands at the very heart of selling a company's products and services. Build a brand and they will come. Later on, in chapter ten we'll talk about the fact that in business or in life, "Nothing happens until somebody sells something." One could easily proclaim the new marketing mantra to be "Nothing happens until somebody brands something." We are literally infatuated with brands. We don't buy athletic shoes, we buy Nikes. We don't buy jeans, we buy True Religion. We don't buy a smart phone, we buy an iPhone. We don't just ride a motorcycle, we ride a Harley. We don't buy tape, we buy Scotch tape. We don't make photocopies, we Xerox. We don't use cotton swabs, we use Q-tips. We don't buy adhesive bandages, we buy Band-Aids.

A company's products and services can be readily copied – but an authentic brand cannot be readily duplicated, because it resides in the very heart, mind and soul of its customers or users. A "passion" brand can become part of a customer's DNA. It's the reason that Apple users, for example, are like evangelists or a tribal community that would rather fight than switch brands. Simply put, authentic brands offer value added and a clear and definitive reason to buy one product over another – even at a price premium.

Key Elements of Branding

There are several key elements that a company must consider when building its brand. It all starts by taking personal inventory and answering some inside/out questions:

1. What business should we be in? (Who are we?)
2. What do we stand for? (What are the company's core values?)
3. What makes us unique? (What are the company's "demonstrable" differences?)
4. Why should people care? (What is our cause beyond our business profit-making paradigm?)

> *What you make people feel is just as important as what you make.*
> —BMW television commercial

Creating Share of Mind

Authentic brands tap into our emotions, which in turn, greatly influence our buying decisions. When brands create share of mind, share of market will likely follow. Need examples? Apple has share of mind; Toshiba does not. Harley Davidson has share of mind; Suzuki does not. BMW's Mini Cooper has share of mind; Mitsubishi does not. Nike has share of mind; Asics does not. Amazon has share of mind; Barnes and Noble does not. Tiny chocolate company Godiva has share of mind while giant Mars chocolate does not. Sub-Zero refrigerators has share of mind; Samsung does not.

A great example of creating share of mind is NASCAR (National Association for Stock Car Racing). Amazingly, NASCAR, not baseball, basketball, or golf is the second most popular sport in America – standing only behind the NFL. Why? NASCAR fans are religiously loyal. They are fanatical followers that totally identify with their race driver of choice. They know everything there is to know about the driver, almost to the extent that the driver becomes an integral part of their extended family. As if attending a family reunion, NASCAR fans will travel on long road trips to support their "family member." This high level of passion translates directly into NASCAR fans backing their favorite driver's corporate sponsorships and endorsements.

Capturing the Aura and Personality of the Brand

A company's branding story should be part of its genuine make up. It should emanate from authentic roots or be part of its very heritage. In Hollywood circles, this would be called the "back story." Eddie Bauer founded his company because he almost died during a severe storm in the great outdoors. Planet, Inc.'s line of green household cleaning products was founded by a fisherman named Stefan Jacob, who wanted to clean up the Canadian waterways.

Authentic brands conjure up a kind of generic top of mind vs. back of mind awareness. When you think facial tissue you naturally think of Kleenex. When you think search, you automatically think Google. In fact, Google has become a verb. When you think online books – you think Amazon. When you think cool designs and easy to use innovations, you think Apple. I'll go a step further. When you think Boise State University, you think of the bright blue artificial turf on their football field. What started out as a point of differentiation has become the key part of the university's identity and its rising football fortunes.

As mentioned earlier, great brands resonate in the heart, mind and soul of their customers. The best brands often provoke genuine feelings and a clarion call to action. Think Nike's tagline of "Just Do It." Avis: "We try harder" Army: "Be all you can be." Apple's landmark tagline urging us to "Think Different".

Communication Keys to Build a Brand

Our marketing consulting firm, BrandMark, Inc. has created and executed a plethora of marketing plans for Fortune 500 corporations, mid-size companies and start-ups. What we've learned from our experience is that there are essentially four communication keys that allow a company to successfully build its brand over time. It's important to note that great companies hit all four communication key cylinders.

The four communication keys are:

1 The Name

2 Features/Benefits/Demonstrable Differences

3 Product or Service

4 Unique Way You Market

We can further illustrate the importance of communication keys by looking at an Apple case study and the ways they build their legendary brand loyalty.

1. Name – Apple symbolizes an organic, evolving system of knowledge, conjuring up Newton and the discovery of gravity.
2. Product or Service – Cool innovative products designed with integrity and ease of use.
3. Features – Courageous innovation, visual awe, incomparable ergonomics, simplicity and concierge type customer service.
4. The Unique Way We Market – Building an almost tribal community of evangelists that has a deep-rooted connection to the company. Apple owners would rather fight than switch.

A great example of a company hitting its communications keys on all cylinders was the Cabbage Patch Kid. Here's a doll that didn't look, feel, or smell any differently from any other dolls. Yet, the doll was one of the hottest Christmas toys two years in a row. Woe to thee that could not put this doll under the Christmas tree!

What made the doll so desirable? Simple. The Cabbage Patch Kid hit all the communication keys right on target. First of all, it had a memorable name: Cabbage Patch Kid. Second, it had a unique feature: it came with adoption papers. Third, the product was "demonstrably different," in that each doll was prepackaged with its own name. Fourth and most important was the unique way the doll was marketed—you didn't just buy a Cabbage Patch Kid, you adopted it! This distinguished the Cabbage Patch Kid brand from other doll and toy brands.

In the whole of recorded history, there will never be another such as you. Each of us is a miracle in uniqueness.

— Pablo Casals

Building Your Personal Brand

Each of us marches to the beat of a different drummer.
— Anonymous

Taking Charge of Your Own Brand

Just like a CEO of a company, you are in charge of your own personal brand. OK, let's face it, you're not Apple. You're not Google. You're not Nike, but you are in charge of an even more important brand called – get this: Me, Inc. Personal brand building is a process that offers your uniqueness to the outside world. It packages your attributes and characteristics in a way that allows you to stand out in a crowd. Personal branding enables you to separate yourself from the rest of the pack. In essence, your personal brand is a precise calling card of what you stand for and how others perceive your attributes, skills and values. Your good name should stand for your core values like integrity, honesty and loyalty, to name a few. What you do for others beyond yourself will go a long way in making your personal and professional mark. Brand building creates a pulpit for who you are and what makes you unique that creates value for others. Here's a punch line: You want to buy stock in a valuable company? Then take personal stock and make an investment in the most valuable company of all – Me, Inc.

It's important that your personal brand be aligned with your true calling and purpose in life. It must be consistent with the talents and contributions you have to offer the world. We all need to do some personal brand building. Ask yourself:

- What positive service do I offer to the planet?
- What talents, strengths, or character traits make me unique?
- How do I market myself so the perception people have of me is aligned with the value I offer to the outside world?
- What does my good name stand for?

Today's mighty oak is just yesterday's nut that held its ground.
— David Icke

What Do You Stand For?

A key element of personal branding is the positive perception people have of what we stand for. For instance, Dr. Martin Luther King Jr. stood for racial equality. Walter Cronkite stood for journalistic integrity. Comedian Bob Hope will always stand for entertaining our homesick troops overseas. Earvin "Magic" Johnson is perceived as a winner both on the basketball court and for the good things he does for the urban community. Tony Robbins is admired as a great personal motivator. Steve Jobs was widely known for leadership, innovative designs and dynamic product marketing.

Having a good personal brand creates value for those around you. Your good values, unique personality, skills/talents, and accomplishments go a long way in differentiating you from those who do not possess your unique traits and capabilities. One of my mentors, Bill Ball, never finished high school. But he shared with others his best individual trait—his personal integrity. He used to say, "Your word is your bond. It is your torchbearer. Do what you say you're going to do or fix it. Your talent by itself will not make you a success. But the combination of talent and integrity will always allow you to stand out from the crowd."

It's important to remember that building your personal brand is a process. It doesn't happen overnight. Your personal brand represents the consistent things you do day in and day out that allows others to perceive your true value and uniqueness. But it takes time to have other people see the value in your personal brand. To build a strong personal brand, you need to intensely focus on what you do that offers value. You need to build a bond of trust with those around you. Trust, as you know, is not given automatically, it's earned the hard way—over time.

Only a mediocre person is always at his best.
—Somerset Maugham

You Have to Specialize

One of the ways you can personally brand yourself is through the art of specialization, or narrowcasting. This is your ability to hone and narrow the scope of who you are and what you represent. Don't try to be all things to all people. I call this "avoiding the clock-radio syndrome." When you purchase a clock radio, you sure as heck know you're not getting the best clock and you most certainly know you are not getting the best-sounding radio either. Don't be a clock radio! Pick something you're great at and go for it with gusto.

In business, one of the biggest differences between Europe and the United States is that in the States we specialize far more than our European counterparts. One of Europe's top job titles is called "Managing Director." This title would not fly in the States because it denotes a generalist versus a specialist. In our country, if you have a problem with your heart, you go see a heart specialist. If your company needs a turnaround, you see a corporate turnaround specialist. I myself am known as a brand-rebuilding specialist.

In their splendid book *The Brand Called You*, Peter Montoya and Tim Vandehey point out the various benefits of specialization:

- Differentiation. You set yourself apart by doing a few things well—not by trying to be all things to all people (that is, the clock-radio syndrome).
- Presumed expertise. When you tell people you are a specialist in something, they naturally think you have specific skill sets in that area.
- Perceived value. Simply put, specialists can demand more money. It's sort of like a special on the menu. If you tell people the seafood pasta is your house specialty, people will not only order it—they'd be willing to pay more for your special entrée.
- Understandable benefit. Your personal brand becomes more memorable when it focuses around a few very clear benefits. People are more likely to see value in something that they readily comprehend.
- Focused on strengths. If you specialize in things that you enjoy and do best, you'll do better work and probably make more money doing it.

Montoya and Vandehey tie a nice ribbon around personal branding: "There's only one you. No matter where you've come from or what you've done, you're unique. When you thread your personality, passions, and history into your brand, you're making yourself stand out from any other brand in the market—even if others have exactly the same skills and training as you."

Revel in Your Uniqueness

Let's pause here for a moment and talk a bit more about uniqueness. In the market section in chapter two we talked about pinpointing our strengths. Again, strength is defined as a strong or valuable attribute. However, uniqueness allows us to stand out from the crowd. Uniqueness allows us to be demonstrably different in the way we display or flaunt our strengths. Lady Gaga is a talented singer and songwriter, but what makes her unique is her captivating stage presence.

Steve Jobs of Apple was more than a CEO; he was an impassioned leader of a community of "Apple Speak" admirers.

Personal brand building is similar to building a corporate brand: you have to get out there and market your uniqueness. In fact, you should revel in your uniqueness. I learned this firsthand while traveling to China in the early 1980s. This was the real "Red China" of over twenty years ago. There were no Coke machines, no luxury hotels. This was the China of great mystery and adventure!

One of my boyhood dreams was to visit the Great Wall of China, one of the Seven Wonders of the World. But on the day I arrived at the Great Wall, it was extremely cold—ten degrees below zero. Due to high, gusty winds, my Chinese hosts strongly suggested that I postpone my trek up the wall. Unfortunately, I was returning home bright and early the next morning. So despite my host's weather warnings, I decided to climb the wall in the blustery cold.

Climbing the wall was such a thrill I hardly felt the chill. In fact, I was the only person to brave the elements that day. Or so I thought. The fact is, I wasn't alone. An elderly Chinese man proudly sporting a worn-out ABC Sports cap, which he claimed he received during the Ping-Pong diplomacy era, greeted me at the top of the wall. He spoke to me in perfect King's English, asking, "Do you like your hair?" To which I quickly responded, "Not really. Why do you ask?" Noting my distinctive strawberry-blond hair color, he explained, "Let me tell you something. Being Chinese and largely dark haired, I am among the most heavily populated peoples on earth. Twenty percent of the world's population is Chinese. There are well over a billion of us. You, however, are one of the most unique species on earth! You see, only one out of every six hundred fifty thousand people on earth has your hair color. You should revel in your uniqueness!" He skipped a few beats, and then countered, "Of course, I'm not just talking about your hair! Each of us is unique in our own way."

Every individual is unique. Think of yourself as a carefully handcrafted work of art. You are not a one-size-fits-all, mass-produced commodity. You are a specially designed custom-made treasure of being. You are an original masterpiece that cannot be replicated at any cost. You are not "rather" or "somewhat" unique. Uniqueness is a clear absolute state. If we weren't unique, there would be little reason for us to exist at all. If we were all the same, our world would be a boring place to live. We'd all be clones. Our world would lack color. It would be like watching all of life's magnificence in black-and-white TV. Author John Powell sums it up nicely: "You have a unique message to deliver, a unique song to sing, a unique act of love to bestow. This message, this one, this act of love has been entrusted exclusively to the one and only you."

Powell tells the story about a wonderful, wise teacher who asked his wide-eyed young students to go out and find a small, unnoticed flower somewhere in town. He then asked his students to put the flower under a magnifying glass to study in detail the veins in the leaves and shades of color in the petals. He asked them to study the symmetry of the flower. He reminded his students that the flower might have gone unnoticed and unappreciated if they had not found and admired it. The teacher then made the connection between flowers and people. People are a lot like flowers. Each one is different, carefully crafted, and above all, uniquely endowed. But you have to spend time with them to know this. So many people in this world go unnoticed and unappreciated because no one has taken the time to admire their wonderful uniqueness. Our uniqueness allows us to live in a multidimensional world; it allows us to appreciate the complementary capabilities and varying talents of people around us.

One day our marketing team was working on a new marketing plan to help turn around our consumer electronics company that had fallen from its former market leadership position. In meetings, our new chief financial officer lamented the fact that our marketing group wasn't paying enough attention to the financial part of the marketing plan. I looked at him in bewilderment and said, "Well, now, if we as marketing people did everything right when it came to finances, there would be no need for you and your unique financial talent." Our CFO smiled that knowing smile of his and said, "Carry on. I'll be here when you need me."

We all have unique talents to contribute to the world. Unlike other species, all human beings are different and extraordinary in some way; we have different personal traits, different backgrounds, memories, talents, and characteristics. That's why when we take those inkblot tests, some of us see the young maiden while others view the same inkblot as the old hag. That's why to some, the wine glass is half empty, whilst to others the same glass is half full.

One of the reasons that many people have a passionate connection to wine is that a fine bottle of wine is unique in that it transports us back to that special place re-living that unique moment in time… with that special someone. A fine wine re-connects us with life's memorable experiences that are often stored in the mind's eye. In some ways, wine is like life itself. Just like us, each bottle of wine is unique because it tends to reinvent itself each year as it matures and evolves in the bottle. In this respect, even the same bottle of wine is constantly changing, depending on how it was stored and when we drink it. Just like us, a great bottle of wine revels in its own uniqueness, striving to achieve its full-bodied potential.

We are all special. We all have something unique to offer. Your very life because of who you are has meaning.

—Barbara DeAngeles

Respecting Your Uniqueness

If we want to be all we can be in life and move ourselves towards our true calling or purpose, it's important that we respect our uniqueness. There are several ways to do this. First, we must internalize that each of us is extraordinary in our own right. I once asked a business colleague what he feared most. He replied: "My biggest fear in life is to be ordinary versus extraordinary." Secondly, we need to clearly define our uniqueness. What do we do best that can add value to others? Finally, we need to accept, and therefore respect our uniqueness. In doing so, we will have more respect for ourselves and our abilities.

One of Apple's ad campaigns saluted the uniqueness in all of us. Let me hit on some key phrases: "Here's to the crazy ones. The misfits. The rebels. The troublemakers. The round heads in the square holes"... The ad closes with... "because the people who are crazy enough to think they can change the world are the ones that do. Think different." So be unique! Dare to be different. But in your difference, make a difference that you were here on this planet.

Even a small difference can count for a lot. One day an old man was walking along the beach in the early morning and noticed the tide had washed hundreds of starfish on the nearby shore. Up ahead in the distance, he spotted a boy who appeared to be gathering up starfish one by one and tossing them back into the ocean. He approached the boy and asked why he spent so much energy doing what seemed to be a waste of time. The boy replied, "If these starfish are left out here like this, they will bake in the sun, and by this afternoon they will all be dead." The old man gazed out as far as he could see and responded, "But, there must be hundreds of miles of beach and thousands of starfish. You can't possibly rescue all of them. What difference is throwing a few back going to make anyway?" The boy held up the starfish he had in his hand and replied, "It's sure going to make a lot of difference to this one!"

Make a Difference

I was part of the team that launched Planet Inc., a line of environmentally safe household cleaning products that also clean terrifically well. The product line was distributed not only in health food stores but also in major supermarkets like Gelson's, Vons, Ralphs, and Safeway.

The original founders of Planet, Stefan Jacob and Allen Stedman, developed a product cleaning formula that was hypoallergenic and safe for the environment and aquatic life. The product is never tested on animals. In a small way, the company is making a big difference on this planet we call earth. Other companies like Ben & Jerry's reach out to make a difference. Although Ben & Jerry's ostensibly sell ice cream, they also serve humanity by giving a percentage of their profits back to charity.

You don't need to be a corporate entity to make a difference in this world. People from all walks of life are making a big difference on a daily basis. We need to look no further than our heroic firefighters, police officers, educators, doctors, and health-care professionals. They all make a difference—each and every day.

It's particularly wonderful to note that you're never too young to recognize the importance of making a difference. By the age of thirteen, Craig Kielburger had done more to change the world than most of us ever will. While reading the newspaper he came across an article about a twelve-year-old boy who escaped from a Pakistani factory where he had been shackled in a carpet-weaving room and forced to work inhumane hours every day. The boy's parents had sold him into slavery when he was only four years old. He was paid the paltry sum of three cents per day.

Craig was appalled. How could children be treated this way in our day and age? Craig looked into the problem and discovered that few North American organizations had focused in this area. Accordingly, Craig and a group of his friends started faxing questions to groups throughout the world and the Free the Children organization was born.

Craig felt compelled to visit these countries and see what child slavery was like. His parents gave him permission to spend seven weeks visiting India, Bangladesh, Thailand, Pakistan, and Nepal with a twenty-four-year-old Asian friend. Among other places, they visited an Indian fireworks factory where ten-year-old children were frequently injured, maimed, or killed due to a lack of safety precautions.

In the years following Craig's first trip, his student-run organization has made great strides. They have helped alert the world's media to the problems and freed or rehabilitated literally hundreds of child slaves. Craig's group was also instrumental in promoting the rug-mark marketing emblem for handwoven rugs certifying that the carpet was produced without using child labor.

Free the Children groups are operating in sixty schools in rural areas of India. They are also building or reconstructing thirty-two schools in South America, providing milking animals and sewing machines to destitute families so they no longer have to depend on their children's income to survive. Along the way, Craig has met with such world leaders as the Dalai Lama and Pope John Paul II.

Utilizing her passion and talents for dancing, Sohini Chakaborty is helping former child prostitutes in India regain their sense of dignity and self-respect. Chakaborty utilizes inspiring dance movements as a psychotherapy tool that allows victims of trafficking and violence to express their sense of joy, happiness and well-being. She launched her company called Kolicata Sanved, (Sanved is Sanskrit means empathy) that conducts dance classes in women's shelters. To date, Sanved has directly helped over 5,000 young women, including over 2,500 former child prostitutes, regain the self esteem that will serve them well as they go back into their communities.

Chakaborty has multiplied herself by training other women who live in outside shelters to become dance therapy instructors. The ultimate goal is not just to teach people to dance, but to allow them to blossom into strong individuals with an uplifting spirit fostered by a newfound sense of self respect.

Nancy Brinker has always been a high achiever and humanitarian. She was U.S. Ambassador to Hungary, served on several high profile corporate boards and received the Presidential Medal of Freedom. Beyond these distinguished accomplishments, perhaps her finest accomplishment was to start a foundation to help cure breast cancer in honor of her sister Susan, who died from the ravages of this dreaded disease. The foundation started the Susan Komen Race For A Cure, which has over 1.5 million global participants. Nancy used her marketing savvy to come up with the now famous "Pink Ribbon" symbol, which reminds donors of the human faces lost to breast cancer. Komen later partnered with businesses to display her eye-catching "Pink Ribbon" logo on their products. Komen used her cause related marketing skills to encourage corporations to be aligned with an important humanitarian mission. Is there something you've always wanted to do to make a difference for others? Take the first step.

SEVEN JUMPSTARTS TO BUILD YOUR PERSONAL BRAND

1. **Define your purpose** – List the things that matter most to you. Get in touch with your core values and what you truly stand for.
2. **Be authentic** – Be clear on who you are and who you are not. Build a reputation that represents the real you.

3. **Live a life of integrity** – Say what you mean and mean what you say. Admit your mistakes and learn from them – and move on.

4. **Respect and revel in your uniqueness** – Remember you are a one of a kind work of art. There's nobody else like you on this planet.

5. **Make a difference** – Strive to make a difference that you were here on this planet by finding a cause bigger than yourself.

6. **Specialize** – Don't try to be all things to all people. Be great at something vs. just mediocre at a lot of things. Avoid the clock radio syndrome at all cost.

7. **Market yourself** – you have to get out into the real world or market your uniqueness. Don't compromise here; stay consistent with your core values.

Executive Summary

This chapter focuses on building a brand over time. Communication keys provide the ways in which a company can be demonstrably different or unique from the competition.

Just as a company builds its brand, we as individuals should endeavor to build our own personal brand as well. We have to get out in the world and market our uniqueness. We need to package our personal attributes and characteristics that make us stand out from the rest of the crowd. To be a strong personal brand, we should strongly consider focusing on what we do that offers value to others.

We talked in chapter two about pinpointing our strengths, but uniqueness goes beyond strength. Our uniqueness allows us to stand out by displaying our strengths in a way that is demonstrably different.

Time to Reflect

How are you unique or demonstrably different?
Have you made a positive difference in helping others?

CHAPTER 7

Expand Your Reach

Creating a Legacy

The only thing you take with you when you're gone is what you leave behind.
—John Allston

In life, reach is all about reaching out to help others so that we can formulate and eventually create our own living legacy.

In marketing parlance, "reach" is the medium you use to transport or deliver your message to your target audience. As Canadian writer Marshall McLuhan said, "The medium is the message." In short, the medium you select to broadcast or get your message out to the outside world is just as important as the message itself.

Until the technological revolution of the mid-to-late 1990s, most companies stuck to the tried-and-true traditional media mix that included TV, radio, newspapers, magazines, direct mail, and billboards. Today the traditional media needs to be integrated with the new media brought about by technological advances. Social networking sites like Facebook and Twitter, blogs, and user-generated content like Google and YouTube are shifting the balance of power from the company to the customer. Utilizing the seemingly unlimited communities across the web, consumers are "chiming in" and providing their own perspective on everything from a company's products to customer service, to the company's latest marketing strategies.

In today's world, when marketers try to control the message about its product or service, customers tend to view the message as biased and self-serving. But when a third party tweets, writes a blog, or an online review, it's viewed as more trustworthy. In fact, a survey conducted by Forrester Research indicated that customers trusted the purchase advice of strangers online more than a company's traditional TV and print advertising campaign.

The New Social Media

By the time you read this, there will be new technologies that provide new modes of connectiveness that foster interactive communities, including word of mouth, more immediate response, and instant access to a company's products and services. Like it or not, companies need to know that the days of exclusively relying on a 30-second spot or a cleverly written radio campaign are over.

The evolution of social media gives companies both the opportunity to engage more deeply with their existing fans and converse with new potential target audiences. The new media platforms also allow the brand to respond rapidly to those who might have had an unpleasant experience with the brand as well. To be sure, top-down, one-way exchanges are long gone. They have been replaced by open and honest two-way communications with both the company and customer emphasizing responsiveness, quality and value. In his book, *The Thank You Economy*, Gary Vayerchuk contends companies that harness the word-of-mouth power provided by social media platforms will pull away from the pack and profit in today's ever-evolving marketplace.

New technology often ushers in rapid change. On January 25, 2011 the world witnessed it's first e-revolution. A group of young Egyptian protestors leveraged the galvanizing tools of social networking to overthrow the corrupt regime of Egypt's dictator, Hosni Mubarek. Facebook, Twitter, You Tube, and blogs were used to share collaborating content that enabled Egyptian protestors to take the streets and in just 18 days overthrow a dictatorship that had oppressively stood for 30 years. Young Egyptian hero, Wael Ghonim, who masterminded the "2.0 Revolution" reveals the secret to the rapid yet largely peaceful revolution: "I've always said if you want to liberate a society give me the Internet and Facebook."

As new technology continues to emerge, we have to continually educate ourselves. As Mark Twain once quipped, "I've been through many years of schooling, but I never let it get in the way of my education." As of this writing, eighty percent of the American population is online. At the dawn of the Internet age, the web was something you read – now increasingly, with platforms like YouTube, it's something you watch. Hardbound encyclopedias are all but dead. To date, Google is answering 88 billion queries worldwide per month. Twitter, 19 billion per month, Yahoo 9.4 billion and Bing 4 billion. Unfortunately, ardent letter writing has become archaic. We now have email, tweets and instant text messages. Woe to the English language as we once knew it! Our media is rapidly shifting from the home centric, to mobile devices like iPhone and Android smart phones, iPods, and iPads. And don't forget this: these days there's an app for just about everything.

Not having a Facebook page in today's world is the equivalent of not having a website in the year 2000. The number of Facebook users worldwide is growing exponentially. Presently one out of every dozen people on this planet has a Facebook account. Over 75 languages are represented, not yet including China, which is almost one fifth of the world's population and will no doubt soon get on board. Facebook members have surpassed the population of the US, Indonesia and Brazil. Users constantly recommend goods and services to their friends. Research data from E-marketer reveals that seventy percent of Facebook users said that a friend's referral would highly increase their chances of purchasing one product or service over others. No wonder just about every corporation in America is jumping on the Facebook bandwagon.

An integral part of the new media revolution is viral marketing. This is a multiplier technique that takes full advantage of pre-existing social networks to produce significant increases in both brand awareness and eventually sales. Viral marketing is so termed because the information within the social network tends to spread like a wildfire virus. Think of it like a ripple effect, where one person tells another about your unique product, service or brand. One of the most well known viral campaigns was the Subservient Chicken viral video by Burger King, which received over 20 million hits. Nike found similar success with its most valuable puppet viral videos featuring NBA superstars LeBron James and Kobe Bryant. The "Let's Say Thanks" campaign created by Xerox allowed customers to send thousands of heartfelt messages to our military forces overseas.

Today more than ever, the customer's voice needs to be heard. One of the best ways to engage the customer is creating a social media campaign. The list that follows will guide you in addressing the key elements in social media markets. Awareness, Inc., a company well versed in creating social media software for their clients, largely inspired these elements.

Key Elements in the Adoption of Social Media Marketing

1. Invite Customer Feedback – Converse with your market.
2. Stimulate a Passion – Create evangelists.
3. Avoid "Not Invented Here" Mentality – Allow customers to be part of your product planning department.
4. Encourage Voting – Let the customer rank features and benefits they like best and least.
5. Create a Loyal Community – Build and reward loyalty through loyalty clubs.

6 Develop a Peer Support Community – Help each other with solutions.
7 Build Subscriber Community – Engage more deeply with subscribers who pay an additional modest fee (i.e. ESPN's Insider).
8 Create Exciting Corporate Events – Build and maintain the buzz.

Integrating Traditional and New Media Strategy

One could easily make the argument that social engagement via the new media is more beneficial than the interruptive old media advertising; however, it is clearly in the company's interest to integrate old and new media to gain maximum exposure. After all, not all of us live our entire life online or in front of screens; it just seems that way. Some companies might shy away from social media marketing because they fear loss of control of their message. They miss the point here. By integrating traditional media with social media, you can remain in charge of guiding your core message while setting the stage for customers to engage and share their opinions with their family and circle of friends. Simply put: you can guide your corporate message without totally controlling it.

Although the new social media can be great for virally speeding your message, it has one potential shortcoming: people don't necessarily view or hear your message in the same positive light as you had hoped. This is where traditional marketing shines; it can lay the important foundation of information and guide it as it circulates to the social network community. By integrating traditional and new media, you increase the clarity of your message, add frequency, and maximize both efforts.

The old media versus new media debate is long and pointless. The key is to balance the freeform interactive-ness of social media with the consistent strategic message fostered by traditional media. Properly integrated, you create the best of both worlds. Tom Cuniff writing for *Media Blogger* puts it this way, "It's time to get past thinking of media as old or new. TV is the 'view' medium where we sit back and hope to be entertained. Digital is the 'do' medium. Generally, we're trying to get something done." Cuniff suggests we stop pitting new against old and think about how we can create a feedback loop and make 1 + 1 = 11.

The highly-watched TV show *American Idol* is a great example of integrating old and new media. It's traditional media because it is broadcast in primetime on the Fox Network. Its social media because of the plethora of voter downloads, tweets, blogs, and chats, which emanate from the broadcast and heighten the overall interest of the show. By integrating the traditional and the new media, American Idol has become a media happening – an experience way beyond a mere TV show.

The greatest danger of our new technology isn't that machines will begin to think like people, but that people will begin to think like machines.

—Anonymous

Connectiveness Leads to Disconnection

Now is perhaps the proper time to ask ourselves whether this plethora of new technology, chock full of screens, Google, YouTube, smart phones, emails, tweets, chat rooms and blogs are the greatest tools ever devised—or something that sucks the time and marrow out of our hearts and souls. Author William Powers poses these questions in his engaging book entitled: *Hamlet's Blackberry: A Practical Philosophy for Building a Good Life in the Digital Age.* In his book, Powers talks about the conundrum of connectiveness. Digital devices serve to enrich our lives in many ways, but the more connected we are, the more disconnected we seem to be from the real world. It becomes harder to find those quiet spaces, those face-to-face special moments that can make life more meaningful. The new connectiveness seems to rob us of up-close and personal time. Our screen and digital devices enable us to perform countless tasks, but somewhere along the way we're losing something of great human value. It's called depth... the sheer enjoyment of intimate, joyful engagement that life has to offer. As mobile phones unit sales soared from 500 million to over 5 billion in the past decade alone, we need to strike a balance between screen and depth. Here's an astounding stat. The Nielsen Company reported in 2010 that the average American teenager receives 2,272 text messages per month! I'm not sure whether this will enhance our kid's writing skills! I rather doubt it. On the other hand, another way to look at it in a positive light, is that we are creating a new global language, where the digital symbols kids are using to text and tweet can be understood universally regardless of whether you are in the United States, Indonesia, India, England, Philippines, Korea or Kenya.

Ever since Marshall McLuhan wrote that the "medium is the message" we have been trying to strike a balance between depth of the human experience and technology. But in today's fast-paced digital world, we might want to consider putting ourselves on a digital detox as we endeavor to restore some balance. We don't want a world that is so neatly organized and arranged that we miss the depth of the human experience. Here are some thought starters to accomplish that delicate balancing act:

- Find your special spot or quiet zone to restore your inner space. It can be in your house, garden, or in a serene wooded settling.

- Read a real book – the old kind with a binding and pages you can actually turn.
- Declare a screen-free day or weekend with your family.
- Go on quiet walks without your iPhone, Android or Blackberry in hand.
- Schedule two times a day to read and send emails.
- Go to a sporting event without your mobile phone. Don't look at the large screen at the ballpark – actually watch the game live – supposedly, that's why you went to the game in the first place.

While social networks can help us escape from the humdrum, depressive mind state of these uncertain times by helping us "get out" and get connected, let's not replace real interactions with digital sound bites. Take the quality time to share your authentic self with others.

> *The giver receives, the receiver gives.*
> —Ron Suskind

Creating a Legacy in Business

Leaving a lasting legacy is something that all good businesses strive to achieve. There are several ways companies can create a legacy in a business context.

- Creating a sense of community. One effective way companies reach their target audience and establish a corporate legacy is by creating a sense of community. This can be accomplished by creating loyalty or membership programs that reward customer loyalty with higher discounts, special gifts, expedited service, and other exclusive offers. Membership in these clubs clearly has its privileges. Frequent-flyer programs offered by the airlines are a great example of this. The more you fly, the more you fly free. The more you fly, the less you have to wait in line. A company like American Express has successfully reached out to create an online community that target customers and gain insightful feedback on their products and services.
- Event marketing. A well-planned event can also allow a company to reach out and build community and loyalty among its target customers. Event marketing can be indirect by sponsoring an athletic contest, fashion show, chili cook-off, beauty contest, or any other event that is consistent

with the brand's image and target audience. That's why you see so many beer companies reach for their twenty-one-to-thirty-five demographic by sponsoring marquee events for their age group including pro-volleyball tours, concert tours, and loads of football games and NASCAR auto races.

- Reaching out beyond target customers. A good company's reach should extend beyond media and loyalty clubs. It's important that a company reaches out to the community at large by participating in social, charitable, and community causes. In an age of lightning-fast sound-bite-driven public opinion, it's more important than ever for companies to become good corporate citizens. Many top companies achieve their citizenry by giving back through charitable donations, setting up foundations, or creating their own community or charitable programs. These donations, foundations, or programs usually support causes near or dear to the company's leadership and corporate culture.

- Media, event sponsorship, and club memberships fulfill a sense of community and promote brand loyalty for companies. Increasingly, companies are reaching out beyond the balance sheet. They are realizing that it is just as important to reach out to help make the world or community a better place to live. By developing "cause marketing" programs through endowments, foundations, and other socially responsible and charitable works, a company can reach not only their customers but also the world community. By improving and enhancing the lives of others, good companies are not only forming a responsible corporate culture, but a legacy of their own.

The true meaning of life is to plant trees under whose shade you don't expect to sit.

— Nelson Henderson

Creating a Legacy

I am what survives me.
—Erick Erickson

Creating a Living Legacy

Earlier in the book, we talked about how true success always involves reaching out to others beyond ourselves. We discussed Ralph Waldo Emerson's broader, more encompassing definition of success. We talked about creating more meaning, not just more money. On a personal level, reach is doing what you do best to reach out to make the world (or just one person) better because of your actions. It's about taking what you do well and creating a positive rippling effect that will help others—beyond yourself. Life can also be likened to an echo. We often receive back from what we put in and sometimes, much, much more.

Just as businesses extend their reach and establish their legacy by giving back to the community, an important part of a good life plan involves reaching out and improving the lives of others. If you can extend the good things you do to have a positive effect on others, you are beginning to form your own legacy. Legacy is not a matter of chance—it's a matter of choice. It's about reaching out to touch the lives of others. It's not about desiring more for just yourself—it's about desiring the best for the entire world around you. Author Herman Melville explains, "We cannot live only for ourselves. A thousand fibers connect us with our fellow men; and among those fibers as sympathetic threads, our actions run as causes, and they come back to us as effects."

Our legacy is like a torch that we pass on to future generations. It is the ultimate reach. It gives our life meaning that lives on beyond our lifetime. Our legacy allows us to leave a trace, however small, that we were on this earth. In a sense, our legacy gives us a large or even small part of personal human history. Creating your legacy is a win-win situation. We commit to fulfill the needs of others and we in turn receive the feeling of fulfillment. We give value and we feel more valued. In his enlightening book *Philegatia: Living a Vision, Leaving a Legacy,* Glenn E. Young-Preston sums up legacy succinctly: "It's truly a case where the giver becomes the receiver and the receiver becomes the giver."

> *The measure of a human being is not their deeds,*
> *but in the legacy they leave.*
>
> —Scott Shuker

Most people think of a legacy as solely something we leave behind after we've long passed from this planet. The fact is, you have to lay the foundation while you are living to secure your legacy after you've departed. To use an analogy, a bamboo tree when nurtured hardly grows at all until its fifth year. Then it sprouts up mightily two-and-a-half feet a day, until in six weeks, it can grow to be ninety feet tall! The bamboo tree growth requires no magic. In its first 5 years, it develops miles of roots beneath the ground. The growth is not readily apparent, but the foundation has been laid for the future growth of the tree. Just like a sprouting bamboo tree, living legacies are not formed overnight. They have to be crafted over time while you are still alive and kicking. Your legacy is comprised of those things you achieve and the values you stand for while you're on this earth. For example, Gandhi sought a nonviolent independence for India while he was still alive. Kennedy never actually saw man go to the moon, but he had the vision to think big when he was alive. Dr. Martin Luther King, Jr. had a dream on earth that is still in the process of being fulfilled. In short, your legacy equals the sum of the life you actually lived before you pass on. I can still hear the words of Ralph Waldo Emerson echoing in my ear: "To know that even one life has breathed easier because you have lived. This is to have succeeded." Remember, your life is a masterpiece. The good things you do now will have a positive rippling effect on others. Make your mark now.

> *The deeds of this life are the destiny of the next.*
>
> —Rick Warren

Developing Your Personal Legacy

Creating our personal legacy can come in several different forms.

Raising Children – We all get a lot of joy in watching our children grow up around us. We watch them as they develop in variations of our own character or likeness. When you stop and think, our kid's lives, accomplishments, and contributions to society are inexorably linked to our own legacy. We revel in the success of our children. When things don't go well, we feel their pain as if it were our own.

Remember, however, there's no written guarantee that your children will reflect your value system in a positive way. The apple doesn't always fall near the tree.

Don't automatically expect that your children will follow in your footsteps or share your same value system. You need to make your own mark. Don't try to live your life vicariously through your kids. If you do, you could be setting yourself up for a short-lived legacy.

A family had a genuine antique vase in their home that had been handed down through several generations. It was a real treasure that was kept on the mantel as a special object of enjoyment. One day the parents returned home to be greeted at the door by their teenage daughter. "Mom and Dad," said the daughter, "you know that antique vase that you told us had been passed down from generation to generation?"

"Yes," answered the parents.

"Well, Mom and Dad,… our generation just dropped it."

It's my personal belief that sometimes we exert too much pressure on our kids or grandkids to carry on our legacy, traditions, or other vital interests, such as keeping our company thriving long after we're gone from this planet. Even if your immediate family carries your torch, it is probably unrealistic to think that succeeding generations will necessarily carry the same torch into their future. The nature of our life cycles dictate that each new generation is different, and with these differences comes change. But one thing is resoundingly clear—a good legacy has the potential to be passed on to future generations to make the world a better place to live.

Work – For many of us (especially those without children), work is often the most significant way to create a legacy. All of us—whether we're business executives, doctors, lawyers, designers, scientists, writers, truck drivers, or street sweepers—want our work to be recognized and appreciated. Good architects want to design buildings that are timeless and enduring. People in health, education, and social work hope that their work as nurses, educators, and counselors will create a legacy of enriched lives for generations to follow. Look, let's face it: we can't all win a Super Bowl or a Nobel Peace Prize, but our good work and deeds can certainly make a meaningful positive statement.

When it comes to meaningful work, I always think about my sister Karen. Karen is a nurse. But she has been referred to by many as an "angel of mercy." She often finds herself working with terminally ill patients. She helps her patients die with dignity. She, like other wonderful nurses, provides both physical and spiritual comfort to her patients. Comfort comes in many different forms. Sometimes she just listens to her patients; sometimes she makes a bed more comfortable, or a pillow fluffier, a room lighter or darker. Most of all, Karen says it's about "dying in peace and comfort." It's about letting terminally ill patients believe that something good will happen. The key to helping other people, she says, is "not being afraid to die yourself." My sister's legacy, like that of so many other nurses, will be that she provided dignity and comfort to those that needed it most.

Screenwriter Phil Alden Robinson, who wrote the screenplay for the movie *Field of Dreams*, made a wonderful personal statement when he was nominated for an Academy Award and lost. In a TV interview, a reporter asked him if he was disappointed that he didn't win the Oscar for best screenplay. Robinson replied that he had already won his Oscar. His award came from the hundreds of letters he received from sons telling him that he helped them reconnect with their fathers.

It is in spending oneself that one becomes rich.

—Sarah Bernhardt

Charitable Causes/Giving Back to the Community – The premium ice-cream maker Ben & Jerry's created the Ben & Jerry's Foundation. Its mission is to make the world a better place by working toward the elimination of the underlying causes of environmental and social problems. In addition to this ambitious mission, the company conducts socially aligned sourcing. The company believes it can drive social change through the power of everyday business decisions. This includes buying milk and cream from socially and environmentally responsible vendors. Ben & Jerry's also operates a Partner Shop program where Ben & Jerry's Scoop Shops are owned and operated by community-based nonprofit organizations. These ambitious examples of reaching out to the community are totally consistent with the 1960s activism culture practiced by the company's founders.

Our legacy may include donating not only money but time to causes that we believe have enduring value. These causes may include some of the following:

▶ Preserving the history and legacy of others

▶ Knocking down racial barriers

▶ Preserving our environment

▶ Helping make sick people laugh

▶ Contributing to our inner-city urban communities

▶ Serving as an ambassador for peace and freedom around the world

▶ Encouraging and enhancing the vitality of the arts

- Dedicating yourself to helping find a cure for a dreaded disease
- Providing a terminally ill child with a summer camp of joy

Steven Spielberg may just as likely be remembered for his preservation of the Holocaust survivors' legacy, via video, than for his Academy Award–winning films. In 1994, after filming the movie *Schindler's List*, Spielberg founded the Survivors of the Shoah Visual History Foundation. The foundation's mission is to videotape, collect, and preserve the testimonies of Holocaust survivors and witnesses. As of this writing, the Shoah Foundation has collected over fifty thousand eyewitness testimonies in fifty-seven countries and thirty-two languages. The foundation is totally committed to ensuring a worldwide, effective, educational use of its archive. While the foundation continues to conduct interviews, the focus has shifted to cataloging the testimonies and eventually making them accessible to the world. Spielberg took his talents and kicked it up a notch for a higher cause.

Jackie Robinson was a great overall athlete and Hall of Fame baseball player, but his real legacy is that he paved the way for others to follow. In 1947, when he came up to the major leagues with the Brooklyn Dodgers, it was a historic move that ended decades of discrimination against minorities in major professional sports. Robinson's legacy, however, clearly transcended baseball. He later became an outspoken leader in civil rights, a socially responsible corporate executive, a civil servant, and a major figure in national politics.

In 1973, a year after he died, his wife, Rachel, founded the Jackie Robinson Foundation. The foundation continues Jackie's fight for human dignity by supporting college-bound minorities and poor young people in developing their potential. The foundation carries out the courageous leadership that was the essence of Jackie Robinson's life.

The late Paul Newman's legacy has been much more than that of a superstar actor. His company, Newman's Own, offers among other products a line of salad dressings, spaghetti sauces, popcorn and even dog food. Every single cent of the company's after-tax earnings goes to charity. Newman's Own has given more than $300 million to charitable causes ranging from the Hole in the Wall Gang Camp for terminally ill children to the Scott Newman Center for drug and alcohol abuse – named after his only son, who died young of an accidental overdose. The company is also active in education and drought-relief programs in Africa.

Newman's Hole in the Wall Gang Camps were founded as nonprofit residential camps ingeniously designed as a Wild West hideout in northwestern Connecticut. More than 135,000 children with cancer or serious blood diseases come to Newman's eleven camps each year, free of charge. These camps provide children with camaraderie, fun, and a renewed sense of just being a kid.

Newman's legacy lives on through the continued efforts of the Newman's Own Company and his often stated feelings on philanthropy. "The concept that a person who has a lot should hold his hand out to someone who has less is still a human trait."

Similarly, hip-hop mogul Russell Simmons is highly motivated by his belief that hip-hop can be a powerful and inspiring change agent. Simmons chairs several nonprofit foundations that promote financial literacy and the need to vote among our younger adult population. Simmons feels that hip-hop is helping others to transform the American dream into a living reality. "I want to contribute more to earth than I take away from it," says Simmons. Likewise, Bono, the lead singer for the epic rock band U-2, uses his great influence to draw attention to poverty around the world and build a greater global response to the HIV/Aids epidemic spiraling across Africa.

Mentoring – Being a mentor is one of life's higher callings, especially for those who are approaching midlife or beyond. The great satisfaction in mentoring is that you can help develop others to become all they can be.

Mentors give, but they also get great satisfaction back from sharing their knowledge and skills and watching others grow because of this sharing. Ralph Waldo Emerson said, "It is one of the most beautiful compensations of this life that no man can sincerely try to help another without helping himself." True mentoring is not about making your dreams happen—it's about making the dreams of others happen. Beware of trying to mentor those who don't want to be mentored! The result will be more like Professor Higgins in *My Fair Lady* than *Tuesdays with Morrie*. There are many people out there hungry for your wisdom and expertise— be receptive. Be there for them when they need you.

On a personal level, I've always had wonderful mentors. They allowed me to be all I could be and reined me in only when it became absolutely necessary (that's just before you make a complete fool of yourself). My mentor at Motorola, Ed Reavey, was the one who originally taught me the Twelve-Point Marketing Plan discipline—on the business side. My other mentor, Don Mainwaring, taught me how to apply the plan back to life in general. Both mentors gave me the original foundation for this book. When I asked what I could give them back in return, they both echoed the same thing: "give back by being a good mentor to somebody else."

Everyday Good Deeds – Little things mean a lot. A legacy can be born out of doing lots of good things for people everyday. They can be small things like making time to listen or being a friend in a time of need. It can be as simple as making someone laugh so they temporarily forget about their pain or illness. It could be the good values you share with others, or the occasional dollar you throw into a tin cup. It could be the call you make to your sick aunt. Legacy doesn't necessarily mean you have to achieve monumental history or book-worthy accomplishments.

In the enduring Christmas classic *It's a Wonderful Life*, we come to recognize that George Bailey (played by Jimmy Stewart) truly had a wonderful life because of the little things he did everyday that touched and influenced other people's lives in a meaningful way. We're reminded through this wonderful Christmas classic that every man's life is important, especially when he makes a positive impact on the lives of others.

> *A rock pile ceases to be a rock pile the moment
> a single man contemplates it,
> bearing within him the image of a cathedral.*
> —Antoine de Saint-Exupéry

Searching for a Higher Meaning

Look at what you do and search for a higher meaning. That reminds me of the story of the Two Bricklayers. A journalist was interviewing people and asking them about their jobs. The journalist came upon a bricklayer and asked him what he did all day. "Can't you see!" said the bricklayer. "I mix mud, water, and straw all day for fourteen hours a day. Sometimes when I get bored, I mix water, mud, and straw just to relieve the repetition." Then the journalist moved on to the next worker who was apparently doing the exact same thing. "Excuse me, what is it that you do?"

"Why, can't you see?" exclaimed the worker. "I'm building the foundation for the most beautiful cathedral on earth!"

They are both bricklayers—but one man has put his job into the context of a higher meaning. He was building cathedrals, not merely laying bricks.

When Apple founder Steve Jobs was trying to recruit John Sculley, the president of Pepsico, he tried to appeal to Sculley's sense of a higher purpose and legacy. Sculley asked Jobs, "Why should I leave this great job at Pepsico?" Jobs stared straight at Sculley and said without skipping a beat, "Do you want to spend the rest of your life selling sugared water, or do you want to change the world?" Of course, Jobs, at the time, was talking about his dream of placing a personal computer in everyone's home. Inspiring author, Guy Kawasaki asserts that enchanting people like the late Steve Jobs, Richard Branson and Jeff Bezos sell much more than their products and services – they sell their dreams. "Enchanters," according to Kawasaki, "sell their dreams for a better future, cooler social transactions, a cleaner environment, a heart-stirring driving experience, or the future of publishing."

> *The use of money is all the advantage there is in having money.*
> —Benjamin Franklin

Even banking can be taken to a higher level of meaning. Muhammad Yunus won a Nobel Peace Prize for pioneering a totally new category of banking known as "micro-credit." This innovative banking concept grants small loans to disadvantaged people who would not normally qualify for conventional bank loans. The program has aided millions of Bangladeshis (mostly women) to buy everything from fishnets to cell phones to livestock in order to start up their own small business. Anyone can qualify for a loan, which averages around 200 U.S. dollars. This small amount of money can go a long way to lifting people out of poverty while greatly enhancing their self-esteem. Yunus has helped spawn similar micro-credit entities in other parts of the world that has fostered a spirit of independence versus dependence among the poorer peoples of the world.

As Yunus points out, the strategy of micro lending is the polar opposite of conventional banks who generally lend money only to those that need it least. Yunus sums it up succinctly. "If the banks lent to the rich… I lent to the poor. If banks lent to men… I lent to women. If banks required a lot of paperwork… we're illiterate friendly. The micro-credit program proved that if you give people a stake in their community, they will respect and treasure it because they own it."

Personally, my prime motivation in writing this book, although certainly not comparing myself to a Nobel Prize winner, was to give something back. If the same marketing-plan process I used to steer companies in the right direction can be reapplied to help others, it will allow me to feel that I've made a positive impact on others. Maybe in a small way, writing this book is part of my contribution—a small part of my legacy to help others who are on the same journey as me. Maybe part of my living legacy will be to make meaning as well as money.

In his introduction to his best-selling book *What Should I Do with My Life?*, author Po Bronson adds his perspective on legacy: "We want to know where we're headed—not to spoil our own ending by ruining the surprise, but we want to ensure that when the ending comes, it won't be shallow. We will have done something. We will not have squandered our time here."

We pass on our personal torch to future generations by reaching out to others. Start now to make your contribution to the world around you. When you do, you have the potential to leave behind a legacy that will live long after you are gone.

It's never too late or too early to achieve your living legacy. Grandma Moses took up painting at 76 years of age. On the other side of the spectrum, hockey great Sydney Crosby started practicing signing autographs at the early age of seven.

SEVEN JUMPSTARTS TO CREATE YOUR LIVING LEGACY

1 **Define your core values** – Decide what you stand for and correspondingly what you will not stand for.

2 **Define what matters most** – Get in touch with your vision or purpose bigger than yourself.

3 **Write your own epitaph or obituary** – How do you want to be most remembered and by whom?

4 **Pinpoint where your legacy will come from** – Sometimes history makes the man, but in most cases your legacy will come in four areas: your family, charitable giving, everyday good deeds, or in many cases your work. Pinpoint a specific area and live your legacy.

5 **Find a higher meaning** – Understand your basic skill sets. Do what you do well and like the bricklayer, view your job in a higher context.

6 **Watch an inspirational movie** – One good way to get in touch with your legacy is to watch a movie that inspirers you to help others. Movies like *Blindside*, *The Pursuit of Happiness*, *It's a Wonderful Life*, *Schindler's List*, *Gandhi*, and *The Color of Purple* might help lead you to your legacy trough.

7 **Create a rippling effect** – Visualize how your good deeds and core values can add value to a succession of others after you have left this planet.

Executive Summary

Chapter seven deals with the traditional and new social networking mediums that a company utilizes to reach its target audience. Beyond the media, good companies extend their reach by getting involved in the community, donating to charities, or setting up foundations to support special causes. Through these philanthropic endeavors, a company reaches out to their customers and the community at large.

On the personal side of the ledger, we are reminded that true success always involves reaching out to people beyond ourselves. Reach is about doing what you do best to make the world a better place. The ultimate reach is to achieve a living legacy. Legacy is like a torch that we pass on to future generations. Our legacy reserves for us a small piece of personal human history. Legacy can be achieved in different forms: raising children, giving back to the community, our work, mentoring, and just plain everyday good deeds. Whatever we do in life, we should reach out to others to achieve a higher meaning or purpose. It's never too late to achieve a living legacy.

Time to Reflect

If you died tomorrow, what would be your legacy?
Would you be satisfied with this legacy?

CHAPTER 8

Build A High-Impact Advertising Campaign

Reawakening the Creativity Within You

> *All children are artists. The problem is to remain an artist once we grow up.*
>
> —Pablo Picasso

In life, this sector is all about re-awakening and unleashing the creative spirit inherent in all of us. On the business front it's about how a company clearly communicates its heart and soul in a compelling way that reaches its target customers.

An effective ad campaign literally builds on the first seven points of the marketing-plan process, enabling the company to show a consistent presentation to the target customer. This footprint or look allows the company to build a lasting consumer impression over time.

The most important thing you need to know about the advertising and creativity section is that it's the eighth point of the marketing-plan process, not the first. Many companies want to start here. But you can't start a marketing plan with an advertising campaign. A great ad campaign is a natural outgrowth of the prior planning steps. Think of the marketing-plan process as a veritable symphony, with each part integral to the success of the whole.

A great "ad" campaign requires these seven key elements:

1. Vision: The ability to see the end result by focusing on a clear, concise purpose.

2. Creative impact: Creating a message with impact that punches through loud and clear.

3. Presentation dynamics: It's not just what you present; it's the way you present it.

4 Reach: Spreading the word to the target audience in the most effective and efficient manner.

5 Frequency: Creating as many favorable impressions as many times as economically possible.

6 Integrating traditional with new media to create a positive word-of-mouth campaign.

7 Buy in (take action): Make no mistake about it—the ultimate objective of any good advertising campaign is to get people to buy into your product or service. Advertising legend David Ogilvy used to say, "If it doesn't sell, it isn't creative."

Classic Ad Campaigns

A strategic advertising campaign can create a whole new brand category. Bob Garfield gives us a few classic examples from his top 100 advertising campaign list. Before the DeBeers mining company opined "A diamond is forever," the association between diamonds and romance and wedding engagement was not even on our mind, never mind in our hearts. Years earlier, Clairol turned a category on its head with the "Does she, or doesn't she?" campaign. During the sexual revolution of the 60s, this was a tantalizing question even if the ad was supposedly just talking about hair coloring. Remember the classic line, "Only her hairdresser knows for sure."

Volkswagen was really thinking big with its "Think Small" campaign, which opened up a whole new compact car category in the United States. Miller's "Taste great, less filling" campaign opened a whole new light beer category.

More recently, Apple's "Get a Mac" campaign punched through and took market share from Microsoft. The genius in these comedic spots was in the casting. Mac guy, Justin Long, portrayed a cool hip younger version of Steve Jobs, while PC guy was personified by John Hodgeman, a less fit, couch potato-like, pasty-skinned geek with all sorts of Windows operating system issues. Apple accomplishes the feat of looking cool and laid back, while unmercifully skewering its hopelessly out-of-date rival Microsoft.

The instant classic Dove soap campaign for real beauty was launched after Dove conducted a global study of how women felt about themselves. The study concluded that among most women the definition of beauty had increasingly narrowed and was almost impossible to attain. The survey found that only two percent of the women around the world consider themselves beautiful. Only five percent thought of themselves as pretty, while just nine percent saw themselves as attractive. Over eighty percent thought that the media and advertising set an unrealistic and unachievable standard of beauty. When it came to body image, women from all countries seemed largely unsatisfied with themselves. Seventy-five percent of women polled thought the media could do a far better job in showcasing more diverse attractiveness, including shape, size, age, and color.

Armed with their information, Dove created its "real beauty" campaign to start a societal change. The company concluded that women would feel more beautiful if the stereotypical views of beauty were widened. Rather than use highly paid professional models, the campaign used "real" women of various ages, shapes and sizes to promote discussion about the narrow beauty standards and images set by society. Famous photographer Annie Leibowitz was the artist behind the print and TV commercials, which celebrate the beauty of older and plus-size women. The result? A simple basic soap like Dove had sales that soared off the charts.

Mini's "Let's Motor" campaign tuned in on the joy of driving and created an alternative culture of driving called "Motoring" where both product and the heart of the driver resided in a synergistic way. The company used social network marketing and memorable events including belting a Mini Cooper on top of an SUV to bang home its "Let's Motor" message. Its website encouraged us to design and customize our own Mini – interior and options. Print ads and billboards featured clever copy that went beyond simply getting from point A to B. An example: owning a Mini "is like riding a lightening bolt bareback." People took notice. The result was a long waiting list for the smallest car in the world.

These successful campaigns clearly reached their target customers, communicated their strategy in a creative and often fun way, and resulted—more often than not—in increased sales.

Memorable Taglines

To be effective, advertising taglines or slogans must offer emotion, passion, and a clarion call to action. A slogan needs to forge raw emotion in order for it to stand out and be memorable. A great example is of the overnight delivery message of FedEx. It's not just about getting there… it's more like when it *"absolutely, positively"* has to get there that adds to the emotional appeal of the tagline. You could think of BMW as a driving machine or "The *ultimate* driving machine." Barrack Obama's successful bid for the presidency went beyond change to "Change we can believe in." This tagline connected the emotional dots that exist on the more creative right side of the brain.

Beyond the classic Avis tagline of "We try harder" are some other taglines that resonate with the consumer.

Motel 6 – "We'll leave the light on for you."

M & M's – "Melts in your mouth, not in your hand."

Las Vegas – "What happens in Vegas, stays in Vegas."

Budweiser – "This Bud's for you."

New York Times – "All the news that's fit to print"

US Army – "Be all you can be."

Reno, Nevada – "The biggest little city in the world."

Smuckers – "With a name like Smuckers, you've got to be good."

Mercedes Benz – "Engineered like no other car in the world."

Seat Belt Safety – "Click it or Ticket."

Charmin – "Please don't squeeze the Charmin."

Planet – "Today's Solution For The Next Generation."

Word of Mouth

Perhaps the most effective form of advertising is by word of mouth: one person telling another that something is good about your product or service (of course, it could also be bad). Word-of-mouth advertising creates a "whispering campaign" that can bode well or ill for you or your company. In today's world, whether you ask or not, you're going to get feedback. So you might just as well know what people are saying about you or your product or service.

In life as well as business, you are in large part how you are perceived. Many business and personal reputations have been enhanced or tarnished by a positive or negative word-of-mouth whispering campaign. How you eventually decide to act on this feedback largely depends on the respect or lack of respect you have for the person who is imparting the information.

In today's virtual world, chat rooms, blogs, Twitter, Facebook and other forms or social network media provide ample forums for customer feedback. Facebook, with more than 800 million members and counting, allows consumers to give feedback on a grand scale and create a community far beyond any corporate website.

Word of mouth is all about creating a buzz for your product or service. Online or offline, word of mouth can differentiate your company and allow it to stand out from the rest of the competitive pack.

Buzz marketing is often augmented by creating a memorable event. Greenpeace created a buzz for climate change by developing a programmed event where two Minnesota men attempted to cross the North Pole on foot and by canoes. Ongoing website reports by the explorers got people in the U.S. Congress talking about and focusing on the need to protect our environment.

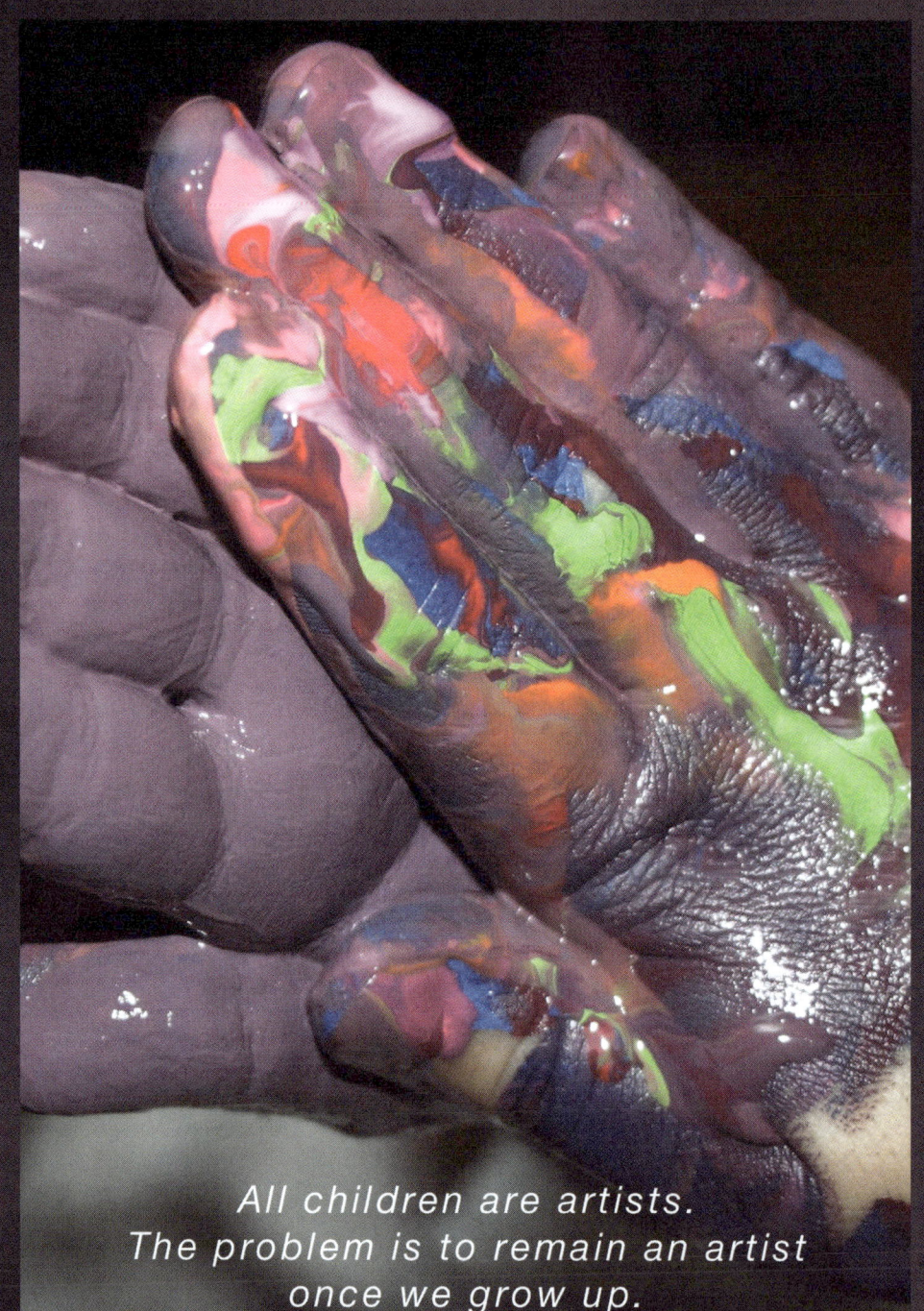

*All children are artists.
The problem is to remain an artist
once we grow up.*

— Pablo Picasso

Reawakening the Creativity Within You

Capturing Your Personal Creativity

Just as a good advertising campaign captures the heart and soul of a company, our innate creative talents allow us to share our own special DNA, vision, and creativity with the outside world. The key question is, "How do we unleash this creativity?" How do we overcome our internal barriers and reawaken the creativity that resides in all of us?

In business or in life, there are no easy shortcuts. Before you can create personal impact, leave a lasting impression, and share your creative heart and soul with the outside world, you need to complete the first seven steps of your life plan. As a refresher course, let's review these important steps:

- Define who you are
- Capitalize on your strengths
- Discover the authentic you
- Find your personal niche
- Reinvent yourself
- Build your personal brand
- Create your legacy

Advertising icon William Bernbach sums up the importance of making a lasting impression in business or in life: "the truth isn't the truth unless people believe in you, and they won't believe in you if they don't know what you're saying, and they can't know what you are saying if they don't listen to you, and they won't listen to you if you're not interesting and you won't be interesting unless you say things imaginatively, originally and freshly." Later in this chapter we'll talk about how we as individuals can punch through loud and clear by presenting ourselves in a dynamic way—allowing our voice to be heard above the noise.

> *The real part of conversation is not to say the right thing in the right place… but to leave unsaid the wrong thing at the tempting moment.*
>
> —Dorothy Neville

Concise Communication

When you come right down to it, advertising and for that matter, much of life revolves around clear and concise communication. The danger in talking about good communication is that it often falls on deaf ears because it seems like a cliché.

I'm reminded of the famous scene from Woody Allen's hilarious movie *Take the Money and Run*. Woody is attempting to rob a bank, but the bank teller can't read Woody's scribbled writing on the hold-up note. Accordingly, he sends Woody to window number nine to get his hold-up note endorsed by the bank's vice president. Moral? The written word is precious, but only if you can read it.

Powerful Punctuation

Pablo Picasso once wrote that he viewed punctuation "as the fig leaf that hid the private parts of literature." However, good punctuation can be highly powerful in the communication process. I recently came across this gem from an English professor who wrote the words, "A woman without her man is nothing" on the chalkboard and asked his students to punctuate it correctly.

All of the males in the class wrote, "A woman, without her man, is nothing."

Are you ready for this?

All the females in the class wrote, "A woman: without her, man is nothing."

Punctuation is all-powerful… it can change the meaning of the written word in this case, probably for the better.

Sometimes even an unintentional pun can help you punch through and communicate your empathy for another person's plight. That reminds me of the time I was talking to a business colleague to set up a dinner meeting to which he replied, "I'll be dietary restricted over the next few days because I'll be going in for a precautionary colonoscopy." To which I readily replied: "I fully understand the importance of having that fully behind you." My colleague almost fell off his chair with laughter, but he greatly appreciated my deep concern.

It's no secret that good communication is often the key to a good relationship. It's been said, "the real art of conversation is not only to say the right thing at the right time – but also to leave unsaid the wrong thing at the tempting moment." Amen. We've all been there… but when will we ever learn?

The intuitive mind is a sacred gift and the rational mind is a faithful servant. We have created a society that honors the servant and has forgotten the gift.

—Albert Einstein

Left Brain/Right Brain

In discussing creativity, it makes sense to delve a bit deeper into the two types of individual mind-sets or different ways of thinking. Logical or left-brain people tend to view things differently than creative or right-brain people. The left-brain/right-brain concept was developed from the research done by psycho-biologist Roger W. Sperry, who discovered that human beings have two very distinct ways of thinking. The following table illustrates some of the key differences of our left-brain/right-brain ways of thinking.

LEFT BRAIN	RIGHT BRAIN
Uses logic	Uses feeling
Detail oriented (looks at parts)	Big-picture oriented (looks at whole)
Objective	Subjective
Uses numbers and facts	Uses imagination
Reality centered	Fantasy centered
Conservative	Risk taker
Pragmatic	Intuitive
Rational	Creative
Thinks step-by-step	Thinks outside the box
Connects the dots	Connects the seemingly unconnected

Although you often hear people say I'm a left-brain person or a right-brain person, it's important to note that creativity (the right brain) resides in all of us. In fact, we're born with a significant amount of right-brain expression. Just observe a child's total sense of wonderment. Watch how they play make-believe games or how they tinker with their toys. Marvel at their finger-painting creativity that always seems to find a special place on our refrigerator door. Think about a child's wonderful ability to transport themselves to a world of fantasy.

Tim Brown, IDEO's CEO, underscores this very point in his creativity presentation at the TED Conference. He asked each conference attendee to draw a simple picture of the person sitting next to them. The net result was lots and lots of laughter and a bit of embarrassment and outright fear of judgment by peers. However, when kids were asked to do the same thing, they would show a delightful sense of fun and childlike wonderment with no fear or peer pressure attached. Ever notice how children find simple delight in playing with opened gift boxes on Christmas morning? To kids, mere boxes offer an infinite set of creative possibilities.

> *Genius is childhood recovered at will.*
> —Charles Baudelaire

Creativity Diminishes as We Get Older

Our school system today reinforces left-brain dominance with its highly structured curriculum and overreliance on timetables, multiple listings and class rankings. It's structured that way because eighty percent of the population is left-brain dominant, while only twenty percent is right-brain focused. There's no wonder why so many famously creative people like Michelangelo, Einstein and Thomas Edison had trouble making good grades in school.

Unfortunately, research studies by researchers and authors McCormick and Plugge show that we lose a lot of our childlike creativity as we get older. In fact, our propensity to generate original ideas reduces from 90 percent at age five to 20 percent at age seven. Regrettably, by the time we reach adulthood, creativity remains in only two percent of our entire adult population. One of the reasons our creativity seems to be diminishing is that today's society tends to use our left brain more than our right. Today's educational system seems to focus on mathematics, language, and logic. Our left brain also comes heavily into play as we deal with the everyday chores of life, including balancing the checkbook, handling administrative duties, or just going through all the political red tape at work.

> *Don't make the perfect the enemy of the good.*
> —Voltaire

Creativity and Perfection

There's this wonderful story where two old buddies are discussing marriage.

"How come you've never married?"

"Well I guess I just haven't found the perfect girl yet."

"Surely you met at least one girl you wanted to marry."

"Yeah," I did meet one perfect girl."

"Well why didn't you marry her?"

"Simple, she was looking for the perfect man!"

Julia Cameron, in her classic book *The Artist's Way*, suggests that when it comes to creativity, we should not try to be too much of a perfectionist. Most of us fear that we won't write the perfect book, the perfect screenplay, make the perfect presentation, throw a perfect party with perfect guests, hit that perfect note, or perform that perfect audition. Let's face it: there will always be room for improvement in any creative endeavor. Very few of us nail a masterpiece on our first try. The world of creativity is chock-full of revisions, rewrites, and if-at-first-you-don't-succeed type scenarios. But at some point, you have to fish or cut bait. Any film editor will tell you that a movie is never cut perfectly. Any author will tell you a book is never really completed. An artist will tell you that their painting was never really finished—they just ran out of canvas. But at some point, even creative people have to meet the reality of deadlines or they'll never be able to share their creativity with the outside world.

Consider the quintessential Renaissance man, Leonardo da Vinci. He was an all-purpose creative talent as a sculptor, painter, engineer, architect, and inventor. He was not just a jack-of-all-trades—he actually mastered all of them. But Leonardo had a big flaw—he had a hard time finishing his projects. He had so many projects going at once, he had difficulty completing any single endeavor. His lack of focus prevented him from ever achieving financial independence. His failure to discipline his creative talents also deprived the world of a lot of his true greatness. Remember: your art and creativity are only a gift when you actually finish what you start.

When it comes to creativity, perhaps Julia Cameron asks the core question: "what would I do if I didn't have to do it perfectly?" Do you have an answer?

If you have a voice within you that says, "you cannot paint," then by all means paint, and that voice will be silenced.

—Vincent van Gogh

Reawaken Your Creative Spirit

So where am I taking you here? Simple. Don't put your creativity on hold! Don't live life vicariously in the creative dreams of others. Stop telling yourself it's too late. Unlock your own creativity—now. Let the creativity that resides deep within your veins flow freely. Regardless of how you do it, it's important to reawaken the creativity that lies dormant within you. For instance, if you always wanted to learn how to play the guitar, take lessons now. If you always wanted to paint, buy some paint, brushes, and an easel and start painting. If you always wanted to be a mentor, find somebody who needs mentoring. If you always wanted to be a dynamic speaker, get in front of an audience. If you always wanted to be a gourmet cook, take some cooking lessons or invite a few guests over to try your new recipe for Eggplant Parmesan. If you always wanted to climb mountains, start climbing. If you always wanted to write a book or screenplay, start pounding those keyboards. First visualize your creativity and then unleash it to the outside world.

Animator Huck Jones tells us that in order to draw a coyote "you have to have a coyote deep within you and you have to get it out." The people who carve Buddhist figures often claim they look for the Buddha deep inside the wood. In my opinion, you're only a creative person when you are willing to share your creativity with the outside world. In short, feel the fear and unleash your creativity anyway.

All of us have our own form of creativity. Don't let it lie dormant—take action and express your own art form as a gift to the outside world. Famous producer Frank Capra once said, "A hunch is creativity trying to tell you something."

Our right brain is just waiting to be tapped. When your creativity bubbles to the surface, it unleashes an explosion of new ideas, directions and paths that can have a lasting and positive impact on your life.

Presentation Dynamics

When it comes to expressing your creativity, sometimes it's not just what you present, it's the impact you make when you present it. I call this the art of "Presentation Dynamics."

As a young marketing executive with Motorola, the art of presentation dynamics played a pivotal role in securing the approval of my target audience. Let me set the scene for you. Part of my job was to present our annual TV advertising campaign to our top five hundred retail accounts. When it came to advertising, this group was hard to impress. They all envisioned themselves as self-appointed advertising experts. Every year I'd have the same problem in presenting our TV ad campaign to this group. Half the group loved the campaign—the other half hated it. I could never seem to get their total approval. After several years of frustration, I put my own creative plan of presentation dynamics into action at our annual meeting. I addressed the retailer group by admitting that because we were all advertising experts, it made it tough to please everybody. I gained empathy by telling them that it was nearly impossible to gain unanimous approval for something as subjective as advertising. I told them how I really felt by singing them a song that I co-wrote entitled "Everyone's an Advertising Expert." It was a long time ago, but the song went something like this:

"Everyone's an advertising expert. Everyone knows how it should be done and just when you get the thumbs up on what everybody thinks, the window washer peers in and says, you know, that ad really stinks!"

I know what you're thinking, "don't quit my day job." But, you know my little song worked! After gaining my audience's understanding (not to mention empathy) they gave my new ad campaign their unanimous approval. For the first time in my young career, I got to exit stage left with a thumbs up and a thundering round of applause. Again, sometimes it's not only what you present—it's the impact you make presenting it.

The rhetorical beauty of Dr. Martin Luther King, Jr.'s "I Have a Dream" speech in the racially torn Washington D.C. of 1963 is unparalleled. At a time when our language has been reduced to texts, tweets and emails, it's important to understand the sheer beauty and power of a well-prepared speech. In this case… it was a speech that changed the entire trajectory of a nation.

> *Money never starts an idea;*
> *it's the idea that starts the money.*
>
> —W.J. Cameron

The Creative Process

When it comes to harnessing creative ideas there is no right or wrong way. But one thing is clear: creativity is indeed a process. In his now-classic book *A Technique for Producing Ideas,* James Webb Young teaches us to think within a creative process to generate ideas. His outline is delightfully simple, but it works:

1 Gather your information

2 Digest your information and blend it into your mind

3 Sleep on the information

4 Give birth to the idea

5 Put the idea into action in the real world

The very soul of creativity lies with the generation of a relevant and exciting idea. This holds true whether you're a business executive, teaching professional, computer programmer, advertising copywriter, home designer, painter, musician or screenwriter. But facing a dark computer screen or blank sheet of paper can be an intimidating and daunting experience. Even if you think you've never had a creative idea in your life, I suggest you try Young's simple but highly effective process. It will help you break through any mental barriers that might prevent you from unleashing your creativity on the outside world.

Creative Rituals

When it comes to stimulating our creative energy, everybody seems to have their way of doing things. Each of us has rituals that can kick start our creative intensity. Here are some rituals that people tell me they have used to put themselves back into a creative flow and mood.

- Take a shower
- Listen to classical music
- Go jogging
- Take a brisk walk
- Work out
- Take a short nap
- Read passages from a great writer
- Meditate
- Use affirmations
- Work in the garden

- Continue to read
- Have stimulating conversations with people you admire
- Walk on the beach
- Always carry something to jot down your thoughts
- Carry a digital voice recorder
- Make love
- Go shopping
- Splash your face with water
- Continue to write
- Feel the fear - get right back at it!

Discovery consists of seeing what everybody has seen and thinking what nobody has thought.

—Albert von Szent-Györgyi

The Creative Environment

Your environment can have a major influence on your ability to be innovative and creative. The environment around you sets the stage or mood for you to be at your innovative best. The right environment can provide the stimuli you need to get your creative juices flowing.

We can all learn a lot about establishing a creative environment in our home or office from some forward-thinking companies. The 3M Company goes to great lengths to provide a corporate environment that allows its employees to "think outside the box." The company encourages its researchers to spend 15 percent of their time on subjects that interest them. This creative corporate value system has often paid off handsomely for 3M. Perhaps the best example of this is Art Fry. Utilizing his 15 percent innovative free time; Fry came up with the idea of designing an adhesive paper that led to the marketing of Post-it Notes. Fry's idea hit the jackpot and has become one of 3M's most profitable office products. 3M doesn't muzzle ideas—they provide an environment that brings innovation and creativity out into the open.

Google urges every employee to spend 20% of their work time on their own creative projects that will ultimately benefit the company. They also get to reap the financial rewards of their success.

The possible's slow fuse is lit by the imagination.
—Emily Dickinson

It's extremely important to provide an environment that allows people to flaunt their innovative skills and creativity without setting up boundaries. I used to have a boss that set the stage beautifully for his advertising department by saying; "in my department sins of aggression will be more than tolerated, sins of omission will not." I've learned in our corporate brainstorming sessions that setting the proper tone is vitally important for the creative process to flourish. In our creative sessions, there are literally no bad or crazy ideas. Every idea is perceived as a great one. We eventually narrowcast the ideas, rework them, and extend the "best of the best" ideas to real-world applications. We then hitchhike off each other to make the idea even better. By the time we're done with the process, we can't even remember where the great ideas came from—we just know we're ready to put them into motion.

Providing the proper environment has a lot to do with your own personal workspace. Look at the room in your house or office. Do your surroundings stimulate the creativity inside of you? Does your creative workspace get your juices flowing? Does the lighting in your workspace allow you to see things clearly? What about the noise level? Is it conducive to the level or concentration that you need? Do you have enough privacy? Is there artwork, decorations, or colors that will allow the real you to emerge? Do you have a comfortable chair to sit on or a comfortable table to work on? Many creativity experts agree that all these things are important to maximize the creative process.

Let me pass along this one personal insight. If you have passion and a purpose for your work, you can work just about anywhere. Some of the best writers and artists are so stimulated by their work that they can literally block out the world around them. I used to be extremely sound sensitive, but I find when I'm stimulated and in alignment with my true purpose, I don't necessarily need the perfect place to light my creative fire. I no longer need crashing ocean waves or mountain greenery to get in gear. I can now work on a jam-packed plane, a noisy hotel room, or in a crowded Starbucks. The more places you can work, the more productive you can become.

Handling Criticism

If there's one thing that can stop creativity right in its tracks, it's unjust feedback or criticism of our creative efforts. I'm not talking about constructive criticism that allows us to refine our work. I'm talking about nasty, personal, inaccurate, unwarranted and mean reviews, rendered by critics, pundits, and naysayers. Experts say the best thing to do when this happens is strengthen your resolve, jump back on the horse, and resume your creative work. Renowned artist Paul Gauguin was heavily chastised for what his Paris critics called the "sensationalism" of his art. They thought much of his work was surreal and overstated. Yet, it was Gauguin who knew the truth. It was Gauguin who painted the beautiful reality of the pink-hued sandy beaches of Tahiti at sunset when the lighting was surreal and nearly perfect. Because his critics had never traveled to Tahiti, they were unaware of the reality of his native island work. It was only after Gauguin's death that he became one of the most famous and lauded artists of all time.

But sometimes, constructive criticism is absolutely vital for a company to provide an environment where people can flourish—both in our personal lives and in the workplace. One of my biggest concerns working with my corporate creative teams is that they sometimes lose sight of the marketing strategy by trying to be too artsy or too cute. It's important to be creative, but you can't lose sight of the fact you're trying to sell stuff. This is where solid constructive criticism comes into play.

When it comes to handling criticism, just remember this: it's just another part of the creative process.

On a personal level, I'm happy to say that when my first book *A Marketing Plan for Life* originally came out, it hit the Amazon best-seller list in several categories. In the old days, if somebody didn't like your book, they would have to take painstaking trouble to write a letter and buy a stamp just to give you their feedback. But in today's digital world, the feedback is instant – no need for a stamp. Although the feedback on my initial book was overwhelmingly positive, it was the negative comments that I wanted to answer first and defend my point-of-view. I had to quickly understand this one undeniable fact: you're not as good or as bad as people say you are! In short, if you want to be continually creative, you can't be thin skinned. Learn to handle the heat or you'll be left out in the cold.

I don't like writing... I like having written.
—Dorothy Parker

Creativity Begins With A Vision

When you stop and think about it, when does creativity actually begin? When a writer types the lead paragraph of his book? When a painter first marks his canvas? When a sculptor first feels the clay in his hands? When a child takes their crayons and scribbles on the kitchen wall? I submit creativity actually begins when the author, painter, sculptor, or child envisions what will ensue. The vision or idea of what will be created is the lead part of the creative process. An image or vision of the final book has already been conjured in the author's mind – all that remains is the skill to finish writing the book. That's perhaps why famed columnist Dorothy Parker when she was asked if she loved writing once quipped, "I don't like writing... I like having written."

It's important to distinguish here the difference between a visionary and a dreamer. A dreamer is someone who has big ideas but is not willing to take the risk to share them. A dreamer is always lamenting the fact that he or she thought of the idea years ago – but a visionary actually makes things happen. A visionary sees solutions when others don't. A person of vision is willing to take the right risk and stick their neck out to effect change and make things happen.

Vision is perhaps the best expression and manifestation of our creativity. Our vision provides a direction and purpose to create an attractive and attainable snapshot of the future. Our vision can inspire a single work of art or encourage an entire group of people to reach new heights. Are you a person of vision? Can you see the forest through the trees? Can you visualize the end result before it actually happens? Visionary people often use "creative visualization." They visualize the end result long before it happens. We'll talk more about this mental rehearsal process in chapter ten.

Most of the world's greatest creators, inventors, and artists are true visionaries. Mozart was so attuned to his vision that some say he could actually see and hear the music in his heart, mind, and soul before he wrote it down.

Michelangelo was known to have said that he could see his completed work of sculpture in a huge block of marble—long before he began chiseling away at it. All he really needed to do was chisel out his vision.

Steve Jobs was perhaps our country's most brilliant visionary. He created cool, elegant, personal tools that changed our lives and placed a treasure trove of music, information and entertainment at our eager fingertips. His volcanic creativity allowed us to channel our innate creativity into areas we had never dreamed before. He made going to a retail store an exciting and memorable experience. He did all this while creating a barrel of wealth for Apple and its stockholders. At the time of his passing Apple was literally the most valuable brand in the world. But perhaps Jobs will be most remembered for his vision to create, as he aptly put it, "bicycles for our mind."

In the entertainment world, perhaps no performer in recent years embodies creative vision more than Lady Gaga. She seems to be three steps ahead of everyone else. She has created an over-the-top stage presence that is a delightful blend of David Bowie, Michael Jackson, Queen, Madonna and a bit of Grace Jones rolled into one. "When I'm creating music," Gaga said, "I can already envision how the music will blend in with my on stage presence, including my wardrobe, stage props and extravagant hairdos." Gaga has the ability to be totally outrageous without scaring off corporate sponsors. As of this writing, *Forbes* magazine lists Gaga as #1 on its celebrity 100 list of the most powerful people in the entertainment business.

> *Creativity might be as much found in a first-rate chicken soup as it is in a third-rate painting.*
>
> —Abraham Maslow

Creative Impact

Because we ourselves are all creations, being creative comes with the territory of being a human being. Even if we don't receive the accolades or the label, we are all creative people. We all have the innate ability to leave an indelible mark or unique footprint in the sand of time. All of us have the need to create.

Perhaps the most satisfying part of creativity is the positive impact it can have on others. It could be as simple as creating a sensational deep-dish apple pie or making up an entertaining fairy tale to help put your kids to sleep. It could be a great book, a brilliant screenplay, or just creatively rearranging your living room furniture to create more space. It can be a magnificent painting or finding a shortcut on the way home. The point is, unleash and reawaken the creativity within you. Don't be afraid to go through the creative process. Struggle. Harmonize. Bemoan. Gather information. Meditate. Incubate. Redo. Reshape. Share jubilation. It's all part of the creative process.

We all have a masterpiece inside us just waiting to come out. So what are you waiting for?

SEVEN JUMPSTARTS TO UNLEASH YOUR CREATIVITY

1 **Rekindle your child-like wonderment** – Let your creative spirit flow without worrying about peer pressure or criticism. Remember what it was like when you were a child and just starting to etch your finger paintings on the fridge. Rekindle the curious beginner's mind you had as a child.

2 **Envision the end result** – Before you start to write, paint, sculpt, make a chocolate cake, or hang the beautiful drapes you just made, have a vision of what you want to create first.

3 **Use it or lose it** – Creativity is like a muscle; if you don't use it, you'll lose it. If you've always wanted to paint – buy some easels, paint and brushes, and get started. If you always wanted to write, have a vision and start pounding the keyboard.

4 **We are all creative equals** – Remember: you don't need to write a best-selling book or hit number one on the musical recording charts to be creative. You can be creative by decorating your living room, planting a garden, cooking a gourmet meal, creating business solutions, or solving a problem within the family. Bring creativity to your daily living – no need to wait for the sound of the trumpets to arrive.

5. **Don't wait for perfection** – There will always be reason for improvement in any creative endeavor. Any screenwriter will tell you no movie script is ever perfect. An artist will tell you no painting is ever really finished – they just ran out of canvas. Ask yourself: "what would I do if I didn't have to do it perfectly?"

6. **Handle the heat** – Remember you're never as good or bad as people say you are. Handling criticism and having to confront your fears is an integral part of the creative process.

7. **Celebrate!** – Learn to celebrate both big and small things. Like writing a chapter of your book or learning a new guitar cord or getting an "A" on your exam. Take a step back and reward yourself by smelling the roses of your accomplishments.

Executive Summary

This chapter reinforces the point that great advertising comes from a well-conceived total marketing plan. A great ad campaign is a natural outgrowth of the prior seven steps of the planning process. You need to complete points one through seven before you are truly ready to present your company's creative message to the outside world.

Similar to a great ad campaign that captures the heart and soul of a company, our innate creative talents allow us to share our special DNA, vision, and creativity to the outside world. We are all born with right-brain creativity, but research shows that we lose a lot of our childlike creativity as we grow into adulthood. It's not that we lose our creative skills; it's just that we need to reawaken the creativity that resides in us. We should not let fear of failure or lack of perfection put our creativity on hold. If you've always wanted to paint, start painting now. If you always wanted to write a book or screenplay, start pounding those keyboards. Find a creative environment that suits you. Don't overreact to unjust criticism. Harness your creativity and share your vision with the world around you.

Time to Reflect
Have you put your creativity on hold?
Do you have a masterpiece within you just crying to get out?

CHAPTER 9

Plan Your Distribution

Investing Your Time and Energy Wisely

*Things that matter most should not be
at the mercy of things that matter least.*
—Johann Wolfgang von Goethe

In life, distribution is all about investing quality time with quality people and putting yourself in the best position to succeed.

In business, distribution is about deciding where to sell your product or service while remaining consistent with the business you're in. When planning your distribution strategy, it's important not to stray off course. It's about being selective in choosing where to sell your product or service. If you want to maintain a high-end positioning for your product, you should probably think twice about selling at a discounter like Wal-Mart. Likewise, you're not likely to see Tiffany selling in the jewelry section of a mass-marketing retailer like Sam's Club. The fact is, when it comes to distributing your product and service, like it or not, you're often judged by the company you keep.

Bricks and Clicks

The world of business distribution has been turned on its head with the advent of online stores that are rapidly challenging the existence of traditional brick and mortar retailers. For instance, in the video retail business, the Netflix "direct to your mailbox" approach has redefined movie distribution and has caused the demise of not only mom and pop video stores, but the bankruptcies of former video giants like Blockbuster and Hollywood Video. Netflix has taken things even a step further by incorporating instant view on your computer and TV.

When it comes to innovative online distribution, Amazon clearly leads the way. Launching with books and music, and eventually evolving into everything from refrigerators to diapers, Amazon has singularly challenged the traditional practice of brick and mortar retailers. Amazon's overall acceptance and customer loyalty has created a highly successful distribution channel for thousands of companies that want to sell their products online. Amazon offers customers an immense selection of products in their corridor of interest, oftentimes with free shipping, allowing the company to be highly competitive with any traditional retail store.

In auto retailing, CarsDirect has changed the way we buy cars. By logging onto the company's website, you no longer have to suffer the indignity of waiting at the car salesperson's desk for the skullduggery promise: "Let me check with my sales manager to see if there's anything more I can do for you." Today, to buy a car, you don't even have to walk into the car dealership; just log onto CarsDirect.com and within minutes you'll have a series of car pricing quotes from multiple dealerships dying to have your business. No more hassle – just the facts. All you have to do is decide the color and accessories and drive off the lot in your shiny new car.

While many people feel totally comfortable with online purchasing, a good percentage of the population is still more comfortable with personal face-to-face attention that is the heart and soul of reputable retailers like Nordstrom, Trader Joe's, Wegman's Markets, Panera Bread, and of course Apple stores. Although Apple nationally has its own online store, it now has over 350 brick and mortar stores that render an up-close and personal retail experience for its ardent and loyal customers. The Apple stores feature a genius bar where people can get just about any technical problem resolved on the spot. Apple Stores also render a friendly concierge-type customer service, normally found only in posh hotels and resorts. Apple has both sides of the distribution coin totally covered.

De-Marketing

Sometimes a product or service is "de-marketed" or unevenly distributed to create a buzz and positive word-of-mouth for your company's product or service. De-marketing is a fancy Harvard term for people wanting something more when it's not readily available to them. For instance, when Red Bull enters a market it strategically limits its number of retailers versus mass distributing the product. Likewise, new restaurants often limit the number of reservations at the outset to create a "tough to get in" buzz.

I had my own de-marketing story. When I was attending college in New England, Coors beer was only distributed in seven western states. Because Coors was not readily available in our region of the country, it quickly became the cult beer of choice at our fraternity parties. It came to this; if we had Coors at our frat parties, it would be the party of choice on campus. So every Thursday we would send a 25-year-old perpetual student (who wasn't going to class anyway) to Kansas to bring back the beer for our weekend beer blasts. This went on until my junior year, when Coors started to distribute nationally. Once Coors went national, it was no longer the cult beer of choice. We had to find other more imaginative ways to get the best-looking girls to attend our frat parties.

Long Tail Distribution

In today's digital world, the Internet is constantly creating new distribution channels. The traditional 80/20 rule states that 80% of your business will come from 20% of your customers or products. The Long Tail distribution concept popularized by Chris Anderson in a 2004 *Wired* magazine article challenges the long held 80/20 rule. The Long Tail concept argues that products in low demand, or those that have a relatively low sales volume, can collectively render a market share that rivals or exceeds the relatively few current blockbusters or bestsellers. Research indicates that a significant number of Amazon's sales come from obscure hard-to-find books not readily available in brick and mortar retail stores. An Amazon employee once described the Long Tail concept in a basic way: "We sold more books today that didn't sell at all yesterday, than we sold today of all the books that did sell yesterday." Beyond Amazon, some of the most successful companies in the world have leveraged the Long Tail as a key component in their distribution strategy including NetFlix, Google, Yahoo!, and Apple's iTunes store.

However, it is only fair to point out that Wharton School researchers, professor Serguei Netessine and doctoral student Tom F. Tan argue that the Long Tail approach holds true in some instances, but not in the majority of cases. The Wharton researchers contend that when a company factors in valuables such as costs, against the potential gain of single niche product offerings, mass appeal products still rule the roost of profitability. Suffice it to say that the landscape of distribution is changing significantly in today's digital world.

Be Where the Business Is

Another element of distribution is that you want your products or services to be sold in locations where the majority of business is most likely to occur. You want to put your company in the best position to maximize its sales. In short, you want to be where the action is. I personally had the misfortune to explain to our board of directors at a well-known boat company that our sales were excellent—except in places where there were large bodies of saltwater. That was highly unfortunate since we were in the business of selling boats. I subsequently explained that the hulls of our boats could not hold up to saltwater over the long term, therefore limiting our sales to freshwater lakes and reservoirs. The fix was simple: modify our hulls and increase sales by being able to sell our boats to both saltwater and freshwater regions. In short, position yourself to be where the business is.

Life is not measured by the breaths you take, but by its breathtaking moments.

— Michael Vance

Investing Your Time and Energy Wisely

*If you want to be a rose,
don't plant yourself in the desert.*

—Stuart Emery

Position Yourself to Succeed

On a personal level, just as a company needs to distribute wisely to maximize sales, we as individuals need to put ourselves in the best position to succeed in life. We, like companies, need to get close to the action. For instance, if you aspire to be a great actor, perhaps you should consider moving to New York or Los Angeles to see how your talent stacks up against the competition. If you want to be a country singer, you might consider Nashville to get closer to the heart of the country music business. If you have a great online business idea, consider moving to Silicon Valley. Distribute yourself wisely – put yourself in position to score and hit your goals.

Personal distribution is also about exercising quality time management. It's about investing not just spending quality time with quality people. It's not just about going through the motions, it's about investing your time on those things that matter most – not the things that matter least. It's about taking timely action. It's not spreading yourself so thin that you can't deliver on the promises you made to yourself and other important people in your life. It's about utilizing your time wisely pursuing your true purpose or calling in life.

The Power of Positive Energy

Distribution is also about spending your time with people who support you. As a child growing up, actress Jodie Foster was surrounded by positive feedback from her family and friends. Upon accepting the Academy Award for best actress, Foster held up her Oscar statuette and proudly proclaimed, "This is for my mother, who told me as a child that my finger paintings on the refrigerator were really Picassos."

No matter how much money we have or how much fame we've achieved, we all need to be around people who give us positive energy. Frank Sinatra was seventy-eight years old and still selling out all his concerts. On one particular night, in front of a packed audience, Sinatra couldn't remember the words to one of his standard songs—*All or Nothing at All*. Try as he might, the words would not come to the aging superstar. Now, in his younger days brimming with confidence, Sinatra would easily brush this off with a self-deprecating joke and move on to another song. But at seventy-eight, and in the twilight of his career, Sinatra seemed totally embarrassed––to the point that he told the packed house, "I'm very sorry… maybe I shouldn't be doing this anymore." As the star was about to shuffle off the stage for probably the last time, a voice in the highest section of the balcony rang out, "That's OK, Frank, we love you anyway." Then another voice echoed, "We love you, Frank." And then another voice rang out, "Come on back, Frank, we love you." Then almost in magical unison the entire audience gave him an enormous standing ovation. The teary-eyed star, obviously emotionally moved, came back on stage and sang the song he couldn't remember with the verve, poise, and passion of a fabulous talent in his prime. The positive energy Ol' Blue Eyes received from his audience pulled him through on a night when he really needed encouragement to stay focused on the moment.

Spending quality time with quality people who mentor, motivate, and encourage you has always been an important element in achieving true success. Unfortunately, the reality of life doesn't always allow us to associate with positive-thinking people all of the time. However, we can certainly make a concerted effort to identify those people who give us the most energy in pursuing our goals, dreams, and aspirations. A high-achieving professional friend of mine has a simple but effective way of achieving this. He writes down those people who make his PE (positive energy) list. Those who send off negative energy make his NE list. His goal? Spend as much quality time as possible with the people on his PE list. He personally used this PE system to help make a remarkable recovery from life-threatening cancer. He surrounded himself with positive-energy people who encouraged and motivated him to beat the disease. He won his bout with cancer in part because of the support system around him.

> *Never allow someone to become your priority while you remain their option.*
>
> — Mark Twain

Attracting like-minded, positive people will allow you to break any cycle of negativity that saps you from achieving your goals or dreams. In her book *Positive Energy*, Judith Orloff talks about different types of energy vampires that try to suck you emotionally dry. She points out the "drama queen" who tries to wear you out with her melodramas. The "sob sister" who is always whining about something, the "blamer" who tries to transfer the blame to you and finally, the "go-for-the jugular" type that is always trying to put you down. Now that you've a got the characteristics and a handle on these vampires, don't let them drain you. Simply stay away from them, don't listen to them, or set clear time boundaries of toleration. It's been said that the essence of love is not just having someone you can live with, but rather someone you can't live without.

A Question of Timing

When it comes to distribution, proper timing is everything. In a legendary ad campaign for Paul Masson wine, actor Orson Welles holds up his wine glass proudly and proclaims: "We'll sell no wine before its time."

Without a clear understanding of time and how to invest our time wisely, we'll have difficulty in achieving our goals, dreams, and aspirations. For starters, as A. Roger Merrill and Rebecca R. Merrill discuss in their illuminating book *Life Matters*, two types of time exist. There's chronos time—a Greek word meaning chronological time. *Chronos* time is linear; no minute is worth any more than any other minute. Time just marches on. The clock dictates the rhythm and beat of life. A key question in chronos time would be how many hours did you work today?

The other type of time paradigm is called *kairos* time—another Greek word that means appropriate or quality time. Here time is something to be experienced. It's not how much time you spend; it's what you do with your time that matters. The essence of kairos time is in the value of the time, not in the numbers or hours spent. So the key question in kairos time is not so much how many hours you worked, but what quality things did you accomplish with your time? Did you invest your time on those things that mattered most?

Investing Time on What Matters Most

In her famous Villanova commencement address, Pulitzer Prize–winner Anna Quindlen recounted the words Senator Paul Tsongas spoke when he decided not to run for reelection because he was diagnosed with cancer: "No man ever said on his deathbed I wish I had spent more time in the office."

Pastor Rick Warren, in his book The Purpose-Driven Life, reinforces Quindlen's sentiments:

"I have been at the bedside of many people in their final moments when they stand on the edge of eternity and I have never heard anyone say, "Bring me my diplomas, I want to look at them one more time. Show me my rewards, my medals, that gold watch that I was given." When life is ending, people don't surround themselves with objects. What we want around us are people—people we love and have relationships with. In our final moments, we all realize that relationships are what life is all about. Wisdom is learning that truth sooner than later. Don't wait until you're on your deathbed to figure out that nothing matters more."

Listen up a minute. Even as I write this book, I'm on the same journey as you. I am finally beginning to recognize that the key to time is not just to spend it, but to make a wise investment in it. Unfortunately, we often have a big gap between what is really important and how we actually spend our time. Here's the wake-up call: you'll never find time for anything important unless you make a commitment to make the time.

After years of primarily spending my time on making money, my own book got me thinking about how I could reapply my passion and marketing acumen to a higher meaning or level. I always dreamed about running a Christmas festival for underprivileged kids. I wanted to share my own childhood memories of the warmth, joy and festive spirit of the holidays. I contacted the Boys and Girls Club in my area and together with my multi-talented business partners, we put on a charitable holiday event called Yule Fest. The three-day event captured the childlike wonderment of the holidays replete with a tree lighting ceremony, Christmas puppet show, magic show, chocolate dipping demonstrations, and gingerbread houses galore. We even brought in a snow making machine so California kids could frolic in snow that most of them had never experienced. It was the kids themselves that made the event memorable. They formed a Christmas choir that sang at our charity dinners and made ornaments for sale in an open air market. The major benefit of the Yule Fest event is that we raised thousands of dollars to support the Boys and Girls Club's lunch and education programs. But there was clearly a side benefit I hadn't counted on. On my way to thinking I was going to give these kids a special Christmas, they gave me my best Christmas ever! This is a Christmas classic case of the giver becoming the receiver.

> *Don't say you don't have enough time.*
> *You have exactly the same minutes and hours per day that were given to Helen Keller, Pasteur, Michelangelo, Mother Teresa, Leonardo da Vinci, Thomas Jefferson, and Albert Einstein.*
>
> —H. Jackson Brown

By now you're recognizing there's a big difference between linear time management and quality time management—between spending time and investing time. Dr. Dan Baker points out in his book, *What Happy People Know*, that each of us has exactly the same amount of time as the richest and most powerful people in the world. Even the wisest person has only twenty-four hours in a day. It's what we do with that day that counts. Baker concludes that "time is not a tyrant. Time is the great equalizer."

Life offers us the precious gift of time. But time is fleeting and mysterious. None of us really know how much time we have left. That's why the gift of time is the most valuable gift you can give another person. Pastor Rick Warren explains: "Time is your most precious gift because you have only a set amount of it. You can make more money but you can't make more time. The most desired gift of love is not diamonds or roses or chocolates. It is focused on attention."

> *If you want to make good use of your time, you've got to know what's important and then give it all you've got!*
> —Lee Iacocca

Too Busy Working to Find the Time

I was spending a delightful evening at a trendy restaurant in New York with a business associate of mine. Let's call him Don. He was an executive with a large apparel company. After several glasses of wine, Don started to lament that his personal life was almost in a shambles. He knew he wasn't spending enough quality time with his wife and two young kids. He also mentioned that he had a passion for golf and that he wished he had more time to improve his golf game. In short, he wanted to spend more quality time on the important things in his life, but he just couldn't seem to find the time because he was so busy working. Listening intently, I asked him to draw two pie charts on the napkin in front of him. (Come to think of it… how trendy could this restaurant be if they were using paper napkins?)

On one pie chart, I urged him to jot down how he would like to invest his time. As I looked at Don's pie chart, naturally a big percent of his pie was spending more quality time with his family; another slice of pie had to do with improving his golf game. Still another had to do with maintaining health, and yet another related to spending more quality leisure time. What was interesting was that his present job was only an average slice of the pie. The kicker came when I asked him to write another pie chart that revealed how he was actually spending his time.

How Don would like to spend his time.

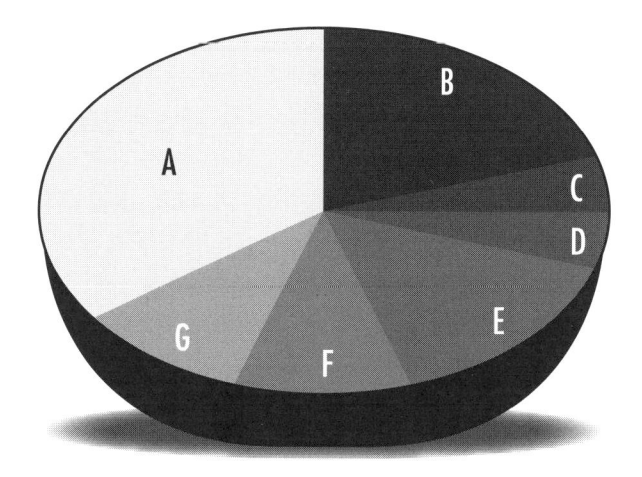

A Family
B Present Career
C Golf
D Quality Leisure Time
E Health
F Friends
G Financial Portfolio

How Don is actually spending his time.

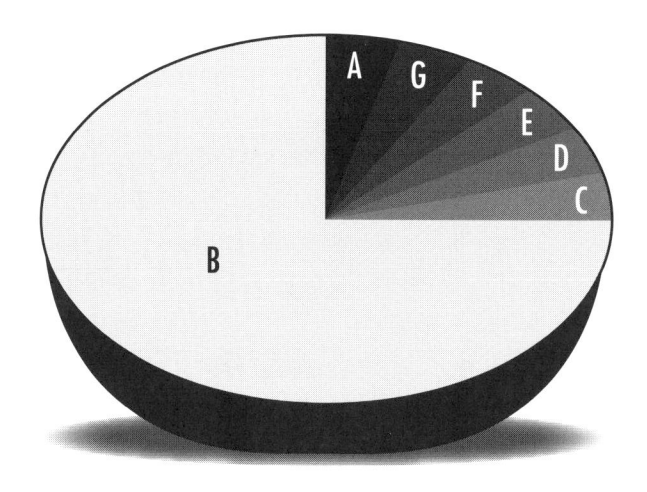

A Family
B Present Career
C Golf
D Quality Leisure Time
E Health
F Friends
G Financial Portfolio

You guessed it! His present job occupied the vast majority of his pie with virtually no time left to focus on what mattered most to him. As we parted, I asked Don to think hard about his time commitments.

A year passed and I lost contact with Don. I knew he'd left his company, but I didn't know where or how to find him. Then out of the blue he phoned me. We met for dinner, and Don explained that he had moved to a smaller company and was happier than he'd ever been. Although his new executive position paid him somewhat less money, it was less stressful and afforded him quality time to spend with his wife and young kids. By the way, his golf game was vastly improved after he spent a week playing golf in Hawaii. He took his wife and kids, of course.

I asked Don what was the catalyst for his change. He looked at me in amazement and said, "Are you kidding?" Then he pulled out a crumpled, wine-stained napkin out of his wallet, revealing the two pie charts. Don't ever underestimate the power of a paper napkin!

> *Life is not measured by the breaths you take, but by its breathtaking moments.*
>
> —Michael Vance

Getting a Real Life

In the introduction to this book, we made it clear that you are more than just your work, career, or possessions. Again, your work is what you do—not totally who you are. Besides, you'll also be better at your work if you create a fuller, more purposeful life—a life of meaning, a life that goes beyond being just an executive, a lawyer, nurse, a teacher, a student, police officer, or whatever you do for a living.

Anna Quindlen puts it in proper perspective for all of us: "Get a life, a real life, not a manic pursuit of the next promotion, the bigger paycheck, the larger house. Do you think you'd care so very much about these things if you blew an aneurysm one afternoon or found a lump in your breast? Get a life in which you notice the smell of saltwater pushing itself on a breeze over seaside heights. A life in which you stop and watch a red-tailed hawk circle over the water or the way a baby scowls with concentration when she tries to pick up a Cheerio with her thumb and first finger. Get a life in which you are not alone. Find people you love and who love you."

Quindlen advises us not to waste our days, our hours, and our minutes. To think of life as a terminal illness, because if we do, we'll live it each day with gusto, joy, and passion. If we do that, we'll cherish the journey, not just the destination. We'll live life the way it was meant to be lived—with each day being a gift. Perhaps the greatest gift of all is the gift of time: time for a sick friend, time to mentor, time to share, and time to love.

Let's take time out for a moment and talk about another gift we need to give ourselves and that's "time off." We need to take quality time for ourselves. It's important to re-charge our batteries once in a while. We tend to brag about not taking a vacation and keeping our nose to the grindstone. But it's vitally important to take time off for both you and your family. Ultimately, it's good for your company too—because your mind will be more refreshed, allowing you to see things more clearly upon your return. The net result is often better creativity and productivity.

> *Know the value of time; snatch, seize*
> *and enjoy every moment of it.*
> *No idleness, no laziness, no procrastination.*
> *Never put off till tomorrow what you can do today.*
>
> —Chesterfield

Time Is Fleeting

Time is one thing we cannot recycle. There's an Egyptian proverb that proclaims: "time never gets tired of running!" I don't mean to be morbid, but we have only so much time left in our lives. In fact, if one were to divide an average lifetime into thirds, many baby boomers born between the mid-1940s and early 1960s are approaching the last third of their lives. Now stay with me on this, and I'll make it come alive for you. In fact, let's try to boil our life down to heartbeats.

- ▶ If a person lives to an average age of seventy-eight years old, he will have more than 3 billion heartbeats in his lifetime. That's an average of 40 million heartbeats in a year.
- ▶ At fifty-five years old, this person has approximately 800 million heartbeats left in his life… or about 27 percent of all the heartbeats in his entire lifetime.
- ▶ At forty-five years old, this person has approximately 1.2 billion heartbeats left in his life… or about 40 percent of all the heartbeats in his lifetime.
- ▶ At thirty-five years old, this person has approximately 1.6 billion heartbeats left in his life… or about 54 percent of all the heartbeats in his lifetime.

We have only a limited number of heartbeats. It's up to us to decide how to use them. Andy Rooney summed it up best when he said, "Life is like a roll of toilet paper—the closer it gets to the end, the faster it goes!" Too many of us realize the importance of time only when we have very little of it left.

Life's Best Teacher

Michael A. Singer, in his riveting book *The Untethered Soul*, explores the notion of death. It is truly a paradox that one of the best teachers in life is the mere knowledge that all of us will die at some point – we just don't know when or how. Wise people embrace the reality, inevitability and downright unpredictability of death. Singer asks us to visualize having a big argument with your mate and leaving with the argument still hanging in the air. Singer implores us to ask ourselves the following question: "How would I feel if they were no longer here? What if you knew it would actually be the last time you saw them?" Singer paints the following verbal scenario: "Imagine an angel comes down from heaven and says, 'Straighten up your affairs. Tomorrow you will be coming to see me.'" If you knew it would be the last time you'd ever set eyes on those that matter most to you, how would you treat them and how much love and affection would you shower on them? If you knew that you or someone close to you was going to die in the next four weeks, how would your priorities change? Who would you reach out to? The punch-line is clear: reach out now to those that matter most to you.

Perhaps the best seminar I ever attended was a two-day event that actually ended a day early. At the end of the first day, the seminar leader asked us to imagine that we had only two days to live. He asked: "Who would you call and what would you say?" As we uncomfortably started squirming in our seats pondering the answer to this vital question, our seminar leader simply said; "This seminar is over a day early – make those calls now and tomorrow to those that matter most to you." Seminar dismissed.

When you stop and think about it, death should not be a morbid thought. On the contrary, death is the greatest teacher we have in life. We should not get in a tizzy over death… instead we should let the very omnipresence of death help us to live life more fully. Singer reminds us that "we don't really need more time before death; what you need is more depth of experience during the time you're given." If you don't live a life of meaning and purpose, it doesn't matter how long you live.

There's a great story that author Jeffrey Davis tells in his book *1,000 Marbles*. A fifty-five-year-old person has about a thousand Saturdays left to live in their lifetime (provided they live to be seventy-five years old). To commemorate this he suggests that we go out and buy one thousand marbles (or pieces of candy for that matter) and place them in a clear plastic container. Every Saturday take one marble out and throw it away. When you watch your marbles diminish, you can more readily focus on the important things in life.

By the way, what are you doing this Saturday? Going out to dinner? Playing on the beach with your kids? Taking in a great movie? Inviting some close friends over for a barbecue? Make every day count—especially Saturdays. Ask yourself this question: When was the last time I did something that I've never experienced before? There's nothing like watching your time here on earth run out to help you focus on what really matters most. Benjamin Disraeli once said, "Life is too short to be little."

Time is one resource we cannot regenerate. The message rings clearly. Spend time; invest your time now on things that matter most to you. Don't wait to take that romantic trip to Venice, Italy. Don't wait to tell your kids you love them. Don't wait until you're too old to enjoy trekking the foothills of the Himalayas. Don't wait to start your own company. Your time is now!

Start now to invest your time on what matters most. Author Michael Josephson tells us how our days will be measured: "What will matter is not what you bought, but what you built, not what you got, but what you gave. What will matter is not your success, but your significance. What will matter is not what you learned, but what you taught!"

SEVEN JUMPSTARTS TO IMPROVE YOUR TIME MANAGEMENT

1. **Define what matters most.** If you don't take the time to define what really matters most, you'll always have a big problem with time management. Invest your time wisely on your "A" priorities, not the "B's" and "C's."

2. **Investing quality time.** Remember it's not how many hours you spend in chronological time, it's the quality and value of time spent that counts.

3. **Avoid energy vampires.** Spend as much quality time as possible with positive, upbeat people. Avoid people who waste your time and zap you of the focus and energy you need to pursue your goals, dreams and aspirations.

4. **Identify time wasters.** Write down those things that contribute to wasting your quality time. These time wasters could include: TV, surfing the Net, phone calls, texting, constant shopping, commuting, and spending non-quality time with energy zapping people.

5. **Delegate more.** Learn to delegate at work, in community service, and at home with your family. Free yourself up to go to your strengths. Don't spend your quality time trying to patch work quilt your weaknesses.

6. **Avoid multi-tasking.** It's been said that if you chase two rabbits, you'll not catch either one. I know that women tend to be better multi-taskers than men. But recent studies show that it takes our brain twice as long to focus when we switch back and forth between priorities. Stay focused and pick up as many as two extra hours per day.

7. **Take time out.** Remember to make the most of your time. Taking a walk in the fresh air, jogging on the beach, or relaxing on a mini-vacation will revitalize you and rekindle both your creativity and productivity.

Executive Summary

Chapter nine centers on the distribution part of the marketing-plan process. In business, distribution is about being selective where you sell your product or service. You are not likely to see Tiffany being sold at the jewelry section of Wal-Mart. In business circles, you are often judged by the company you keep. Distribution is also about efficiency and time management.

On a personal level, we're talking about spending quality time with quality people. It's not just about time management—it's about quality time management. It's about spending and investing time wisely pursuing your true purpose in life. It's not about spreading yourself so thin you can't focus on the things that matter most in your life. We're reminded to spend time with people who send off positive energy, people who encourage us to fulfill our goals, dreams, and aspirations.

The chapter concludes with a dose of reality. Time is fleeting. Time is one resource we can't regenerate. The message is crystal clear: spend time now on that which matters most to you.

Time to Reflect

*Are you currently investing quality
time on the things that matter most to you?
What are you waiting for?*

CHAPTER 10

Achieve Your Sales Goals

Reaching Out to Make Your Personal Goals a Reality

Goals are dreams with deadlines.
—Diana Scharf-Hunt

The next point in the marketing-plan process is sales. On the business front, we have to sell our products, services, programs, concepts, and even an idea or two occasionally. To paraphrase Arthur H. "Red" Motley, former publisher of *Parade* magazine, "Nothing really happens in business or, come to think of it, in life until somebody sells something." Even a starving artist has to sell something, sometime! Most of all, we have to sell ourselves in order to make things happen.

In our business or professional lives, we live in a world where setting goals and sales targets are an integral part of running a business. It is not uncommon for sales people to have weekly and monthly sales goals, quarterly sales targets, and annual sales reviews. Good companies review these goals for validity each quarter, at the very least. Business goals are often readjusted to conform to the swings or moods of the marketplace.

Sales people recognize that goal setting is "business as usual." In the corporate sales world, it's a commonplace way to monitor progress. Those who sell understand the importance of reaching their goals.

Hitting goals and exceeding them is the lifeblood of any salesperson. At our marketing consulting firm, BrandMark, Inc., we developed a sales incentive program for our clients called DreamMaker. The program linked the salesperson's quotas and incremental sales targets with their personal dreams. For example, if a 41-year-old salesperson always dreamed of attending the Chicago Cubs baseball fantasy camp, they could fulfill their dream by exceeding their pre-established company sales quota by, say, 30%. The more expensive the dream, the more the salesperson would have to sell. One lady on our sales staff wanted to attend Le Cordon Bleu gourmet cooking school in France. To realize her dream, she needed to increase sales beyond her original quota by 60%. Our DreamMaker program offered several major benefits to our client companies. First, it tied the company's sales quotas with a salesperson's dreams. Secondly, it created incremental business. Thirdly, it served as a great employee retention vehicle. After all, who would want to leave you and go to another company when you're helping them fulfill their personal dreams?

Sales Mirrors Life

The primary attributes of a good salesperson in many ways mirrors the characteristics that are necessary to succeed in the game of life. Sherry Buffington, CEO of NaviCore International, Inc. guides us in outlining the key personal attributes of outstanding sales performers.

1. **Goal oriented.** Good sales people thrive on setting – then hitting or exceeding their quantifiable goals.

2. **Competitive drive and spirit.** Sales people are highly competitive and love to celebrate victories, both big and small. It's not hard to understand why many outstanding sales achievers are former athletes or love sports. They are filled to the brim with competitive drive and spirit.

3. **Empathy.** High sales achievers have a lot of empathy for their customers or clients. They care deeply about rendering their customers the best service possible.

4. **Integrity.** The best salespeople will not sell their customers something they don't believe in themselves. They know that people buy valuables from people they value.

5. **Ability to shut up and listen.** If there's one trait that all good salespeople possess, it's that they are great listeners. They are good at reading people and understanding their genuine needs.

6. **Self esteem.** Outstanding salespeople don't take the no's seriously. They view the no's as a mere gateway to a yes.

7. **Not afraid to fail.** Even the best of salespeople get turned down 7 out of 10 times. Great sales people have the ability to overcome rejection and the perseverance to close the sale.

Sales and Perseverance

The sales process has a lot to do with perseverance. Perseverance is often the key difference in separating those who achieve versus those who do not. Our tenacity allows us to overcome adversity and the choppy waters that the storms of life present. As mentioned earlier, my mother often echoed the old Irish expression, "Never judge a sailor on a calm sea."

One of my favorite tales of perseverance and tenacity involves the building of the Brooklyn Bridge. In his award-winning book *The Great Bridge*, author David McCullough chronicles the twenty years of effort it took to build this architectural masterpiece.

Before the building of the bridge, the trip across the East River from Manhattan to Brooklyn was an arduous one—there were just too many boats on the water in the summer months, and during the frozen winter, the trip became nearly impossible. In 1863, engineer John A. Roebling drafted plans for a bridge. Although Roebling had a great reputation as a bridge engineer, many reputable engineers doubted that the bridge could be built. Others thought that the bridge's innovative suspension design would sway too much in heavy winds.

In 1869, President Grant approved the plans to build the Brooklyn Bridge. However, a month later, John Roebling died from complications stemming from an accident. His son, Colonel Washington Roebling, took over as chief engineer. By then, political corruption added to the skepticism that the bridge could be built. In 1872, after some real progress, Washington Roebling was struck with decompression illness, which occurs due to the high pressure in the bridge construction's underwater enclosures. The disease rendered him partially paralyzed. He also lost the use of his voice. It was then that his wife, Emily, began assisting him as her husband watched construction of the bridge through his bedroom window. Later, Emily took complete charge of the project and saw the completion of the bridge in 1883. When the bridge finally opened in 1883, it was heralded as one of the most magnificent construction projects of the nineteenth century. Now that's perseverance!

We've all had moments in our lives when we had to call on our powers of perseverance. As the senior marketing vice president of an eyewear company, I tried to reach a licensing agreement with Laura Ashley Limited for Laura Ashley Eyewear—and was turned down more than twenty times! Then one day, I sent a fax to the company's London headquarters telling them that I was going to be in England with my partner and would like to see them concerning the potential licensing deal. After conducting our initial business in London, we went out for a quick pint at a London pub. It was time to head over to Laura Ashley's headquarters. But my partner, who is a kindhearted soul, took a wrinkled fax from Laura

Ashley out of his attaché case. It read, "Dear Mr. Fried, Thanks for informing us of your intent to come to London. Don't come now. Don't come ever. Don't come. We're not interested."

Undeterred, I said, "Let's go anyway." After all, we were already in London. Not knowing that Laura Ashley's corporate headquarters was only five minutes away from the pub, we were taken on a one-hour taxi ride by a crafty cabbie. That one-hour delay allowed us to catch Laura Ashley's managing director, who was alone in the office, burning the midnight oil. In the meeting, we convinced him that we could create incremental licensing revenues while protecting the integrity of the brand. That impromptu meeting led us to closing one of the biggest business licensing deals of my career. That success had nothing to do with being smart—it had everything to do with perseverance. There's an Italian proverb that goes something like this: "He who endures conquers."

Sales executive John Barnickel told me that several years ago his medical equipment company lost a major hospital contract. He paid a visit to the hospital's decision makers to see if he could salvage the contract. It seemed hopeless since a new contract had already been signed and would go into effect in several weeks. The undeterred Barnickel fired for effect and asked if the hospital would consider making just one more major purchase prior to the old contract expiration date. The decision maker quipped: "Put something in front of me." Several days later, Barnickel received a purchase order for over $1 million dollars of medical equipment. When it comes to sales or life, persistence pays off. The worst people can say is "no!"

As my mentor once told me, you should never stop asking for the order. In fact, a marketing study conducted by the University of Notre Dame revealed the following:

- ▶ 44% of all salespeople quit trying to land a client or customer after only one sales pitch
- ▶ Another 24% quit after the 2nd try
- ▶ Another 14% quit after the 3rd try
- ▶ Still another 12% quit after the 4th try

Here's the punch line: 94% of all salespeople have given up by the 4th try. But research shows that 60% of *all sales* are made *after* the 4th try. This amazing statistic shows that 94% of all sales associates don't give themselves even a chance to sell 60% of the potential buyers. That means that 60% of the potential customers are being left at the table!

To be successful at sales… you have to hang in there; you have to have tenacity. You have to have perseverance.

Former U.S. President Calvin Coolidge put persistence in perspective, when he said, "Nothing in the world can take the place of persistence. Talent will not; nothing is more common than unsuccessful men with talent. Genius will not; unrewarded genius is almost a proverb. Education will not; the world is full of educated derelicts. Persistence and determination alone are omnipotent. The slogan 'press on' has solved and will always solve the problems of the human race."

> *Ah, but a man's reach should exceed his grasp, or what's a heaven for?*
>
> —Robert Browning

Think Big!

When it comes to sales, we have to think big. My mentor always reminded me, "It's just as easy to sell a cabin cruiser as it is a canoe! Customers ask the same two questions: 'How much is it?' and 'Is it going to sink?' " It takes the same amount of effort, but the reward for selling a cabin cruiser is greater than selling a canoe, so don't be afraid to reach out and work on the big things. Go after the big fish!

FedEx chairman and CEO Fred Smith is the very personification of one who thinks big. He also knew how to sell himself. While a student at Yale, Smith wrote a term paper proposing a unique global freight and package delivery system. He thought the behemoth U.S. Postal Service was ripe for the taking. Smith was right. He created FedEx, which today is one of the world's largest package-delivery companies. One of the proudest moments in Smith's career came when the U.S. Postal Service decided to add FedEx drop boxes in post offices around the country. Fred Smith succeeded because he had a big vision and was willing to take the necessary risks to make his vision a reality. But the primary reason he succeeded is that he wasn't afraid to fail. He wasn't afraid to take on the vulnerable U.S. Postal Service.

Never judge a sailor on a calm sea.

— Old Irish Expression

Reaching Out to Make Your Personal Goals a Reality

Focusing on Personal Goals

Most people easily set goals in their business or professional life, but many don't take the time to set goals in their personal lives. To achieve a life that offers personal fulfillment and meaning, it is important that we focus on personal goals as well as professional goals. Our personal goals are the signposts that steer us in the right direction, so we can see the light at the end of the tunnel.

Your personal goals should not be cast in concrete. Just like the ever-changing business marketplace, there could be events in your personal life that cause you to consider adjusting your goals.

As in setting business goals where market conditions often change, it is essential that you revisit your personal goals at least every six months. There's a good reason to do this. Life's triggering events often intervene – events that could affect your goals. These could include a loss of a loved one, a changing relationship, job loss, or an unforeseen calamity. These events could also be positive, like having a baby or getting a promotion and moving to a new and exciting town. Setting goals will help you focus not only on what you "want" to achieve, but will also set a specific timetable for realizing your achievement.

> *You have a gold mine when you have a goal in mind.*
> —Author unknown

Goals Versus Objectives

It really surprises me that most people don't know the difference between an objective and a goal. An objective is general in nature—for instance, I'd like to lose weight. A goal, however, is always, always, always quantifiable—it has numbers and time attached to it. A goal is: I'd like to lose ten pounds in the next six weeks and keep that weight off forever.

Here are a few examples of personal goals to get you off and running:

- I'd like to enter and finish the Los Angeles Marathon next year.
- I'd like to take eight months off and sail around the world starting next winter.
- I'd like to have a baby within two years.
- I'd like to increase my financial portfolio by 10 percent this year.
- I'd like to start a new digital marketing consulting business over the next eighteen months.

It's important that we understand that achieving our personal goals, dreams, and aspirations is inexorably linked to meeting our professional goals. In fact, they're literally joined at the hip. For example, I may want to buy a new house or new car, but it will take me a lot longer if I don't meet my business goals, or increase my stock portfolio, or receive my year-end bonus, or earn that commission check. Adding a new baby to the family might require more income in order to maintain your existing lifestyle.

When it comes to goal setting, try to think of it like this: goals are dreams with deadlines attached to them. Vague goals produce what? Vague results.

If people see themselves as a person they can become, and act as if they are that person, soon they will not be acting.

—Cynthia Kersey

Visualize Success

An essential part of succeeding is putting yourself in the proper mind-set to succeed. Motivation experts suggest that in order to reach a goal, you must visualize the end result. Literally, you must "see" the reaching in your own mind before you actually arrive at your goal. People who succeed often make "mental rehearsals" —they script themselves for success. That's why you often see Olympic downhill skiers using "creative visualization," seeing themselves perfectly executing each gate on their way to a gold medal. Top-selling real-estate brokers visualize the "sold" sign going up. (However, the best brokers see themselves already spending their commission check on a shiny new car!) Likewise, highly trained karate experts visualize the end result by "seeing through the brick" on their way to smashing it in half.

Sometimes, the ability to "see" the end goal is the difference between success and failure. In the 1950s, endurance swimmer Florence Chadwick set a goal for herself that was going to be tough to meet. She was already the first woman to swim the English Channel in both directions. Now, at age thirty-four, her goal was to become the first woman to swim from Catalina Island to the California coast. On that Fourth of July morning in 1952, the sea was like an ice bath and the fog was so dense she could hardly see her support boats. Looking ahead, Florence saw nothing but a thick wall of fog. Her body was numb from the cold. She had been swimming for nearly sixteen hours. Sharks cruised toward her, only to be chased away by her support boat's rifle shots. Against the current of the icy, choppy sea, she struggled on while millions watched on national television.

Alongside Florence in one of the boats, her mother and her trainer offered shouts of encouragement. They urged her on by telling her she didn't have much farther to swim. But all Florence could see was a dense layer of fog. Florence was not known for being a quitter. But with only about a half mile to go, she asked to be pulled out of the freezing water. After thawing out her body she told a reporter, "Look, I'm not excusing myself, but if I could have seen land I might have made it." It was not fatigue or even the icy water that defeated her. It was the fog that blocked her vision. She was unable to see her goal.

Two months later, she tried the same swim again. This time, despite the same thick fog, she swam with her focus intact and her goal clearly pictured in her mind. She knew that somewhere behind that fog was land and her goal. Not surprisingly, this time she made it! Florence Chadwick became the first woman to swim Southern California's Catalina Channel, eclipsing the men's record at the time by two hours. Her mantra: Even if you can't "see" the end of your journey, always keep your goals in sight.

It's been said the former champion golfer Jack Nicklaus never stepped up to address the golf ball before picturing the perfect golf shot in his mind's eye. Shakti Gawain, in her bestselling book *Creative Visualization*, teaches us that where attention goes, energy tends to flow. Albert Einstein extolled, "Imagination is everything. It is the preview of life's coming attractions."

Picture yourself succeeding in your mind's eye… then persevere to make it happen.

> *The arrow that hits the bull's-eye*
> *is the result of one hundred misses.*
> —An old adage

There are many other classic examples of why we shouldn't give up. Take a look at this litany of people who never quit:

- Winston Churchill was the odds-on favorite to become prime minister in his early thirties, but did not secure the position until age sixty-six.
- TV soap-opera actress Susan Lucci finally won her coveted Emmy in 1999 after having lost eighteen times in her bid to garner the award.
- Colin Powell got his first job mopping floors at a Pepsi-Cola bottling company.
- Kurt Warner, NFL quarterback and Most Valuable Player, worked as a grocery-store bagger shortly before joining the St. Louis Rams and winning the Super Bowl.
- Albert Einstein was four- years-old before he spoke and seven before he could read.
- Ludwig van Beethoven's music teacher once said of him, "As a composer, he is hopeless."
- Thomas Edison failed more than four thousand times before he successfully invented the light bulb.
- A newspaper editor fired Walt Disney because he "lacked creativity."
- Ted Turner was expelled from college.
- Louis Pasteur was rated as "mediocre" in chemistry by his professors at the Royal College.
- As a young student, Rev. Dr. Martin Luther King Jr. was told by a teacher that he would never be able to speak with enough passion to inspire people to take action.
- Simon Cowell dropped out of school at age 15 and his music company went bankrupt before he created *American Idol*.
- Failing miserably as an out-of-control starting pitcher for the St. Louis Cardinals, Rick Ainkel switched positions to the outfield and has become an excellent position player with a lot of power at the plate.
- At age 30, Steve Jobs was fired by Apple – the company he created. He later came back and under his inspired leadership, Apple became one of the most highly valued companies in the world.

- After being turned down by almost every Hollywood studio, Peter Jackson persevered and finally found a backer in New Line Cinema for his Academy Award winning *Lord of the Rings* Trilogy. His *Return of the King* went on to win a record setting eleven Academy Awards.
- Highly successful novelist John Grisham was rejected by dozens of publishers and sold copies of his first book, *A Time to Kill,* from the trunk of his car.
- Michael Jordan, considered by many as the greatest basketball player of all time, got cut from his high school basketball team.
- The film *Slumdog Millionaire* was not likely to see the light of day when Warner Bros. pulled out of their investment. Fox Searchlight stepped in and the film garnered eight Oscars including best picture.
- Cisco, one of the largest tech companies in the world was turned down by 76 venture capital firms before being funded.
- As a young 22-year-old, Edgar Renteria was a World Series hero with the Florida Marlins. Thirteen years later, though hobbled by injuries, he hit a dramatic three-run homer to lift the San Francisco Giants to their first World Series title in 56 years.

Success is not built on success. It is built on failure.
—Sumner Redstone

Overcoming Fear of Failure

High-achieving people are not afraid to fail. They consider their mistakes as only temporary setbacks or stepping-stones on the road to achieving their goals. Failures are inevitable. Failures indicate a willingness to reach out and take risks. People who achieve their dreams know that failure brings them another step closer to realizing their goal.

In her engaging book *Unstoppable*, Cynthia Kersey says that it's through failure that we ultimately achieve our goals. "Being able to see failure as an opportunity for learning and improvement is critical to becoming unstoppable. People who can't bear a moment of failure have doomed themselves to mediocrity, for they'll never be able to push themselves past a point that is uncomfortable or unfamiliar. Yet it is beyond that place where success dwells."

Sometimes however, you have to watch out for what you ask for – because you just may get it. It's interesting to note that many lottery winners squander their money within 3-5 years after winning it. Many psychologists believe it's because the lottery winners are out of their comfort zone. They simply are not comfortable with their newfound success, so they go back to living from paycheck to paycheck. Here's the punch line: you have to be ready for success or it can take you places you are not ready to go. Historian Arnold Toynbee once opined, "nothing fails like success."

I have a personal story. When my first book hit Amazon's best-seller charts, my publisher immediately asked me to start thinking about writing another book. I said I wasn't ready because I needed to better understand the book I'd just written. You see, I knew I was still on the same journey as the reader and needed to live what I had extolled in my book.

Speaking of nothing failing like success, highly accomplished professional women often have fears about standing out intellectually because of how it might affect their relationships with men. Arianna Huffington, author and founder of the *Huffington Post* relates a story echoed by Maureen Dowd in her book *Are Men Necessary?: When Sexes Collide*. Dowd recalled, "A friend of mine called nearly in tears the day she won the Pulitzer: "Now," she moaned, "I'll never get a date!"

An important part of life is not being afraid to fail. Think of it, Major League Baseball batters go to the Hall of Fame by failing two-out-of-three times! Do the math: you get one hit for every three times at bat, your average is .333, and you're on your way to Cooperstown.

Ralph Waldo Emerson teaches us that the line between failure and success is so fine that we scarcely know when we pass it. In that regard, the difference between a great Hall of Fame baseball player and an average journeyman player is amazingly marginal. If the average player batting a lowly .250 got only two more hits out of every 24 times at bat – they also would be on their way to the Hall of Fame. At one time, Babe Ruth simultaneously held records for most homers as well as the most strike-outs. In fact, when one enterprising reporter asked Babe what he thought about when he struck out, Ruth said, "That's easy, I think about home runs."

In sales as well as sports, three out of ten isn't bad. As mentioned earlier, even the best of salespeople get turned down seven out of ten times. Outstanding salespeople don't take rejections personally – they view them as a gateway to eventual success. Sales people are indeed a special breed. After all, how many people do you know that fail 70% of the time and still call it a great day?

> *You miss 100% of the shots you don't take.*
>
> —Wayne Gretzky

If at First You Don't Succeed...

Sometimes the best stories of persistence and perseverance reside right in your own family. By the time my nephew reached college, Kevin already knew what he wanted to do in life. He wanted to help people with their pain. He wanted to be a doctor.

Although Kevin got good grades in college, he didn't do well when he initially took the Medical College Admission Test (MCAT). He was very disappointed, but decided to get his master's in neuroscience to be in a better position to reapply to medical school. Once again, Kevin failed to achieve a good score on the MCAT exam. Kevin was disconsolate, but refused to give up. He decided to take a job as a medical researcher with the idea that he'd give medical school one last try. But once again, he failed to pass his MCAT exam. No medical school in the country would accept him.

Still unwavering, Kevin decided to apply to a small medical school in the Caribbean Islands. Finally, he was accepted to medical school. Kevin's plan was bold: get straight A's in the small medical school in the Caribbean and eventually work his way back to a good residency position in the United States.

Kevin worked hard in the small foreign medical school and graduated near the top of his class. He applied to many U.S. schools for his residency, but highly respected Stanford was his top choice. There was one small problem: Stanford very rarely accepted foreign students into their program.

During his interview at Stanford, Kevin's quest to get into their residency program, against all odds, struck a respondent chord with his interviewers. They recognized that great doctors know more than medicine—they also understand life and overcoming adversity. They all came to the same conclusion: Stanford needed doctors like Kevin. He was unanimously admitted to one of the best residency programs in the country—ten years after his med school odyssey began.

In summary, failure is just another pit stop on the road to success. All of us are going to fail at times. But we can't permit fear of failure to stymie our efforts to reach our goal. We cannot deprive ourselves from being all we can be. As legendary UCLA basketball coach John Wooden once said, "The man who is afraid to risk failure seldom has to face success."

SEVEN JUMPSTARTS TO FOCUS ON YOUR GOALS

1. **Write them down.** First and foremost, write your goals down. You can write them down in the back of a daily planner, or store them in your computer or smartphone for ready review. Clear, well-written goals are the basic staple of high achievers. A study of Harvard graduates found that after twenty years, the 3 percent of graduates who had recorded their goals in writing went on to achieve more financial success than the other 97 percent combined.

2. **Put them where you can see them.** Place your written goals or picture of the end result on your refrigerator or another highly visible place. It might be an inspirational quote that reaffirms your commitment to achieving your goals.

3. **Recite daily affirmations.** Each day, repeat an affirmation statement consistent with attaining your goal. For example: "today I will continue to move toward the completion of my book."

4. **Go public.** Tell someone whom you respect or admire that you are in the process of achieving a goal. It puts some pressure on you, but it also focuses you on the task at hand. It also adds to your support group.

5. **Use poignant symbols.** Place symbols of your end goal in your office or in your house. For example, if you want to move to Big Sur, show a picture of the waves crashing against the region's distinctive coastline. If you want to take a trip to Positano, Italy find a picture of the enchanting Amalfi Coast to inspire you daily to actually take the trip.

6. **Visualize success.** See yourself succeeding by making mental rehearsals. Try visualizing yourself achieving your goal in your mind's eye long before it actually happens.

7. **Keep positive.** Realizing your goals is largely about having a positive attitude and proper mindset to succeed. It's about understanding that your "IQ" is not as important as your "I can!"

Executive Summary

This chapter points out that nothing really happens in business or in life until somebody sells something. In order to make things happen, we need to not only sell ourselves but to set personal goals that can be quantified. Achieving your business goals is often linked at the hip with making your personal goals a reality. Perseverance is often the key difference in separating those who achieve versus those who do not.

Another key element in the selling process is not being afraid to fail. The lessons of failure often lead to success. Remember, the arrow that hits the bull's-eye is the result of one hundred misses.

Those who are afraid to face failure rarely see success.

Time to Reflect

*Has fear of failure stymied your efforts
to achieve your personal or business goals?*

CHAPTER 11

Analyze Profit and Loss

Tallying Your Personal Balance Sheet

The real measure of wealth is how much you'd be worth if you lost all your money.
— Anonymous

Our personal balance sheet has a lot to do with returning to our core values to enhance our sense of self worth.

On the business front, profitability is a company's just reward for having properly executed the preceding points of the marketing-plan discipline. Profitability creates value for a company, its employees, and its stockholders. Profitability creates jobs, puts food on the table, fosters new product development and allows a company to be a good corporate citizen by giving back to the community. Today the most admired companies are held in high esteem for not only profitability, but just as importantly, for their core values that they stand for. Great companies don't just hang their core values on their wall – they live by them each and every day. In the decade that kicked off the new millennium many large and formerly revered companies drifted from their core values, which led in part to our recent Great Recession.

When money speaks, the truth keeps silent.
— Russian proverb

The Great Financial Meltdown

In 2008 – 2009, a great financial Tsunami rocked the world as we knew it and caused us to take a giant step back to reassess our core values. A plethora of bank, insurance company, and real estate failures triggered the greatest financial meltdown since the great depression of the late 1920s and early 30s. A series of financial calamities ostensibly halted worldwide credit markets, paving the way for unprecedented federal government intervention and subsequent bailout action. Fannie Mae and Freddie Mac, the government-backed entities designed to increase housing credit were both taken over by the U.S. government. Startlingly, the once powerful Lehman Brothers Company failed to find a buyer and had to declare bankruptcy. Troubled Merrill Lynch was acquired at a swap-meet price by Bank of America. American International Group (AIG) the nation's largest insurance company was bailed out with an 85 billion dollar cash injection by the federal government. Several months after these events occurred, J.P. Morgan Chase scooped up the remaining assets of Washington Mutual in what was to become the largest bank failure in U.S. history. Once venerable institutions such as Citi Group ceased to exist as an investment bank and had to crawl to our government, begging for financial aid to stay afloat. On top of everything else, our American legendary automobile companies Chrysler and General Motors both declared bankruptcy.

A people that values its privileges above its principles soon loses both.

—Dwight D. Eisenhower

The major cause of the economic meltdown was rooted in the sub-prime crisis and significantly deflated real estate prices. When the federal government lowered interest rates in the late 1990s, it jumpstarted a housing boom that lasted throughout the next decade. Skyrocketing increases in prices of U.S. homes, coupled with a period of government deregulations, allowed formerly unqualified buyers to get mortgages (especially for second homes) that they really couldn't afford. Banks, almost cavalierly, issued risky sub-prime mortgage loans that started with artificially low "variable" interest rates that increased dramatically after the initial sign-up period. That was fine and dandy for real estate speculators, as long as housing prices continued to rise. But when the housing bubble burst at the seams in early 2007, it caused a calamity in real estate markets. As home prices fell off the roof, many homeowners failing to keep up with their payments lost their homes in foreclosure. Accordingly, banks and mortgage lending institutions lost hundreds of billions of dollars when they were forced to write-off their risky mortgage loans. These write-downs forced many of our financial institutions to the brink of insolvency––with many major firms having to declare bankruptcy. These failures started a chain reaction, precipitating a crisis of consumer confidence that eventually led to the biggest stock market collapse in our nation's history. Many so-called "safe harbor" 401(k)s were down by fifty percent or more.

As customer confidence continued to wane and retail buying was at its lowest ebb, the nation witnessed still another financial scandal in early 2009. Bernie

Madoff pleaded guilty to 11 federal crimes and admitted that he created a Ponzi scheme defrauding investors of twenty billion dollars. On top of everything else, unemployment crept up to its highest double-digit level in years, forcing us to re-evaluate our values and rethink issues ranging from our career path to our once venerable institutions that were now seemingly built on quicksand.

Jerome Kohlberg Jr., from the private equity firm of Kohlberg, Kravis, Roberts and Company, addressed the breakdown of values in corporate America: "All around us there is a breakdown of values. It is not just the overpowering greed that pervades our business life. It is the fact that we are not willing to sacrifice for the ethics and values we profess. For an ethic is not an ethic, and a value is not a value, without some sacrifice to it. Something given up, something not taken, something not gained."

If you tell the truth, you don't have to remember anything.

—Mark Twain

Big Recession Causes a Small Business Boom

It's quite interesting to note that the great recession actually caused a boom in small business start-ups. When people lose their jobs, they begin to rethink their career path and want to take hold of their own destiny. History has proven when everybody else is hunkering down it's the best time to go on the offensive. Need proof? Companies like FedEx, Microsoft, CNN, MTV and Wikipedia were all started during recessionary times. The Kaufman Foundation released a study citing that more entrepreneurs started up new businesses in the troubled times of 2009 than at any time in the preceding 14 years.

Some companies thrived in the chaotic decade of 2000 – 2010. These well run companies stuck to their core values and their profitability continued to soar even in turbulent times. *Forbes* magazine compiled an annual list of the most admired companies and here (as of this writing are a few corporate gems from that list).

Apple

When Steve Jobs returned to take over the reins of Apple after nearly a dozen years in exile, the company was literally teetering on bankruptcy. Thirteen years later, even as the company's CEO reins have passed to Tim Cook, Apple has a market cap of 390 billion dollars as I write this, making it the world's most valuable tech company. Over the years, Apple has redefined itself from personal computers to one of the world's largest consumer electronics companies. It is well on its way to becoming a significant factor in eBooks as well, with the introduction of iPad and iBooks.

The Apple brand has become a cultural phenomenon in the corporate world. The brand is so powerful that its customers are like evangelists that have acquired true religion. Apple users would rather fight than switch to a competitive product. Considered by many as the most innovative company in the world, Apple tends to build the future into its current products. For the past decade, the company has introduced a series of platforms including: the Mac OSX, the iPhone OS, iTunes, new retail stores, the App Store, and the iPad. These innovations will create a launching pad for innovative Apple products in the future.

What makes a company like Apple so innovative is not that it creates a new mousetrap from scratch, but that it designs and markets the existing mousetrap better than its competition. Although the product is at the very cornerstone of everything that Apple does, savvy marketing is the key to the company's almost mythical rise to success. Apple has literally created its own "Apple-speak" language that appeals to everyone who desires to be a creative person.

Innovation and functional design is another key element in Apple's success story. The company cultivates its followers with integrity in design that makes the product almost iconic. Apple often seeks design inspiration from outside the world of technology. For instance, the design for iPad came from studying sleek kitchen appliances and a multitude of auto designs such as Porsche. Even Apple's retail stores are designed more like an inviting Four Seasons Hotel concierge service than a bland outlet acting as a purveyor of products.

When it came to product innovation, Steve Jobs didn't overreact to the whim of the customer; he used their input as inspiration, rather than direction. In this regard, Jobs often liked to quote car-maker Henry Ford, who once opined: "If I had to ask the customers what they wanted, they would have told me a faster horse." When it comes to Apple, its classic ad campaign "Think Different" shows that innovative action goes well beyond mere words.

Southwest Airlines

At a time when many airline carriers are struggling to stay alive, Southwest Airlines continues to flourish with its no frills service, enviable safety record, and a history of on time flights. In fact, as of this writing, Southwest has grown into the largest airline in the world by number of flights and has posted a profit for 37 consecutive years. This great track record was achieved in an industry that historically has trouble making a profit. The company can also boast that it has the fewest customer complaints of any airline in the sky. One of its stated goals is to make flying fun again. The company thrives utilizing a successful business model that involves flying multiple, short trips into convenient and less costly airports of major markets. Unlike other airlines that charge baggage fees, Southwest still allows two pieces of baggage to be checked free.

Southwest believes the best way to succeed is to treat employees with the utmost respect and give them the latitude and encouragement they need to do their jobs well. They must be doing something right as they continuously make the *Forbes* "Best Companies to Work For" list.

Procter & Gamble

Your bathroom, kitchen pantry and laundry room is likely heavily stocked with Procter & Gamble's legendary billion-dollar brands, including: Tide, Dawn, Downey, Duracell, Gillette, Crest, Oral-B, Pringles, Iams, Head and Shoulders, Olay, Pantene, Pampers, and Charmin. Here's a staggering stat: every man and woman on earth spends an average of twelve dollars per year on P&G's products! That's true… you read that right.

P&G now aims to turn its 80 billion-dollar behemoth company into a more nimble growth company over the next decade by reaching outside the United States into developing countries such as China, India and Africa. The company's ultimate strategy is to convince people of relatively modest means to buy P&G products that will improve their day-to-day lives. The company is also making a concerted effort to reach out more to male customers as well as females – especially with its Gillette brand of products.

The key to P&G's strategy is diversity: "we're never going to be able to serve the needs of 5 billion consumers if we are not diverse ourselves" proclaimed P&G's CEO, Bob McDonald.

Amazon

An authentic icon of the Internet era, Amazon is the world's largest online retailer and purveyor of books. Founded in the mid-1990s by dynamic CEO Jeff Bezos, books were just the start of something big. The company eventually spread its wings and expanded beyond books to include CDs, movies, toys, furniture, household cleaning products, groceries, jewelry, beauty products and clothing. Incidentally, it's interesting to note that the company was named Amazon after the world's largest river. The company's logo type is an arrow that stretches from "A to Z." The ultimate goal is to offer every product in the alphabet. It seems that Amazon is well on its way to realizing its goal.

During the 2008 economic meltdown when most companies were hunkering down, Amazon went on the offensive and launched the first electronic book reader called Kindle. In essence, the company created a whole new eBook market with books being sold at a discounted price. Amazon's invention turned the traditional publishing business upside down and brought a string of competition into this newly created segment – most notably the Apple iPad. By 2010, sales of eBooks on Kindle outnumbered the sales of hardcover books for the first time ever – sending another wake-up call to the once venerable publishing industry that was soundly asleep at the switch.

Amazon has always offered a unique "consent marketing" paradigm by following up with its loyal customers in their corridor of interest. It goes something like this: Thank you for buying the latest book on Winston Churchill. Did you know Amazon has thirty other books and five movies on Churchill? We already have your credit card. Click here. It certainly appears that Amazon will be clicking on all cylinders for years to come.

Berkshire Hathaway

If there is a CEO one could admire for his wisdom, integrity and generosity, many would pick Warren Buffett who runs Berkshire Hathaway, a highly profitable investment company with sales over 100 billion dollars. Buffett is currently the world's third richest man with an estimated 47 billion dollar fortune. In 2006, he pledged to give away 99 percent of his wealth to the Bill and Melinda Gates Foundation and other family charities. He has helped convince dozens of U.S. billionaires, including media mavens Barry Diller and Ted Turner to give at least fifty percent of their fortunes to charities.

Buffett has made his fortune at Berkshire Hathaway by implementing a basic conservative investment approach. First, Buffett only invests in companies that are easily understood with formidable long-term prospects. Secondly, the companies must be operated by honest and competent people. Finally, the company or its stock must be available at a very attractive price.

Utilizing this approach, Berkshire Hathaway's core holdings include corporate stalwarts such as American Express, Coca Cola, Kraft Foods, and Wells Fargo. The company also owns Geico Insurance Company, Fruit of the Loom, and the Acme and Justin Boot brands.

When the U.S. economy went into cardiac arrest in 2008, Berkshire Hathaway was one of the first companies that stepped up and supplied liquidity into our financial system. At the very peak of the crisis, Berkshire Hathaway poured

15.5 billion dollars into the financial system by purchasing stock in cash-strapped companies such as Goldman Sachs, General Electric, and Wrigley. In 2009, it acquired the remainder of the BNSF Railway that it didn't already own.

Buffet's investment philosophy should be taught in all business schools as well as the school of life. Here's a sampling of his wisdom when it comes to investing:

- "It's far better to buy a wonderful company at a fair price, than a fair company at a wonderful price."
- "A financial or corporate system that holds no one accountable is a bad system. Hire people who already love what they do."
- "I don't look for the seven-foot bar… I look for the one-foot bar I could step over."
- "We do not view our company itself as the ultimate owner of our business assets… we view our company as a conduit through which our shareholders own the assets."

Buffett believes that a business should be run profitably but also with integrity. It takes 20 years to build a reputation and only 5 minutes to ruin it," claims Buffett. Clearly words of wisdom that we can all heed. Despite the great line from the movie *Wall Street*, au contraire… greed is not good.

Those who stand for nothing fall for anything.

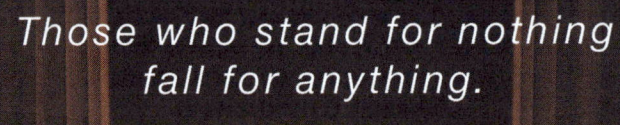

— Alexander Hamilton

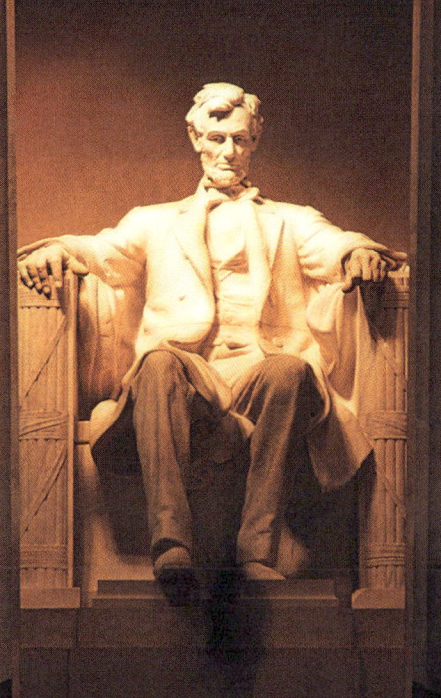

Tallying Your Personal Balance Sheet

Profiting From a Good Value System

Let's talk about your personal balance sheet for Me, Inc. Your personal balance sheet has a lot to do with having a good value system. Good values enhance our self-equity and self-worth. Bad ethics or values lower our sense of self-worth and self-esteem. We as individuals can profit from a good value system. As mentioned in earlier chapters, a key element of knowing yourself is determining what matters most to you. A good value system lays the foundation for what you stand for and truly believe in. Our good values often determine how we act in a given situation, especially in turbulent times—times when life seems to be moving too rapidly or closing in on us. Our good values provide the core stabilization we need to make life's choices based on our authentic sense of self-worth. According to management consultant Jim Clemmer our core values provide us with a stronger sense of personal bottom line. Says Clemmer, "Knowing where we stand on things clarifies what we won't stand for."

> *Seek respect mainly from thyself*
> *for it comes first from within.*
> —Steven H. Coogler

Identifying Our Core Values

Just like these successful businesses, it's crucial that each one of us take the time to identify and clarify our core values. Says my esteemed colleague Dr. Dan Baker: "When we identify these values it gives our life focus and a sense of security—especially during times of chaos and confusion."

Take a look at the core values listed on the next page. Mentally or physically, check off those core values that apply most to you. Later in the workbook exercises section of the book, you'll have an opportunity to narrow down your list.

- ___ Authenticity
- ___ Balance
- ___ Bravery
- ___ Cause centered
- ___ Charitable
- ___ Community oriented
- ___ Compassionate
- ___ Courageous
- ___ Creative
- ___ Dedicated
- ___ Dependable
- ___ Educated
- ___ Empathetic
- ___ Encouraging
- ___ Ethical
- ___ Fair
- ___ Faithful
- ___ Family oriented
- ___ Fitness minded
- ___ Flexible

- ___ Focused
- ___ Generous
- ___ Hard working
- ___ Helpful
- ___ Honest
- ___ Honorable
- ___ Hopeful
- ___ Humble
- ___ Humorous
- ___ Imaginative
- ___ Inspirational
- ___ Integrity
- ___ Inventive
- ___ Joyous
- ___ Kindly
- ___ Logical
- ___ Lovable
- ___ Loyal
- ___ Mentoring
- ___ Open-minded

- ___ Original
- ___ Patient
- ___ Peaceful
- ___ Persevering
- ___ Religious
- ___ Respectful
- ___ Reverent
- ___ Romantic
- ___ Secure
- ___ Spiritual
- ___ Strong
- ___ Supportive
- ___ Thoughtful
- ___ Trustworthy
- ___ Truthful
- ___ Understanding
- ___ Unique
- ___ Uplifting
- ___ Wisdom

Identifying and clarifying your core values gives you a virtual road map that will guide you in making key decisions as you travel through the journey of life. Your values act as a compass that leads you in the right direction and steers you back on course.

When you live up to your core values, you focus on a clearer sense of purpose—one that is aligned with the authentic you.

Rethinking Our Core Values

Not unexpectedly, a new set of American's values has emerged from the ashes of the worst financial crisis since the Great Depression. With double-digit unemployment, a lost decade of stocks, and the worst housing crash ever, it was only natural that we take a step back and reassess our core values – especially the way we think about money and meaning.

American's today are not just cutting back on expenses, we are rejecting a lot of the bling-bling material things that once seemed so important like Mc Mansion homes, fancy jewelry, gas guzzling SUVs, and expensive vacations. Today we are seeking more intrinsic rewards like quality time at home with family, personal growth, good relationships, and giving back to our community. The pendulum is clearly swinging from chasing greed to doing good for others.

There's certainly nothing wrong with the ownership of money, but there is something inherently wrong with money owning you.

> *It's not hard to make decisions when you know what your values are.*
> —Roy Disney

Marketing research polls and a Met Life 2009 study of America's values indicate that Americans are re-calibrating their worth and value of everything from their careers and investments to their happiness and relationships. In short, they are focusing on things that matter most – not the things that matter least.

Surveys indicate that Americans are increasingly moving back to core values. Let's take a look at the chart that I put together below:

WHAT WAS	WHAT IS
Focused on just making money	Focused on making both meaning and money
Big debt	No debt
Net worth	Self worth
Spending	Saving
Showing off our bling	Not flaunting our material wealth
Fancy foreign vacations	Road trips or staying home with family
Retire early at 55 years old	Job security; holding on to your job
Working for a company	Starting up your own company
Viewing your home as a "cash cow" account	Appreciate the home as a place to live
Trusting our once venerable institutions	Trust needs to be earned
Owning several gas guzzling vehicles	Owning fuel-efficient, economic vehicles
About me	About community and volunteerism
Having a good career	Creating life/work balance
Brand name products	Generic products
Supermarkets	Big Box Stores
What was	What is
Maxing out credit cards	Bank debit cards
Focusing on what matters least	Focusing on what matters most

A Silver Lining in the Clouds

Understandably, not all the lessons learned from the economic crisis will stay with us forever. Rest assured, Americans will continue to borrow and spend again when the economy turns around. But enough people have been adversely affected that a return to our intrinsic core values will likely stay with us for quite some time to come. For younger people, experiencing the economic crisis could be transformative as they watched their parents suffer through fiscal trauma.

What lies behind these fundamental value changes could be a real behavior shift in the way Americans view things going forward. In fact, some psychologists believe that the economic turndown might provide a silver lining for the country, forcing us to take a step back and rethink our core value system. "One could easily get the sense that the economic crisis was a long overdue catharsis. A jolt that was needed to reverse a multitude of bad financial habits and destructive attitudes developed over many years," offered Dan Kedlec, a contributing writer for *Money* magazine.

Forming Your Value System

How we formulate our value system has always been the subject of varied opinion. According to many experts, our value system is formed at an early age, often between eight and twelve-years-old. That's why you often hear someone who grew up during the breadlines and the Depression of the 1930s say security-conscious things like:

"Save a penny for a rainy day."

"Eat everything on your plate. There are poor people starving around the world."

"What do you mean… you're a senior in college and you still don't know what you want to be yet?"

However, boomer kids (born between 1946 and 1964) are likely to be far less security minded than their Depression-era parents. Why? Boomers are accustomed to challenging existing institutions and old ideas. Questioning the notion of traditional rocking-chair retirement is no exception. It is very likely that boomers will demand much more than tee times and bingo in their retirement years. The boomer generation seeks experience and discovery as much as the financial security that was often the chief concern of their parents.

Dr. Dan Baker reminds us that our values change as we grow older and go through the winds or passages of life. Here's a chart Baker used at our *Marketing Plan for Life* seminar.

AGE	SOURCE OF VALUES
6–8	Family
8–12	Heroes
12–20	Peers
21 and over	Life's experiences

Looking at his chart and considering my own life, I'd say that Dr. Baker is definitely onto something here. When I was 6 to 8-years-old, my mother was the primary influence in my life, simply because my dad worked long hours at his restaurant. My fiery, red-haired Irish Catholic mother didn't always agree with my dark-haired Jewish father. But they did agree on important things—because they had the same good, solid value system. They taught us at an early age to respect people of various races and religious beliefs. I believe that these core values instilled at an early age helped me immensely in building the international segment of my business career because I was attuned to racial, cultural, and religious nuances. This greatly benefited me later in life to market effectively to other countries.

In my childhood years, I worshiped my baseball hero Mickey Mantle and idolized the New York Yankees. If the Yankees lost or Mantle went hitless, it could literally ruin my day. (I know a lot of you had similar feelings when it came to worshiping your childhood heroes.)

Between the ages of 12 and 20, I was not unlike most of us—I wanted to fit in, so I joined various clubs and fraternities to be one of the guys. In the years that followed my twenty-first birthday, I was definitely influenced by my life's experiences; from college to various management positions, to my parents' recent deaths, to the fast-paced and ever-changing world events. When I stop and think about it, this book itself is greatly influenced and is a natural outgrowth of my life's experiences and core value system. But as someone once said, "My ultimate goal is to be as good a person as my dog already thinks I am."

Dawna Markova, in her riveting book *I Will Not Die An Unlived Life*, offers this enlightened perspective on our core values: "Your values are an activating intelligence in your life, guiding you toward the noble tasks that are yours alone to do. There are moments in all our lives that reveal these values. Their significance lies in not only what meaning we make of them, but also what we allow those moments to make of us."

Your solid core values are like a ship arriving in safe harbor, a beacon to which you can always return, especially in stormy weather and today's turbulent times. Remember, when your outside world reflects your inside world, your sense of value and self-worth will soar off the charts.

It all boils down to this: we are what we value. As Elvis Presley once said, "Values are like fingerprints. Nobody's are the same, but you leave 'em all over everything you do."

Nobody can take away your core values or the essence of being unless you let them. Don't let them.

Balancing Your Personal Integrity Account

Each time you act in accordance with your core values, you essentially make deposits in what authors A. Roger Merrill and Rebecca R. Merrill call your "Personal Integrity Account." This, they point out, is your most important trust account because it reflects the amount of trust you have in your relationship with your authentic self. The more you stay within your core value system, the more you act on what really matters most—the more you deposit into your personal account. The more this account is balanced with core values, the more likely you are to feel a sense of high self-esteem and self-worth.

> *The time is always right to do what is right.*
> —Dr. Martin Luther King Jr.

My personal sense of self-worth was never higher than when I quit an excellent job because, although the job was a lucrative one, the company's values weren't compatible with my own.

One spring, my boss asked me to hire an MBA marketing major from one of the country's top business schools as a summer intern. Let's call this intern Adam. But my boss threw me what I considered to be an unethical knuckleball. He wanted me to lure Adam to the company for the summer (to help out with a big project) by promising a full-time position—then fire him at the end of the summer, regardless of his job performance. I objected strongly to this proposal, to which my boss replied, "I trust you to do the right thing at summer's end." Without hesitation, I answered: "Trust me, I'll do the right thing."

As it happened, we hired Adam as an intern, and he was magnificent in his job. He was well liked and respected by everybody in the company. As the end of summer approached, my boss came into my office and asked if I had let Adam go. I told him that it would be unethical to dismiss such a talented individual, especially when we had promised an ongoing position, and that he would have to fire me first. Instead, my boss dangled a promotion in front of me as an incentive to do what he asked. I refused, and then resigned. My boss urged me to stay, but I told him it was irrevocable.

In the days and weeks that followed, I realized the import of what I'd done. I had no job, no leads, nowhere to go, and a big mortgage to boot. But despite the fears, I felt almost euphoric! I never lacked for confidence, but for the first time in my life I had something more: I had high self-esteem and a true sense of self-worth. When it came down to values, the worst of bosses had just taught me the best of lessons. By the way, it only took me two weeks to land a better position in another company. I guess my rekindled sense of self-worth came through loud and clear in the interview process.

Appreciation in Value

In their thought-provoking book *Inner Security and Infinite Wealth*, Stuart Zimmerman and Jared Rosen remind us that many things can appreciate in value. A stock appreciates in value. Your house might ultimately appreciate in value. Even your baseball card collection can appreciate in value. You can appreciate in value, too. Your self-worth can skyrocket. When you value yourself and when your actions are aligned with your core value system, your sense of self-worth will increase mightily. But more important, you will live a life of enrichment.

> *If you have integrity, nothing else matters.*
> *If you don't have integrity, nothing else matters.*
> —Senator Alan Simpson

Being fully aware of your core values is the key element in making wise choices in your life. Whether it's buying a house, choosing a partner, or making career decisions, your core values come into play. Your value system is the starting point and ending point for all the important decisions you will make in your life. Sometimes, however, we can lose sight of our core values or not factor them in enough during our decision-making process.

My friend Bill was being heavily recruited by a large company based in Arizona. Bill's new career opportunity seemed almost too good to be true. As it turned out, it was. Everything seemed in order. A great financial package? Check. A sunny climate? You bet. A great benefits package? Ditto. Exciting products? Once again, check. A boss who had integrity? No.

During the interview process, Bill's potential boss told him several lies, including the fib that the company's new product line would roll out earlier than anticipated. Bill knew from a previous interview that the new products would likely be delayed for more than a year. He also noticed that the company continued to run ads proclaiming that the new products were "coming real soon." The boss also highly inflated the company's sales projections, which were directly tied to Bill's potential bonus package. Although he came away feeling his potential new boss would not necessarily honor his commitments and probably lacked integrity, Bill accepted the job anyway. Maybe he was blinded by the lure of the Arizona sun. You probably guessed the rest of the story. Bill resigned less than a year later when his boss demanded that he run an unethical ad campaign regarding the still-to-be-delivered new products. Bill failed to realize that when your boss lacks the core value of integrity, every other potential benefit is built on quicksand.

Net Worth Versus Self Worth

After the Dot-com crumbling of 2000-2002 and economic crisis of 2008-2009, it was easy for us to fall into the time-honored trap of allowing our net worth to determine our self worth.

It was especially tough to gaze at our computer screens when our stocks or 401(k)'s plummeted to fifty percent of their former value. That paled in comparison to losing our jobs and finding it even tougher to get another one. It was painstaking to see the value of our home decline, or even worse to lose our home to foreclosure. When crises like these hit, we not only feel demoralized, we feel devalued as a person. It's times like these that we need to constantly remind ourselves that how much money we have isn't the totality of who we are, or even who we can become. It's been said that "the real measure of wealth is how much you'd be worth if you lost all your money". Self worth and net worth are clearly different animals, but we tend to join them at the hip. Net worth is defined as your assets minus your debts. In essence, self worth is being worthy of self esteem or respect. Now, it's recognized that we all need to have enough money to pay our bills and keep a roof over our heads, but our values as best-selling author Rick Warren puts it, "should not be determined by our valuables." In fact, it makes far more sense to decide how we can be valuable to others than it does to rank ourselves by our valuables.

But like it or not, we reside in a culture where the term net worth and self worth have become almost synonymous. It's not uncommon to measure our success purely by money or our possessions. In her book *Money Therapy* author Deborah L. Price sums it up succinctly: "Since we often do not feel good about our net worth, our self worth has become devalued and our self esteem deflated." This is because we have not properly appreciated ourselves for being intrinsically valuable in our uniqueness, separate from our net worth. Most of us never really feel we have enough money. The more we have, the more we want. The less we have the more pressure we put on ourselves to measure up which tend to affect our sense of self-esteem. We feel a distinct lack of security. It's only when you realize that our real security lies in those things that can never be taken away that you can continue to feel a high sense of self worth and self esteem.

When you're a person with good character and good values, you are indeed a person of true wealth. Your real currency is measured not just in money, but the inner security you feel when you are a person of true integrity.

When the dust clears, life isn't about the number of zeros in your paycheck, the luxury car you drive, the fancy clothes you wear, or the size of the home in which you live. Your net worth, no matter how large, will never be a good substitute for your integrity and true character. Don't get me wrong, it's good to have security and to be able to afford the finest things in life. But it's who you become and what you do with your wealth to help others that really matters most.

> *When our life becomes a true expression of our values we make our greatest contribution to the world.*
>
> —Cheryl Richardson

Recasting The American Dream

The American dream is clearly not dead. It is still alive and kicking, especially among our valued immigrants who came here seeking the land of milk and honey. What we do need, however, is a refresher course in what made this country great in the first place. Our Declaration of Independence teaches us the values of life, liberty and the pursuit of happiness. There's nothing written in our timeless and great document about four chickens in every pot… two homes for every person and a gas guzzling SUV in every garage.

As bad as the economic crisis was, it will hopefully provide an opportunity for us to recast the American dream. An American dream focuses on values that our forefathers so astutely laid out before us; an American dream focuses on self worth as much as net worth.

SEVEN JUMPSTARTS TO ENHANCE YOUR SELF WORTH

Regardless of the status of your net worth, here are some steps you can take to enhance your self-worth.

1. **Revel in your uniqueness** – Remember… there will never be another you in recorded history. Utilize your unique strengths to bring value and happiness to others.

2. **Take full responsibility** – Take responsibility for your past actions and mistakes, then move on and turn the page. None of us are perfect. So don't be so hard on yourself.

3. **Have a purpose** – One of the real tragedies of life is not to have a purpose. When you have a real purpose to get up in the morning, your self-esteem will soar. Take the time to define your purpose utilizing the exercises that we talked about earlier in chapter one.

4. **Set quantifiable goals** – Well written goals are basic staples of not only high achievers, but people who are happy. Don't forget to set personal goals as well as career goals. Your goals should always be quantifiable; they should have time and numbers attached to them.

5. **Build your personal brand** – You are the CEO of your own personal brand called Me, Inc. When you build your own brand, you are in essence building a pulpit for who you are and the value you bring to others.

6. **Don't limit yourself by the labels** – Remember, what you do is important, but it's not the totality of who you are. You are more than just a butcher, baker, or candlestick maker. You are also a mother, a father, a friend, a person that cares greatly about their community.

7. **Be generous with your time** – Even if you are low on money, you can be generous with the time you spend supporting worthy causes of others. Give your time to the Boys and Girls Club, the local hospital in your area, or some other worthy cause. It will deposit handsome dividends into your self-worth account.

Executive Summary

This chapter hones in on the importance of profitability—but not profit at any cost. Today's business ethics or values are under severe scrutiny. A company's good ethics and business values add greatly to the overall value of the enterprise.

Likewise, on a personal level, our personal balance sheet has a lot to do with having a good core value system. Good values enhance our sense of self-equity and self-worth. A good value system is often accompanied by a higher feeling of self-esteem. Our value system allows us a safe harbor to fall back on, especially in turbulent times. When you live up to your core values, you are focused and have a clearer sense of purpose. When our outer life is aligned with our inner feelings, we put ourselves in a better position to make a contribution to the world. It all boils down to this: we are in essence what we value. In the words of Alexander Hamilton, "Those who stand for nothing fall for anything."

Time to Reflect

Have your core values ever been severely tested?
Do you have a high sense of self-worth?

CHAPTER 12

Establish Targets of Opportunity

Making Your Dreams Come True

*A man is not old until his regrets
take the place of his dreams.*

—John Barrymore

On a personal level, this section of the plan is all about making your dreams a reality. In the business sector dreams are targets of opportunity or visions of future products and services that are in keeping with the company's core competency. In a sense, this is the dream section of a marketing plan.

There are different types of approaches that will help enable a company to grow steadily and create incremental business. When this happens, the goals, dreams, and aspirations of both employees and shareholders are often realized. Let's review a few of the ways companies can realize their targets of opportunities for growth.

New Products and Services

The Walt Disney Company is a great example of layering on new products and services. They started as an animation company, then a movie studio, branched out into theme parks, created a Sunday-night television program, then a licensed product brand. Later, Disney established hundreds of retail stores selling only Disney-branded characters and products. Disney later acquired the ABC Network and ESPN as part of their family entertainment strategy. Then Disney layered on a litany of other channels to the ESPN flagship station, including: ESPN 2, ESPN 360, ESPN 3D, ESPN Classic, ESPN Latin America, ESPN The Magazine, ESPN Game Plan, and ESPN Soccernet. By layering on these additional products and services, ESPN has become the biggest profit center for Disney. Amazon is another good example of generating incremental business via layering on new products. The company went from selling books online, to e-Books to Kindle. The company's additional product offerings include: movies, music, computers, office equipment, household cleansing products, garden supplies, and beauty care. And the beat goes on!

Creating New Divisions

Companies often set up new divisions so they can achieve greater focus in realizing their business goals. Most companies have international divisions that concentrate solely on achieving foreign-market penetration. Other companies set up key account divisions to focus on selling their biggest customers. When I was at Motorola, we set up "new venture" groups that focused on bringing incremental business into the company. GE set up a financing division that could help people pay for products and services over time. The net result was an incremental big profit center for GE. (However, I must point out that this division suffered greatly in the financial meltdown of 2008.)

Striking Key Alliances and Partnerships

Luxury leather-maker Coach collaborated with luxury car-maker Lexus to create a Coach Special Edition car. Eddie Bauer collaborated with Ford to create the Eddie Bauer Edition of Ford Explorer. Starbucks and United Airlines forged an alliance to improve in-flight coffee, while extending the Starbucks brand name into overseas markets.

The Sierra Club partnered with Clorox's Green Works – a line of natural cleaning products to encourage other manufacturers to "green" their product lines. Although the Sierra Club came under harsh criticism for receiving fees for their endorsement, their strategy was to lend their name to a large company that could promote affordable green products to mainstream America.

Luxury auto companies like Lexus and Land Rover have struck affiliations with luxury resorts. Guests get to use their vehicles for free while at the resort in exchange for highly visible auto displays well-positioned on the grounds of the resort.

Mergers and Acquisitions

On the mergers and acquisitions front, one company often hooks up with another to acquire complementary capabilities that will add value or re-energize the acquirer's brand. Oracle purchased Sun Microsystems, giving the industry's largest software division an entry into the server and storage markets. Google bought YouTube and widely expanded its customer base. Amazon went on a shoe, apparel, and houseware-buying spree by snatching up the social networking and customer loyalty expertise of Zappos. In the consumer electronics sector, Panasonic purchased Sanyo to acquire the company's strength in green energy, solar panels and rechargeable batteries. When Kraft acquired British candy-maker Cadbury, the combined company instantly became the global leader in chocolates and sweets.

Creating New Value-Added Streams

Phone companies are highly creative when it comes to creating new value streams, while still staying within the corporate tapestry. When you get your phone bill, you are charged extra for these valued services: call waiting, call forwarding, caller ID, call blocking, speed dialing, and call conferencing, just to name a few. Still other examples of added value streams include luxury suites at sports stadiums and valet parking at major shopping malls.

Licensing

Developing a good licensing program is one of the best ways a company can grow. Licensing should be viewed as a strategic marketing tool to extend the brand into new market categories, while continuing to build brand awareness of the company's core line. While adding new product categories adds to the brand's elasticity, it should also be consistent with the company's brand image and positioning in the marketplace. Ralph Lauren (fashion apparel) moved into top-quality paint. In concert with their licensing partner, Lauren often updated fashion-color palettes on a seasonal basis in the best hardware stores in the country.

The key to licensing is staying true to the brand. After gaining the bebe license for optical and sunwear products, I was asked to present my suggested brand positioning for the collection in bebe's world headquarters near San Francisco. I was met by a highly intelligent and attractive (after all, this was bebe) Stanford graduate who headed up the company's marketing department. I confidently presented my brand positioning as bebe: the eyewear collection for highly confident women offering a hint of sensuality. To which my bebe colleague replied: "We don't offer a mere hint of sensuality, we offer pure unadulterated sensuality which has sold well, from the beginning of time." Obviously, the bible belt is not the main target audience of bebe products… but hey, you never really know.

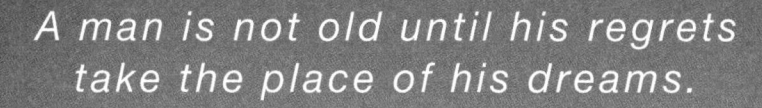

A man is not old until his regrets take the place of his dreams.

— John Barrymore

Making Your Dreams Come True

*Never fear the space between your dreams and reality.
If you can dream it, you can make it so.*

—Belva Davis

Realizing Your Personal Dreams

Just like a growing company, your personal targets of opportunity have to do with realizing your dreams. But it's one thing to have dreams, it's another to have pipe dreams. Similar to any good company, you must make sure your dreams are an integral part of who you are. Your dreams should be aligned with your individual core strengths—as well as with your heart.

Layering on new products and additional targets of opportunity has application on a personal as well as a big business level. If you are an author of nonfiction books, you might consider branching out into writing blogs, magazine articles, newsletters, a newspaper column, or creating your own Web site. These are all logical extensions that can be layered onto your core competency.

In life, we often seek to gain skill sets that others possess that will help us make our dreams a reality. We hire skilled architects and creative interior designers to transform our fixer-upper into a dream house. We retain the services of a stockbroker who lends expertise to establish a financial portfolio that will enable us to fulfill our dreams. By passing on part of the dream work to others, we can more rapidly realize our own dreams.

Both companies and people are able to realize their targets of opportunity (and in a sense, their dreams) by having the courage to create an extended self, while not losing sight of who they are. They create new opportunities for growth, but still stay within the parameters of their core competency. They know how far they can reach to make their targets of opportunity a reality.

One word of caution here: don't reach for something that is unattainable. I might dream of becoming the chief marketing executive for my favorite major league baseball team, but if my goal was to become the chief financial officer, my dream of joining my beloved team would turn out to be a nightmare. Without the necessary skills and interests for the job, I'd be going to my weakness, not my strength. Dream big—but in your dreams don't lose sight of who you are.

The Impossible Dream

U.S. Olympic hockey coach Herb Brooks had a dream that he could guide young amateurs to a gold medal in the 1980 Winter Olympics at Lake Placid, New York. His goal was labeled the "impossible dream," considering his team stood no chance against the experienced, professional Soviet team, which at the time dominated international hockey. In fact, the Soviets demolished the American squad of college kids 10–3 in an exhibition game at New York's Madison Square Garden just one week before the Olympics.

But Coach Brooks convinced his young, inexperienced squad to buy into the impossible dream. In what is now referred to as the "miracle on ice," the Americans stunned the world by upsetting the heavily favored Russian team 4–3. To this day, no single upset in sports history is more fondly remembered in the United States. As the final seconds of the game ticked away, announcer Al Michaels made his now famous call: "Do you believe in miracles? Yes!" The American team went on to secure the gold medal and the hearts of all Americans by beating Finland several days later. Coach Brooks encouraged and motivated his players to believe in their dreams. By doing so, his dreams became their reality. It also became a legendary sports story for the ages.

> *It all started with a dream and a mouse.*
> —Walt Disney

Walt Disney tells his own story about his dreams. His boyhood dream was to draw comic strips. But as a young man, he was strongly advised by a Kansas City editor to give up drawing because he lacked artistic flair and talent. Disney kept knocking on doors, but he was continually rejected. Finally, a church hired Disney to draw some basic publicity material. While working out of an old dingy garage, Disney befriended a small mouse. Disney's new little rodent friend inspired him to create the character of Mickey Mouse. Before long, both Disney and the mouse became part of bigger dreams. You know the rest of the story.

> *Move into your castle in the sky*
> *as if it were your right to do so.*
> —Gene Lundrum

Dreams certainly did come true for Oprah Winfrey, but only after trials, tribulations, and just plain hard work. Oprah was born in humble surroundings in a small farming community in Mississippi. As a child, she was sexually abused and moved to Nashville, Tennessee, to live with her father. As a youngster, Oprah read a lot of books about heroes and heroines that inspired her to have dreams of her own. After attending Tennessee State University, she began working in a Nashville radio and television station. Later, Oprah moved to Baltimore where she hosted a TV chat show called *People Are Talking*. The show became a hit and she was asked to host another talk show—*A.M. Chicago*. Her major competition in this time slot was Phil Donahue, who at the time, literally owned the daytime talk show market. After just a few months, Winfrey's unique, warm, and empathetic personality had won her considerably more viewers than Donahue. Oprah vaulted to first in the TV ratings. Her success catapulted her to national acclaim and a role in Steven Spielberg's 1985 film *The Color Purple*, for which she was nominated for an Oscar for "best supporting actress."

Winfrey then launched the *Oprah Winfrey Show* in 1986. It became a nationally syndicated program. The show remained the number-one talk show for sixteen consecutive seasons—earning 47 Emmy Awards at the time of this writing. Her show became the highest-rated talk show in television history. As her ratings increased, Oprah's subject matter gradually shifted from sensational topics to topics that provided possibilities for people to transform their lives. She began an on-air book club designed to get the country more interested in reading—especially about inspirational subject matter.

Now Oprah literally does OWN the airways (oops… cablelines). To further showcase her philosophy of life, she launched her Oprah Winfrey Network on cable in 2011. From humble beginnings, Oprah has established herself as a person who not only envisions, but enlightens and encourages millions of people around the world to believe that their dreams can also come true. If she did it, so can you.

J.K. Rowling was an unemployed single mother and living on state benefits when she eked out the beginnings of the Harry Potter series on a napkin in a coach class train. Twelve publishing houses rejected her first novel, *Harry Potter and the Philosophers Stone*. Finally, a tiny publisher decided to give her a chance, offering J.K. a small advance against royalties. Talk about making your dreams a reality! The overwhelming success of the Harry Potter series of books and subsequent Academy Award winning movie trilogy made J.K. Rowling the world's second richest woman in entertainment right behind… you guessed it… Oprah Winfrey.

> *The greatest danger for most of us lies not in setting our aim too high and falling short, but in setting our aim too low and achieving our mark.*
>
> —Michelangelo

Whether you're trying to realize your personal dreams or professional goals, it's absolutely essential that we have positive people (also known as good alliances) around us. Football coach Lou Holtz realized his dreams by doing what he did best, namely coach football—but he also had a positive wife who encouraged him to reach out to make his "impossible dreams" happen. In fact, Lou Holtz had an interesting approach to making his dreams come true. He'd write his dreams down from one to one hundred in a book and check them off as he achieved them. When he was only an assistant coach at the University of Minnesota, he dared to dream that someday he'd be the head coach of Notre Dame—arguably the dream job for any college football coach. He dreamed of winning a national collegiate football championship. He also dreamed he'd visit the White House and eventually meet the pope. Some pretty lofty goals, indeed! But Holtz managed to make his dreams a reality.

Here's how he did it: he turned around a losing football program as head coach at Minnesota and was awarded the head coaching job at Notre Dame several years later. While at Notre Dame, he won the national championship, which led to meeting the president at the White House, and later the pope while touring Europe. Holtz wrote his dreams in a book and checked them off as he made them happen. In a sense, his book of dreams became a book of realities.

Dreams are free, so free your dreams.
—Astrid Alauda

Unlock Your Dreams

Following and achieving your dream is not a direct highway. Like any other of life's challenges, there will be potholes and boulders strewn across the road. Once you've defined your dream, go for it. Go for it with all the gusto and positive energy you can muster. The key is to have the courage to keep going. Keep heading in the direction of your dreams and you will make them a reality. The point is: If you can dream it—if you can visualize it—you can do it. As Eleanor Roosevelt said, "The future belongs to those who believe in the beauty of their dreams."

What are your dreams? Can you visualize them? Have you always wanted to write a screenplay or a book? Do you dream of starting your own company with a trusted partner? Do you dream of spending more quality time with your family? Do you dream of setting up a charitable foundation? Sailing around the world? A blissful retirement? Do you dream of being a person who can pull the ripcord and take action on the important things in your life? We all have the power within our indomitable human spirit to make our dreams a reality. If you build your dreams from the heart and pursue them with passion, you can accomplish anything you set out to do. Let me make this abundantly clear: we all need to have a dream. We need to allow our dreams to fly and fly high. Don't put your dreams on a short string. Dream on. Set your dreams free. The real tragedy of life would be not to have a dream at all.

> *For all the saddest words of tongue and pen,*
> *the saddest are these, it might have been...*
> —John Greenleaf Whittier

Don't Let Anyone Attack Your Dreams

Author Monty Roberts calls people who attack your aspirations "dream stealers." When Monty was in high school, his teacher gave the class a term paper assignment on what they wanted to do when they grew up. Monty wrote that he wanted to own a 200-acre ranch and raise thoroughbred racehorses. His teacher gave Monty an "F," claiming that his dream was an unrealistic pipe dream.

You see, Monty came from a very poor family background. His teacher thought no poor boy could ever amass enough money to buy the land… let alone the racehorses. When the teacher offered Monty a second chance to rewrite a more realistic term paper to receive a higher grade… Monty told his teacher, "You can keep the 'F' – I'll keep my dream."

It's a fact of life. There is always going to be someone who will try to steal or hinder your dreams. Don't abdicate your dreams to others who raise their eyebrows. Don't give in to doubting Thomases. There will always be pundits and nay-sayers who sneer and try to discourage you by planting the seeds of doubt. We can't give in to these people. We're not puppets on their proverbial string.

Author and national speaker Larry Hinds tells us that there's always a "thief" that goes around trying to steal our dreams. They try to rob or alter our mental state needed to obtain our goals. These thieves disguise themselves in different forms. Sometimes it's a discouraging parent, a doubting partner or co-worker. Sometimes the thief comes from a friend who doesn't believe you can accomplish your dreams and doesn't want you to get hurt by trying.

Strivers achieve what dreamers believe.
—Jonetta Patton (Usher's mother)

Don't let other people attack your dreams. Don't listen to people who say you're not good enough, tall enough, talented enough, or rich enough. Here is a litany of examples why we should not always listen to our doubters.

- When Steve Jobs of Apple went to Hewlett-Packard to get them interested in his and Steve Wozniak's personal computer, he was turned down summarily because he had yet to finish college.

- Very few so-called marketing experts thought Evian could sell still water for more than two dollars a bottle. After all, who would pay for water that already comes out of a tap?

- Barbra Streisand's mother told her she wasn't pretty enough to be an actress and that she wasn't a good enough singer to be a star.

- A New York publisher actually told James Michener that he should stick to editing and not try to be a writer. Undaunted, Michener wrote his first book, *Tales of the South Pacific*, which won him the Pulitzer Prize for literature!

- As a young man, Leonard Bernstein was constantly harassed by his father to give up his music and go out and get a real job. Years later, after Bernstein became one of America's most successful composers, his dad was asked why he didn't do more to encourage his son. To which his father replied, "Well, how was I supposed to know that he'd grow up to be 'the' Leonard Bernstein?"

- Singer Jennifer Hudson got voted off *American Idol* but went on to win an Academy Award for best supporting actress in her spellbinding performance in *Dream Girls*.

- Autistic high-school basketball manager Jason McElwain dreamed about playing just one minute in one game before he graduated. During the final minutes of the final game of the season, Mc Elwain got his chance. He thrilled the crowd by sinking six long three-point shots. The crowd went wild and carried a jubilant Mc Elwain off the court on their shoulders.

- Some famous acting people went homeless while continuing to fight for their dreams. The homeless list includes the unlikely names of Hilary Swank (who slept in her car,) Jim Carrey, David Letterman, and Charlie Chaplin.

- Lady Gaga's former boyfriend told her she would never amount to anything before she released her debut album *Fame,* which went on to win a Grammy.
- Tennis champion Raphael Nadal's pundits and sports writing critics thought that he could only win on the clay court surface of the French Open. Nadal has since silenced his naysayers by winning major titles on all surfaces including the grass courts of Wimbeldon and the hard courts of the U.S. and Australian Opens.
- After a series of largely unseen horror movies, many people doubted director Peter Jackson's ability to make a mainstream movie hit. That's before he directed a movie trilogy known as the *Lord of the Rings.* His third film in the trilogy, *The Return of the King* won eleven Academy Awards, cementing Jackson's place in cinematic history.
- Russell Crowe failed miserably in his attempt to become a rock star and worked as a bingo caller in a hotel before trying his hand at acting. Crowe went on to win an Academy Award for best actor in *Gladiator.*
- Flaming redhead and Olympic snowboarding and skateboarding champion Shaun White endured two major heart surgeries for a heart defect when he was a child. He has since become one of the most exciting and popular sports figures of his time.
- Andrea Bocelli was told at age 34 he was too old to start singing opera. You know the rest of the story.

Oliver Wendell Holmes summed it up best when he said, "many people die with their music still in them." The real tragedy is when we ourselves allow our dreams to be stolen from us. Stand up for your dreams!

Dreams Are Ageless

There's no age limit on your dreams. As previously mentioned, Grandma Moses didn't start painting until age 76 and painted until the ripe old age of 101. Architect Frank Lloyd Wright finished the Guggenheim Museum at age 92. In a sport where many consider an athlete over the hill by their early twenties, swimmer Dara Torres made the U. S. Olympics team at age 41. Julia Childs didn't take up cooking until age 40, and launched her TV cooking show in her fifties. At age 61, farm worker activist and labor leader Cesar Chavez endured a 36-day fast to call attention to the harmful pesticides affecting other farm workers and their children. In 1994, Chavez was posthumously awarded the Presidential Medal of Freedom, our nation's highest civilian honor.

Does Your Personality Fit Your Dreams?

Martha Beck, in her delightful book *Finding Your Own North Star*, writes about the types of personality profiles that bode well or ill for making dreams a reality. Here's my brief synopsis of each personality:

Chaos Commando

This is a person whose dreams are constantly changing. They come up with a new dream until they get bored again. The net result: a lot of scurrying around and dabbling with very few dreams fulfilled.

Big Dreamer/Little Doer

You know this person. This is the dreamer type that loves sitting in their office planning their illustrious career. On the surface, they seemingly do all the right stuff. They practice creative visualization, do daily affirmations, and write detailed mission statements. They read all the good self-help and motivational books they can find. But in the end—they do nothing. They take no action. The truth is this person is more comfortable in their imagination than they are in the real world. Unless this person learns to take pragmatic action, their dreams will never become a reality.

Rock of Gibraltar

This is the steady-as-a-rock type. They meticulously complete every assignment and mundane aspect of their job. But don't ask this person to do anything but forge straight ahead like a bull in a China closet. Although they get their job done, don't ask them to think outside the box. Don't ask them to come up with new responses or creative solutions.

Realist

This is that wonderful person that keeps track of all the details. This type is great at arranging schedules and following up to ensure every assignment gets meticulously done. This is a person that falls in love with other people's visions. In a sense they live vicariously through others—by helping make other people's dreams a reality.

Dream Maker

I would personally like to add another type of person to the profile list and that's the Dream Maker. The Dream Maker not only has the vision, but they also know how to make things happen. They understand that by accenting the positive aspects of each profile, they'll end up with a team that has complementary capabilities to accomplish wonderful things. The Dream Maker readily understands that the person who can read the road map might not be the best driver. Dream Makers have vision. They can think outside the box, but they also have enough focus and "tunnel vision" to know how to cross the goal line. They know how to take people with different personality profiles to pull the oar in the same direction and sing from the same sheet of music. Dream Makers do much more than dream about building castles in the sky. They actually lay the foundation and orchestrate the building of the castle, brick by glorious brick.

Ask yourself these questions: Which one of the profiles we discussed describes you best? Are you a combination of several profiles? Do you surround yourself with people of complementary capabilities that will allow you to make your dreams a reality? Answering these questions honestly will help you manage your efforts properly to realize your dreams.

> *The tragedy of life is not death, but what we allow to die within us while we're still living.*
> —Norman Cousins

Having the Courage to Fulfill Your Dreams

People who fulfill their dreams have at least one thing in common: they have the courage to act to make their dreams come true. Courage is the lynchpin that will allow you to achieve your dreams. If you don't exhibit courage, you may never have the fortitude to keep following your dreams when things look their bleakest. According to author Peter McWilliams, we must be willing to pay the price for achieving our dreams. We must be willing to come out of our comfort zone. McWilliams writes: "We must be willing to be uncomfortable. Lack of comfort, however, is a small price to pay for actualizing your dreams."

The inspiring story of young Wimbledon tennis champion Maria Sharapova reminds us that the American dream is still alive and kicking even if you were born in Siberia. When Maria was a baby, her family moved to escape the Chernobyl nuclear fallout. The Sharapovas wanted a better way of life for their daughter, so they decided to uproot the family and move to the United States with only seven hundred dollars in their pockets. The parents' dream was that their daughter Maria would be accepted and excel in Nick Bollettieri's famed tennis academy in Florida for youngsters who showed tennis potential at an early age.

On the day the Sharapovas were leaving Russia, Maria's grandmother observed her seven-year-old granddaughter calmly packing and carefully folding her clothes as if "she was preparing for her destiny." Destiny arrived earlier than expected for Maria. At the young age of seventeen, she shocked the tennis world by upsetting the heavily favored Serena Williams to win the 2004 Wimbledon Tennis Championship and subsequently the U.S. and Australian Opens. Maria and her family proved that dreams do come true, but it takes courage and the right risks to turn dreams into reality.

Erma Bombeck puts having courage and having dreams in perspective: "There are people who put their dreams in a little box and say 'yes, I've got dreams, of course I've got dreams.' Then they put the box away and bring it out once in a while to look at it and say, 'yeah, they're still there.' These are great dreams but they never get out of the box. It takes an uncommon amount of guts to put your dreams on the line, to hold them up and say, how good or bad am I? That's where courage comes in." Norman Cousins once said, "The tragedy of life is not death, but what we allow to die within us while we're still living.

One of my all-time favorite movies is *Field of Dreams*, starring Kevin Costner. As a kid, I, too, dreamed of becoming a Major League Baseball player and playing with the greats of the game. In my favorite scene, John Kinsella and doctor Moonlight Graham (convincingly played by an aging Burt Lancaster) have a riveting discussion about a man's dreams. Let me break down the scene for you: Kinsella asks Graham what it was like to play in only one major league game. Graham responds by saying he never even hit the ball out of the infield. The game ended and the season was over. Then the aging Graham responded reflectively, "Back then I thought there'll be other days—I didn't realize that that was the only day."

> Dream as if you'll live forever,
> Live as if you'll die today.
> —James Dean

Timing and Dreams

I'd like to dwell a moment on timing and dreams. Sometimes trying to time things too perfectly can cost you on your dreams. The best time to act on your dreams is now. Look, each of us is given a limited number of heartbeats – so don't squander them on living somebody else's dream. Remember all those wonderful dreams you had when you were younger? The time to act on them is now. As I researched material for this book, I asked people what was the happiest period of their life. Invariably, they answered when they were young and were in school or college. It had nothing to do with money, since most of us didn't have any then. It had to do with the fact that our dreams were still ahead of us, and everything, even the impossible, seemed possible.

Let me share a personal story as it relates to timing and dreams. Ever since I was a young man growing up I dreamed of living in Carmel-by-the-Sea, California. For those of you who haven't heard of or been to Carmel, it's a beautiful seaside town where Clint Eastwood was once the mayor. It lies next to the world famous Pebble Beach Golf course to the north and the legendary Big Sur coast to the south. As I mentioned earlier in this book, I dreamed of living there someday. But my someday never seemed to come. I keep putting my dream on hold until I found the so-called perfect time to act. I didn't comprehend that the perfect time to act is in the now. I was waiting for the perfect price or the perfect interest rate – on both. Anyway, you get the procrastinating picture? I'm happy to say that by acting in accord with my own book, I took the leap to the land of my dreams and am now living in Carmel-by-the-Sea savoring every glorious sunset as if it were my last.

How did I finally take the leap to the land of my dreams? Simple, I finally realized there was never going to be a perfect time to act. If I wanted my dream, I had to stop chasing it. I had to stop being engaged in the pursuit. I simply had to act in the "now".

When it comes to your dreams, don't harbor any regrets that you didn't go for it full-bore. If you do, you'll regret it not only now but later. As Mark Twain tells us, "Twenty years from now you'll be more disappointed by the things you did not do than the ones you did do. So throw away the bowlines. Sail away from safe harbor. Catch trade winds in your sails. Explore. Dream. Discover."

President John F. Kennedy built the new frontier and his dreams of a better America while being inspired by one of his favorite quotes from George Bernard Shaw: "Some people look at the world as it is and ask why. I dream of worlds that never were and ask why not."

Reach out to touch the stars. Have the courage and fortitude to make your dreams a reality. Don't be afraid to stray from the shoreline. But most of all, harbor no regrets.

I'd like to close this final chapter with this exhilarating quote from John Barrymore: "A man is not old until his regrets take the place of his dreams."

SEVEN JUMPSTARTS TO REALIZE YOUR DREAMS

1 **Unlock your dreams** – Get your dreams out of the lockbox. Clearly define them and have the courage to take the right risks to make your dreams a reality.

2 **Avoid pipe dreams** – Make sure your dreams are aligned with your purpose, passion, talent, and strengths. If you have a terrible voice, don't fantasize about a professional singing career.

3 **Act now** – Dreams are not just mercurial flights of fancy. They need to be fueled by continued action to move the dream forward.

4 **Avoid the doubting Thomases** – Don't let anyone attack or steal your dreams. There are a lot of well-intentioned people who will end up robbing you of the positive mental state needed to achieve your dreams.

5 **Tell others** – Tell upbeat people that you admire and respect that you will go all out to fulfill your dream. As mentioned earlier, it puts some pressure on you – but it adds greatly to your support group.

6 **See through the brick** – Visualize the end result of realizing your dreams. See yourself finishing your novel or starting your own business. Karate experts see through the brick on their way to splitting it in half.

7 **Focus forward** - Don't harbor any regrets that you didn't dream big and go for it, full bore. Remember; don't let your regrets take the place of your dreams.

Executive Summary

The final chapter defines the various targets of opportunity or visions of future products and services that will allow a company to grow in the future. In essence, this is the "dream section" of the marketing-plan process.

On a personal level, each of us has our own dreams. It's up to us to make our dreams a reality. There will always be doubters who will try to discourage us from fulfilling our dreams. We have to have the courage and commitment to make our dreams happen. We can't lock up our dreams in a safe-deposit box. They must be free to fly high.

But most of all, when it comes to our dreams, we should harbor no regrets. If we can dream it, we can do it.

Time to Reflect

Do you have great dreams that you have put on hold?
Are you chasing your own dream or are you living vicariously through the dreams of others?
Are your regrets taking the place of your dreams?

EPILOGUE

*Either write something worth reading,
or do something worth writing about.*

—Benjamin Franklin

I must admit that my life has changed dramatically since I penned my bestselling book, *A Marketing Plan For Life*. On my way to helping you discover what matters most, I had a personal epiphany. I discovered myself. I was living a white lie by denying my true calling. You see, the very things I was encouraging you to do were the things I needed to experience for myself. It never really dawned on me that my own book would go a long way in restoring my own life/work balance.

In the introduction of this book, I underscored that I was not just coming along for the ride, but taking the same personal life journey as my readers. I never imagined at the time that I would be taking what amounted to the most exhilarating trip of my life. Eerily, as I wrote each chapter, it seemed to mirror precisely what was going on in my personal life at that moment in time.

For instance, when I was urging you to discover your true calling or purpose, my own purpose came into sharper focus. My gut told me I needed to motivate myself and others, to make meaning as well as money. I needed to spread the gospel that true success always involves others. On my way to exhorting you to become your authentic self, I realized that I was wearing a corporate mask and wasn't the person I always wanted to become.

When I was encouraging you to invest your time wisely and take action on what mattered most, I recognized that I was unconsciously paralyzed when it came time to taking action on those things that mattered most to me. I recognized that many of the important things in my life were put on hold for the sake of a bigger marketing challenge or a fatter paycheck. For me, at the time, it was all about the scorecard, baby! How much… how many… and how fast.

As I was extolling you to reinvent yourself, I hadn't realized I was in the same process of rebooting the direction I would take in my own life.

I was always concerned about my legacy when I died, but now I know it's what I do when I'm living that counts. I realized that the answer to my "living" legacy could be found in the very pages of my own book. Additionally, I confirmed that the process I used to make money for corporate clients could be kicked up a notch to make meaning. And here's the irony: I learned that sometimes you make even more meaning when you make money. (See Oprah Winfrey, Bill Gates, and Robert Redford.) The ability to make money is a talent and a gift but your heart and giving spirit has to be in the right place. Mine wasn't. Now it is, and my sense of self-worth soars with the eagles.

Jumpstarted by my own life/work process echoing in my ear, I pulled my personal ripcord and took the following action on my life plan:

- I courageously (for me) resigned from my lucrative executive post at a company I helped to co-found because it was no longer aligned with my life's purpose and my need to clearly define my living legacy.

- In order to make meaning as well as money, I utilized my marketing acumen to create a Christmas festival to raise money for the Boys and Girls' Clubs. I learned that if the Christmas spirit wasn't in my heart, it's unlikely I'd find it underneath the tree. Additionally, I volunteered my marketing services to the 75-year-old Carmel Bach Festival to layer on a more youthful audience that will appreciate classical music for generations to come. I joyfully went back to my alma mater in New England and helped them market their exciting new vision for the future. Who says you can't go home again?

- We launched into full gear our company called Thirdwind. The new company focuses on motivating people and corporations to define and realize their goals, dreams and aspirations. The company offers a series of books, video courses, seminars, personal coaching and speaking engagements. There's also a "Get A Life" social networking game in the works as well as a collection of inspirational apparel and accessories. Stay tuned for further developments.

- Taking care to make both money and meaning, we continue to serve our clients around the world via our BrandMark marketing consulting firm. The consultancy will offer on-line marketing plan courses to help small companies and small-business owners launch their products, build their brand and reach their full growth potential.

*Life should not be a journey
to the grave with the intention of arriving
safely in a pretty and well-preserved body,
but rather to skid broadside
in a cloud of smoke, thoroughly used up,
totally worn out, and loudly
proclaiming "Wow! What a ride!"*

— Hunter S. Thompson

In closing, I hope this book serves as a catalyst to start you on your own personal journey. A journey of rediscovery, a journey that helps define your true purpose. A journey that reminds you to invest your time on those things that matter most. Remember, as you embark on your journey, the wonderful words of Hunter S. Thompson:

"Life should not be a journey to the grave with the intention of arriving safely in a pretty and well-preserved body, but rather to skid broadside in a cloud of smoke, thoroughly used up, totally worn out, and loudly proclaiming 'Wow! What a ride!'"

PERSONAL EXERCISES

What follows is a workbook-type exercise section linked to each chapter of this book. You'll find challenging but highly fruitful questions that relate to both jumpstarting your business and your life. Answering these questions will be a lot easier if you read the entire book first. Remember, your answers are not cast in concrete. Certainly on the personal side, they probably will change with triggering events that you'll face in your life (e.g. getting married, having children, changing jobs, moving to another area, getting a divorce, and the loss of a parent or family member.) Accordingly, you should revisit your answers every six months to make sure they are still aligned with your true purpose and passion.

To offer you flexibility in answering your business and/or life questions we've developed three options for you to input your answers.

1 Answer the exercise questions at the end of the book on your own notepad and keep them in a drawer or file cabinet for future review. I'm suggesting you don't write your answers in the book so that you can share the questions with your friends and family without influencing their answers.

2 Sign-up at www.ignitingyourtruepurpose.com/exercises and we'll email you a form to fill in your answers. Or if you want to go old school we'll mail you two sets of pre-printed questionnaires. Store the finished questionnaires where they are easily retrievable for future review. Remember, this life planning process is a living, always changing thing. You'll want to revisit these questions from year-to-year.

3 Log on to www.ignitingyourtruepurpose.com. Create a personal profile and you can answer the questions right there. We'll securely store your answers for your future review. That way you'll never misplace your work and have the opportunity to apprise your plan every six months or update whenever inevitable life-altering events suggest that you take another look at your plan going forward.

Once you've registered at www.ignitingyourtruepurpose.com, you'll have the option of joining our online community of others who are on the path to Jumpstart their lives to greater heights.

CHAPTER 1

Exercise 1: Self-Discovery Questions

It takes some courage to tackle the self-discovery questions in this exercise. However, your written answers will help you define who you are, and more importantly, who you would like to become.

A. What really matters most?

List the five things, people, or causes that matter most to you. Try to list them in order of importance. (Sample answers are included to help you get started.)

1 (family)

2 (career)

3 (new career)

4 (community work)

5 (charitable causes)

B. What is your purpose?

Utilizing what you learned from the defining your purpose section earlier in chapter one, write a sentence or paragraph describing your life's purpose: (Example: to motivate, encourage, and mentor others to take action on what matters most to them.) My purpose in life is:

C. What ignites your passion?

List the five true passions in your life. What gives you the most joy? (Sample answers are included to help get you started.)

1 (my young son Michael)

2 (the Los Angeles Lakers)

3 (cooking a great meal)

4 (traveling to Italy's Amalfi coast)

5 (breaking 90 in golf)

D. When were you filled with unbridled joy?

Think about the times in your life when you were filled with unbridled joy. What were the circumstances?

E. When do you lose total track of time?

What are the things that you are doing when you lose total track of time? List them.

F. What were your childhood dreams?

When you were a child, what were dreams and fantasies?

G. Write down your "most admired" list.

Jot down those famous or not so famous people and the reasons you admire them.

Time to Reflect
*Am I currently on a path that will
lead me to my true purpose in life?*

CHAPTER 2

Exercise 1: Hone in on Your Strengths

Knowing your strengths, put a check mark next to those words that define you best. Then, review the list one more time and cross out those words that are definitely not strengths of yours. Remember, go to your strengths and manage around your weaknesses.

___ Acting	___ Encouraging	___ Leading
___ Advising	___ Enforcing	___ Learning
___ Analyzing	___ Evaluating	___ Managing
___ Budgeting	___ Executing	___ Maximizing
___ Caretaking	___ Focusing	___ Mentoring
___ Competing	___ Funding	___ Monitoring
___ Communicating	___ Growing	___ Motivating
___ Connecting	___ Helping	___ Organizing
___ Cooking	___ Imagining	___ Persuading
___ Creating	___ Implementing	___ Pioneering
___ Developing	___ Influencing	___ Problem-Solving
___ Directing	___ Initiating	___ Restoring
___ Editing	___ Innovating	___ Writing

Exercise 2: Take a Personal Snapshot

A. Ben Franklin used this simple plus-and-minus chart, which you'll find useful in analyzing your strengths and weaknesses. Utilizing what you gleaned from Exercise 1, fill in your strengths and weaknesses in the chart below. Remember: do not restrict your strengths and weaknesses to your career. Include your personal traits as well.

Ye Olde Ben Franklin Chart

Strengths (+)	Weaknesses (-)

B. After you have completed your chart, ask five people who know you (not just friends or immediate family) to list your top three strengths and weaknesses. Check if their input is similar to your list. Is what you think of yourself the same as how others see you? (For example, if you thought you were a great leader but others don't, do you need to narrow the gap between perception and reality?)

Exercise 3: Capitalize on Your Strengths

List the ways in which you can best capitalize on your professional strengths to add joy and meaning to your personal life (for example, if you are a good writer or good speaker, you could use your communications skills to benefit others by writing a column for the community paper or lecture at the local college).

Exercise 4: From Good to Great

What is it that you can do as good as (or better than) most?

Exercise 5: Create Your New ID Card

Create a new calling card that goes beyond your job, profession, or business title (for example, Jane Doe: Galloping Gourmet, Eleanor Smith: Designer Extraordinaire).

Name:

New ID:

Exercise 6: Manage Your Weaknesses

List the ways in which you can best manage around your weaknesses. For example, if you lack the necessary computer skills to compete in today's ultra competitive job market, you might enroll in a computer class.

Time to Reflect
*Think about how you can best capitalize
on your strengths and manage around your weaknesses.*

CHAPTER 3

Exercise 1: The Authentic You

A. Describe the person you've always wanted to become. (For example: a person of high moral integrity who helps others in the community? A good father and husband who provides for the well-being of his family?)

B. List the times you feel you compromised the real you for the sake of others, or for that matter a corner office or a fatter paycheck.

C. What masks do you wear at work or at home that prevent people from experiencing the Real You? (The brave mask? The comical mask? The pity-poor-me mask?)

D. Discovering your authentic self: in discovering the real you, it is sometimes easier to articulate that which is clearly not you. Make a two-column list with those things that are clearly not you on the left. You can also list the times and places when you feel least authentic. On the right side, list those things, times, and places where you feel like the real you––the you that shines through.

Once you've completed this exercise you need to take those action steps to close the gap between who you are and who you were meant to be.

Clearly Not Me	The Authentic Me

Exercise 2: Less Is More

Write down the three things you need to have less of to make your life fuller. (For example: fewer e-mails, less time texting on my iPhone, less time surfing the web, less time watching TV or playing video games, less traffic, less work, less distraction.)

Exercise 3: Your Genuine Team

List those people that would make your "All Genuine Team" and the reason that you admire them. For example: Oprah Winfrey for being a positive role model for others.

Time to Reflect

Are you currently the person you were meant to be?

CHAPTER 4

Exercise 1: Taking Action

A. List three times in your life that you regret you didn't pull the ripcord and take action (for example: changing jobs, investing in a stock that has since appreciated, dissolving a bad relationship, etc.).

B. Take action on your purpose. List three action steps you can take now in order to better position yourself toward your true purpose in life (for example: investing more quality time with my family, begin to write my screenplay, contribute more to my community or become a donor to your high school or college).

C. Name three times in your life when your actions spoke louder than words.

Exercise 2: Perfect Timing

List the instances in your life when you let things get away because you tried to time things *too* perfectly (for example, the dream house that got away, the job you didn't take).

Exercise 3: Risk Taking

A. List the three times in your life when you wish you had taken a greater "right" risk.

B. What was the result or outcome of not taking that risk?

C. List the three best risks you have ever taken in your life? (Example: I quit my "going nowhere" job to start up my company.)

D. What was the positive result or outcome of having taken those "right" risks?

E. What risks do you need to take over the next few months to be more aligned with your true purpose in life?

F. Risk taker versus risk avoider: Looking back on your life, list the areas in which you are a risk taker (for example, investing in stocks, gambling). Then list the areas in which you are a risk avoider (for example, relationships, reluctance to change jobs, etc.).

<u>Risk Taker:</u>   <u>Risk Avoider:</u>

Time to Reflect

When was the last time you risked failure for something you passionately believed in?

CHAPTER 5

Exercise 1: Defining Moments by Decades

A. Write down the defining moments in your life by each decade since you were born.

Decade One: (1–10 Years Old)

Decade Two: (11–20 Years Old)

Decade Three: (21–30 Years Old)

Decade Four: (31–40 Years Old)

Decade Five: (41–50 Years Old)

Decade Six: (51–60 Years Old)

Decade Seven: (61–70 Years Old)

Other Decades (If Applicable)

B. Take a step back and review how life's defining moments helped shape or strengthen your character traits. (For example: Making a dramatic recovery from a car accident taught me how to persevere. Getting good grades in school gave me confidence to pursue higher education. Losing my parents helped me cope with tragedy and sorrow.)

C. Looking back, which decade has given you the most joy? Why?

D. Looking back, which decade has given you the most regrets or sadness? Why?

E. What historical or world-shaping occurrence or event has affected your life most? Why? (For example, 9/11, other terrorist attacks, economic meltdown, home foreclosure, stock market bust and boom, technological revolution.)

Exercise 2: Reinventing Yourself

A. List the time(s) in your life that you have reinvented or redefined yourself to better achieve your goals, dreams, and aspirations.

B. If you could make one change in yourself or your life today, what would it be? What is stopping you from making that change?

Time to Reflect

*When was the last time you reinvented yourself
to better realize your goals, dreams, and aspirations?*

CHAPTER 6

Exercise 1: What Does Your Life Stand For?

A. List the ways in which you are "demonstrably different" or unique.

B. Oprah Winfrey's name stands for realizing your dreams and reaching your full personal potential. Dr. Martin Luther King Jr.'s name represents racial equality. What does your good name stand for?

Exercise 2: Specialization/Narrowcasting

What one thing are you truly great at? How can you channel this greatness to make a difference to others? You might want to refer back to Chapter 2 – Exercise 3, Capitalize On Your Strengths.

Exercise 3: Making a Difference

Name three times in your life that you made a positive difference in helping others.

Exercise 4: Your Personal Brand

Write one sentence that describes your personal brand. (For example, I am a person who inspires and encourages others to reach their full potential.)

Exercise 5: Marketing Your Personal Brand

List the actions you need to take to better market your personal brand to the outside world. (Example: Need to update my resume on Linkedin, update my Facebook page, update my wardrobe.)

Time to Reflect

How are you unique or demonstrably different?
Have you made a positive difference in helping others?

CHAPTER 7

Exercise 1: Define Your Legacy

A. If you died tomorrow, what would your legacy most likely be?

B. Would you be satisfied with this legacy? Why or why not?

C. Write down the epitaph that you would like to see imprinted on your tombstone. Start with: Here lies a person who…

Exercise 2: Your Legacy—Where Will It Come From?

Your legacy can come in several forms. Choose the most likely form(s) in which you can best express your legacy. (Please explain.)

A. Family/children

B. Meaningful work

C. Charitable causes

D. Giving back to the community

E. Mentoring or coaching others

F. Keeping a positive attitude toward others

G. Everyday good deeds

H. Other—please explain

Exercise 3: Mentoring

A. Who was the most significant mentor in your life?

B. What positive contribution did your mentor make toward the way you reach out to others?

Exercise 4: Inspirational Ways to Help Others

List an inspirational movie, book, play or piece of art that has inspired you to reach out to help others.

Time to Reflect

If you died tomorrow, what would be your legacy?
Would you be satisfied with this legacy?

CHAPTER 8

Exercise 1: Unlocking Your Creativity

A. The left-brain way of thinking uses logic and is detail oriented, while the right brain uses feeling and is big-picture oriented. Would you describe yourself as predominately a left-brain or right-brain person? What are your major left- or right-brain characteristics? (Refer back to the left brain, right brain section in Chapter 8.)

<u>Left Brain</u>   <u>Right Brain</u>

B. What were the most creative things you did as a child growing up?

C. List the most creative things you have done as an adult.

D. List three creative things you always wanted to do, but always postponed (for example, playing the guitar, taking a cooking class, learning to paint, writing a children's book etc.).

E. What creative things would you do if you weren't afraid of failure, concerned about criticism, or had the need to do things "perfectly" before you finish them?

F. What are the major stumbling blocks that prevent you from expressing your creativity?

G. List three action steps that you can take now to reawaken your creativity (for example, take a gourmet cooking class, guitar lessons, sing in you church choir).

H. Creative heroes: List three people whose creativity you admire most. (Example: Steven Spielberg, Lady Gaga, Pablo Picasso)

I. Setting creative goals: List the action steps that you will take over the next year to rekindle your creativity. As we discuss in chapter ten, your goals should be quantifiable; they should have time and numbers attached to them (for example, I'd like to finish my first book of poems during the next six months and have them published a year later).

Exercise 2: Vision

Are you a person who can see the forest through the trees? Can you visualize the end result before it happens? List two cases in your life when you exhibited vision.

Time to Reflect

Have you put your creativity on hold?
Do you have a masterpiece within you just crying to get out?

CHAPTER 9

Exercise 1: Distributing Your Time Wisely

Before we can distribute our time more wisely, we need to hone in on what matters most to us. We need to know what we want to make time for. Accordingly, check off the things on this list that you wish were a bigger part of your life:

- _____ Overall family fun
- _____ Son
- _____ Daughter
- _____ Wife
- _____ Husband
- _____ Niece/nephew
- _____ Grandchildren
- _____ Relationships
- _____ Career
- _____ New career
- _____ Health
- _____ Cooking
- _____ Quality leisure time (travel, etc.)
- _____ Hobbies (specify)
- _____ Education/self-education
- _____ Community/volunteer work
- _____ Managing your personal portfolio
- _____ Getting more in touch with nature
- _____ Your home or vacation home
- _____ Sports: golf, tennis, mountain climbing, working out, etc.
- _____ Other (please specify)

Exercise 2: Investing Time on What Matters Most

Now that you've discovered what you want to make time for, it's time for you to fill out your own pie charts. Remember each slice of the pie should represent a percent value as to what matters most to you.

How do you wish you were spending your time?

How are you currently spending your time?

Exercise 3: Investing Your Time Wisely

A. If you knew you had only six months to live, how would you spend your time more wisely in the following areas? Would you make any changes? Please briefly explain:

1. Family

2. Relationships

3. Leisure time/travel

4. Financial portfolio or will

5. Career or profession

6. Community or charitable work

7. Other: Please specify

B. If you knew a loved one (a spouse, family member, or friend) had only six months to live, describe how you would treat them differently in their remaining days?

Why not treat them that way right now?

C. If you had only one hour to live, who would you call and what would you say?

D. Identifying Time Wasters

Write down those things or people that contribute to wasting your quality time (e.g. surfing the net, watching TV, texting, energy-zapping people, commuting, etc.)

Time to Reflect
Are you currently investing quality
time on that which matters most to you?
What are you waiting for?

CHAPTER 10

Exercise 1: Write Down Your Goals

Write down your major short-term goals (one to two years out) and your major long-term goals (three to five years out). Remember, goals are always quantifiable: they have numbers and time attached to them (for example, "lose twenty pounds in this year"). Be sure to re-evaluate your goals at least every six months in the categories listed below:

Family Goals

A. Short term (one to two years from today)

(Example: Spend one weekend per month with my aging parents)

B. Long term (three to five years from today)

(Example: Take my family on trips of learning and discovery to Europe and Asia)

Health Goals

A. Short term (one to two years from today)

(Example: Lose ten pounds in year one, another five pounds in year two)

B. Long term (three to five years from today)

(Example: Maintain your 15 pound wight loss with a healthy diet and exercise program)

Career/Professional Goals

A. Short term (one to two years from today)

(Example: Become my company's sales director in year one and vice president of sales in year two)

B. Long term (three to five years from today)

(Example: Start my own business in the area of personal growth and grow the business by 20 percent each year)

Financial Goals

A. Short term (one to two years from today)

(Example: Increase the value of my personal portfolio by 10 percent this year)

B. Long term (three to five years from today)

(Example: Buy a home no later than year five)

Relationship Goals

A. Short term (one to two years from today)

(Example: Spend more quality time with my family and closest friends versus my business acquaintances)

B. Long term (three to five years from today)

(Example: I'd like to be married and start a family)

Personal Growth Goals

A. Short term (one to two years from today)

(Example: Identify my true purpose and passion in life and take action to identify what really matters most to me)

B. Long term (three to five years from today)

(Example: Write a book in the area of personal growth)

Leisure Time and Travel Goals

A. Short term (one to two years from today)

(Example: Play golf once a week)

B. Long term (three to five years from today)

(Example: Take a month off to tour Italy and Spain)

Miscellaneous Goals (Things I Always Wanted to Do)

A. Short term (one to two years from today)

(Example: Learn to play the guitar)

B. Long term (three to five years from today)

(Example: Climb Mount Rainier)

Exercise 2: Perseverance

List the times in your life when you persevered to achieve your goals and an apparent "no" became a yes.

Exercise 3: Fear of Failure

List the times in your life when fear of failure stymied you in your efforts to achieve your purpose or business goals. What would you have done differently?

Time to Reflect

*Has fear of failure stymied your efforts
to achieve your personal or business goals?*

CHAPTER 11

Exercise 1: Your Core Values

A. Take another look at your core values listed in Chapter 11 - "Identifying Our Core Values". It's important that you narrowcast your values to a manageable number—a number you can get your arms around. Accordingly, try narrowing your core values down to those eight core values that matter most to you. These values should capture the true essence of your authentic self. Remember, nobody can take these core values away from you—unless you let them. These values represent your safe harbor, a place you can always come home to when making life's important decisions.

My eight most important values:

B. Is your present job in tune with your core value system?

Explain.

C. Name a time or times in your life when your core values were severely tested.

What was the outcome?

What did you learn?

D. Give some examples of how your core values guided you in a positive way in making important decisions in your life.

E. Have you ever lost sight of your core values in making an important decision in your life?

If yes, what was the outcome?

What did you learn?

F. What good values did your parents instill in you?

G. Given your life's experiences, how have your values changed over the years?

Exercise 2: Self-Worth/Self-Esteem

A. List the times in your life when your sense of self-worth or self-esteem was at its highest.

B. List the times in your life when your sense of self-worth or self-esteem was at its lowest. (What core values did you use to gain or regain your self-worth or self-esteem?)

Time to Reflect

Have your core values ever been severely tested?
Do you have a high sense of self-worth?

CHAPTER 12

Exercise 1: Writing Down Your Dreams

Write down your top five personal dreams that you would like to make a reality. For now, don't worry about prioritizing each dream—just let it flow. Even your wildest dreams count. Remember, we eventually all run out of time. What we can never do is run out of dreams.

Exercise 2: Realizing Your Dreams

Give two examples in your life when you reached out to make your dreams a reality.

Exercise 3: Unfulfilled Dream

Do you presently harbor any regrets for not going all out to fulfill an important dream in your life?

If so, please explain.

Exercise 4: Dream Inspiration

Take the time to jot down a movie, play, book, song, piece of art, or sporting event that inspired or inspires you to realize your dreams.

A. Movie (for example, *The Blindside*, *Field of Dreams*)

B. Play (for example, *Man of La Mancha*, *Phantom of the Opera*)

C. Song (for example, "*Beautiful Day*"–U2; "*Somwhere Over The Rainbow*"–Israel "IZ" Kamakawiwo'ole version)

D. Piece of Art (for example, Michelangelo's David)

E. Sporting Event (for example, the U.S.A. Olympic Hockey Miracle on Ice)

Time to Reflect

Do you have great dreams that you have put on hold?
Are you chasing your own dream or are you
living vicariously through the dreams of others?
Are your regrets taking the place of your dreams?

SUBJECT INDEX

Benefits of a Life/Work Plan	11	Action Speaks Louder Than Words	71
Define the Business You Should Be In	13	Sometime Taking No Action is Action	72
Constant Redefinition	15	Discomfort Leads to Action	73
Defining Who You Are	18	The Perfect Time Is Now	73
Living a Life of Purpose	19	Don't Wait For That Perfect Time	74
Igniting Your Passion	22	Taking The Leap	75
America's Passion with Sports	26	The Right Risk For You	76
Assess The Market	31	A Classic "What If" Story	77
Building on Your Key Strengths	32	Weather the Product Cycles	81
Defining Strength	34	Companies Reinvent Themselves	81
Taking a Personal Snapshot	36	Lifecycles	86
Complementary Capabilities	37	Reinventing Yourself	86
It Takes Two to Tango	38	Winds of Life	90
Don't Avoid Your Strengths	39	Defining Moments	92
Managing Your Weaknesses	40	Looking Back/Going Forward	96
Your Strength Can Be Your Weakness	41	Our Story is Still Unfolding	97
Finding Strength in Weakness	43	Build Your Business Brand	99
Communicating Your Strengths	43	Heart of Branding	99
Don't Let Anyone Talk You Out of Your Passion	44	Creating Share of Mind	100
Go for Greatness	45	Capturing the Aura of the Brand	101
Identify the Target Customer	47	Communication Keys to Build a Brand	101
Authenticity is Key	48	Taking Charge of Your Own Brand	104
Sweet Simplicity	51	What Do You Stand For?	105
Be True to Yourself	53	You Have to Specialize	105
Less is More	54	Revel in Your Uniqueness	106
Masking the Real You	55	Respecting Your Uniqueness	109
Rediscovering Your Authentic Self	56	Make a Difference	109
Traits That Characterize a Truly Authentic Person	57	Expand Your Reach	113
Happiness and Personal Enrichment	58	The New Social Media	113
It's Never Too Late to Be Authentic	61	Key Elements in the Adoption of Social Media Marketing	115
Launch Your Strategy	65	Integrating Traditional and New Media Strategy	116
Unique Competence: Where's the Beef?	66	Connectiveness Leads To Disconnection	117
Build It and They Will Come	67	Creating a Legacy in Business	118
The Right Risk in Changing Strategies	67	Creating a Living Legacy	121
Your Personal Mission Statement	70	Developing Your Personal Legacy	122
A Clear Call to Action: There Is No Try	70		

Searching For Higher Meaning	127
Build A High Impact Advertising Campaign	131
Classic Ad Campaigns	132
Memorable Taglines	133
Word of Mouth	134
Capturing Your Personal Creativity	137
Concise Communication	138
Powerful Punctuation	138
Left Brain/Right Brain	139
Creativity Diminishes as We Get Older	140
Creativity and Perfection	141
Reawaken Your Creative Spirit	142
Presentation Dynamics	142
The Creative Process	143
Creative Rituals	144
The Creative Environment	145
Handling Criticism	146
Creativity Begins With A Vision	147
Creative Impact	148
Plan Your Distribution	151
Bricks and Clicks	151
De-Marketing	152
Long Tail Distribution	153
Be Where The Business Is	153
Position Yourself to Succeed	155
The Power of Positive Energy	155
A Question of Timing	157
Investing Time on What Matters Most	157
Too Busy to Find the Time	159
Getting a Real Life	161
Time Is Fleeting	162
Life's Best Teacher	163
Achieve Your Sales Goals	167
Sales Mirrors Life	168
Sales and Perseverance	168
Think Big!	171
Focusing on Personal Goals	173
Goals Versus Objectives	173
Visualize Success	174
Overcoming Fear of Failure	177
If at First You Don't Succeed…	179
Analyze Profit and Loss	183
The Great Financial Meltdown	183
Big Recession Causes a Small Business Boom	185
Profiting From a Good Value System	191
Identifying Our Core Values	191
Rethinking Our Core Values	193
A Silver Lining in the Clouds	194
Forming Your Value System	195
Balancing Your Personal Integrity Account	196
Appreciation in Value	198
Net Worth Versus Self Worth	199
Recasting The American Dream	200
Establishing Targets of Opportunity	203
New Products and Services	203
Creating New Divisions	204
Striking Key Alliances and Partnerships	204
Mergers and Acquisitions	204
Creating New Value-Added Streams	205
Licensing	205
Realizing Your Personal Dreams	207
The Impossible Dream	208
Unlock Your Dreams	210
Don't Let Anyone Attack Your Dreams	211
Dreams Are Ageless	213
Does Your Personality Fit Your Dreams?	214
Having the Courage to Fulfill Your Dreams	215
Timing and Dreams	217

BUSINESS INDEX

~~~A~~~

ABC Network, 203
Accenture, 58
Acme, 188
Agilent, 81
Amazon, 32, 48, 100, 101, 147, 148, 151, 153, 178, 187, 188, 203, 204
American Express, 118, 188
American Idol, 89, 116. 176, 212
American International Group, 184
Android, 114, 118
Anheuser-Busch, 32
Apple, 13, 32, 48, 56, 65, 77, 81, 82, 99, 100, 101, 102, 104, 107, 109, 127, 132, 148, 152, 153, 176, 185, 186, 212
Army, 38, 67, 94, 101, 134
Asics, 100
AT&T, 55
Audi, 32
Avis, 66, 101, 134

~~~B~~~

Bach, 221
Banana Republic, 50
Band-Aids, 99
Barnes & Noble, 100
Bebe. 205
Berkshire Hathaway, 188
Blockbuster, 151
BNSF, 189
Boise State University, 101
Boston Red Sox, 25
Brandmark, 101, 167, 221

Brooklyn Dodgers, 125
Budweiser, 32, 134
Build-a-Bear, 67
Burger King, 66, 115

~~~C~~~

Cabbage Patch Kid, 102
Cadbury, 204
Cadillac, 15
Calvin Klein, 13, 87
Canyon Ranch, 60
CarsDirect, 152
Charmin, 134, 187
Cheerio, 161
Chicago Cubs, 167
Chrysler, 184
Circus Circus, 83
Cisco, 177
Citi Group, 184
Clairol, 132
Clorox, 49, 204
Coach, 83, 204, 208
Coca-Cola, 51, 89
Columbia University, 89
Coors, 152
Cornell, 40
Crest, 187
Crew J, 50

~~~D~~~

Dawn, 187
DeBeers, 132
DIRECTV, 32
Disney, 13, 203, 208
Dockers, 31
Dodgers, 125
Dom Perignon, 48
Dove, 132, 133

Duke University, 22
Duracell, 187

~~~E~~~

E-marketer, 115
Eddie Bauer, 14, 49, 50, 101, 204
Entourage, 87
ESPN, 13, 116, 203
Evian, 212

~~~F~~~

Facebook, 65, 113, 114, 115, 134
Fannie Mae, 183
Fast Company, 48, 49, 58, 61, 67
FedEx, 32, 42, 133, 171, 185
Florida Marlins, 177
Forbes, 58, 148, 185, 187
Ford, 47, 186, 204
Forrester Research, 113
Fortune, 101
Fox Network, 116
Freddie Mac, 183
Fruit of the Loom, 188

~~~G~~~

Geico, 188
Gelson's, 109
General Electric, 189
General Motors, 184
Gillette, 58, 187
Glaceau, 89
Godiva, 100
Golden Gate Capital, 50,
Goldman Sachs, 189
Google, 13, 42, 65, 66, 117, 145, 153, 204

Gourmet, 37
Green Bay Packers, 37
Greenpeace, 135

~~~H~~~

Harley Davidson, 65, 100
Harvard, 36, 40, 67, 88, 94, 152, 180
Hertz, 66
Hewlett-Packard, 81, 214
Huffington Post, 178
Hyundai, 49

~~~I~~~

Iams, 187
IDEO, 140

~~~J~~~

J.P. Morgan, 184
Julliard, 44
Justin Boot, 188

~~~K~~~

Kindle, 188, 203
Kleenex, 101
Kohlberg, Kravis, Roberts & Co., 185
Kolicata Sanved, 111
Kraft Foods, 188, 204

~~~L~~~

Land Rover, 204
Laura Ashley, 14, 169, 170
Lehman Brothers, 184
Levi Strauss, 31, 32
Lexus, 204
Los Angeles Lakers, 22, 89

~~~M~~~

Majestic Athletic, 50
Marantz Stereo Company, 14
Mars, 100
Marvel, 139
Mercedes Benz, 134
Merck, 81
Merrill Lynch, 184
Method, 65
Mini Cooper, 100, 133
Mitsubishi, 100
MLB, 50
Motorola, 38, 39, 94, 126, 142, 204
MSNBC, 82

~~~N~~~

NASCAR, 23, 100, 115, 119
NBA, 50
NaviCore, 168
Netflix, 151
New Line Cinema, 177
New York Knicks, 93
New York Times, 89, 134
New York Yankees, 196
Nielsen Company, 117
Nike, 58, 65, 67, 68, 99, 100, 101, 104, 115
Nobel, 123, 128
Nordstrom, 32, 49, 152
North Face, 49
Nosal Partners, 44

~~~O~~~

Olay, 187
Oprah Winfrey Network, 209
Oracle, 204
Oral-B, 187

~~~P~~~

P&G, 187
P.A.S.S, 90
Pampers, 187
Panasonic, 204
Panera Bread, 152
Pantene, 187
Parade Magazine, 167
Patagonia, 49
Paul Masson, 157
Pebble Beach Golf, 217
Penguin, 95
Pepsico, 127
Pepsi-Cola, 51, 178
Philegatia, 121
Pisoni Vineyards, 23
Planet Products, 65, 101, 109, 110, 134
Pope John Paul II, 111
Porsche, 50, 186
Post-it, 145
Pringles, 187
Procter & Gamble, 187
Pulitzer, 157, 178, 212

~~~Q~~~

Q-tips, 99

~~~R~~~

Ralphs, 109

~~~S~~~

Safeway, 109
Samsung, 100
San Francisco Giants, 177
Sanyo, 204
Scotch Tape, 99
Seventh Generation, 65
Sierra Club, 49, 204
Smuckers, 134
Soaring Oaks Consulting, 56
Soccernet, 203
Southwest, 32, 186, 187
Stanford University, 40, 56, 179, 205
Starbucks, 146, 206
St. Louis Rams, 176
Sub-Zero, 100
Sun Microsystems, 204
Sundance Foundation, 27
Suzuki, 100

~~~T~~~

Tennessee State University, 209
Texas Wesleyan, 75
Thirdwind, 21, 95, 221
Tide, 187
Tiffany, 151, 166
TNS Financial Services, 59
Toshiba, 100
Treasure Island, 83
Twitter, 113, 114, 134

~~~U~~~

UCLA, 179
United Parcel Service, 15
University of Minnesota, 210
University of Southern California, 60
University of Notre Dame, 170, 210

~~~V~~~

Villanova, 157
Volkswagen, 132
Vons, 109

~~~W~~~

Wal-Mart, 151, 166
Walt Disney Company, 203
Warner Bros., 177
Wharton, 153
Wikipedia, 42, 185
Wimbledon, 87, 215, 216
Wrigley, 189

~~~X~~~

Xerox, 99, 115

~~~Y~~~

Yahoo, 114, 153
Yale, 40, 171
YouTube, 67, 113, 114, 117, 204

~~~Z~~~

Zappos, 204

NAME INDEX

~~~A~~~

Abdul, Paula, 89
Abraham, Daniel, 74
Adams, Samuel, 48
Agassi, Andre, 87
Ainkel, Rick, 176
Alauda, Astrid, 210
Alexander The Great, 59
Allen, Woody, 138
Allston, John, 113
Amalfi Coast, 41, 180, 226
Anderson, Marc C., 23
Anderson, Chris, 153
Aristotle, 78

~~~B~~~

Bailey, George, 127
Baker, Dr, Dan, 60, 96, 159, 191, 195
Baldwin, Faith, 87
Bale, Christian, 87
Ball, Bill, 105
Balzac, Honoré de, 23
Bangladeshis, 128
Banks, Tyra, 89
Barnickel, John, 170
Barrymore, John, 203, 206, 218
Baudelaire, Charles, 140
Bauer, Eddie, 50, 101
Bean, LL, 49
Beck, Martha, 214
Beethoven, Ludwig van, 43, 176
Bennett, Tony, 89
Bernbach, William, 137
Bernhardt, Sarah, 124
Bernstein, Leonard, 212
Berry, Jon, 60
Berthiaume, André, 52, 55
Bezos, Jeff, 48, 127, 148, 187
Blake, William, 55
Bocelli, Andrea, 213
Bodhidharma, 71
Bombeck, Erma, 216
Bono, 126
Bowie, David, 148
Brecht, Bertolt, 90
Bridges, David, 48
Brinker, Nancy, 111
Bronson, Po, 19, 20, 22, 128
Brooks, Herb, 208
Brown, H. Jackson, 158
Brown, Les, 73
Brown, Tim, 140
Browning, Robert, 171
Bryant, Kobe, 115
Buckingham, Marcus, 36
Buddha, 142
Buffett, Warren, 72, 188, 189
Buffington, Sherry, 168
Bushnell, Nolan, 71
Byrne, Robert, 13, 28

~~~C~~~

Cain, Herman, 58
Cameron, Julia, 141
Cameron, W.J., 143
Capra, Frank, 142
Capriati, Jennifer, 91
Carlin, George, 54
Carmel, 74, 94, 96, 221
Carnegie, Andrew, 71
Carrey, Jim, 212
Casals, Pablo, 99, 103
Catalina, 175
Chadwick, Florence, 175
Chakaborty, Sohini, 111
Chalmers, Alexander, 59
Champs-Élysées, 38
Chaplin, Charlie, 212
Chavez, Cesar, 213
Chernobyl, 215
Chesterfield, 162
Childs, Julia, 213
Chouinard, Yvon, 49
Churchill, Winston, 18, 77, 176, 188
Clemmer, Jim, 191
Clifton, Donald, 36
Clinton, Hillary, 88
Coogler, Steven H., 191
Coolidge, Carvin, 171
Combs, Sean Diddy, 87
Cooperstown, 178
Costner, Kevin, 89, 216
Cousins, Norman, 215, 216
Cowell, Simon, 176
Cronkite, Walter, 105
Crosby, Sidney, 129
Crowe, Russell, 213
Cuniff, Tom, 116

~~~D~~~

Dalai Lama, 111
Dante, 23
David, 26
Davis, Belva, 207
Davis, Jeffrey, 163
Dean, James, 216
DeAngeles, Barbara, 109
De Gaulle, Charles, 72
DeVito, Danny, 87
Dickinson, Emily, 145
Diller, Barry, 188
Diogenes, 59
Disbennett-Lee, Rachelle, 45
Disney, Roy, 193
Disney, Walt, 176, 208
Disraeli, Benjamin, 71, 164
Donahue, Phil, 209
Dowd, 178

~~~E~~~

Easterlin, Richard, 60
Eastwood, Clint, 217
Edison, Thomas, 140, 176
Einstein, Albert, 139, 140, 158, 175, 176
Eisenhower, Dwight, 89, 184
Eliot, George, 47
Elwain, 212
Emerson, 7, 8, 24, 31, 45, 121, 122, 126, 178
Emery, Stuart, 155
Erickson, Erick, 121
Eskew, Michael, 15

~~~F~~~

Feather, William, 39
Ford, Henry, 186
Foreman, George, 88
Foremen, 88
Forrester Research, 113

Foster, Jodie, 155
Franken, Al, 88
Frankfort, Lew, 83
Frankl, Victor, 95, 96
Franklin, Benjamin, 40, 128, 220
Fromm, Erich, 56

~~~G~~~

Gaga, Lady, 106, 148, 213, 236
Gandhi, Mohandas, 18, 122, 129
Gardner, Dave, 60
Garfield, Bob, 132
Garry, Maryanne, 97
Gates, Melinda, 88, 188
Gates, Bill, 88, 188, 221
Gauguin, Paul, 146
Gawain, Shakti, 175
Gide, André, 56
Glenn, John, 89
Goethe, Johann Wolfgang von, 36, 151
Gogh, Vincent van, 142
Gold, Stuart Avery, 74
Graham, Moonlight, 216
Grant, President 169
Green, Bill, 48
Green Works, 204
Greenpeace, 135
Gretzky, Wayne, 179
Grisham, John, 88, 177
Guggenheim, 213

~~~H~~~

Hamilton. Alexander, 202
Hanks, Tom, 57
Havner, Vance, 65, 69

Hawthorne, Nathaniel, 55
Heraclitus, 85
Higgins, Professor, 126
Hillary, Edmund, 53
Hinds, Larry, 211
Hodgeman, John, 132
Hoffman, Hans, 54
Holmes, Oliver Wendell, 18, 213
Holtz, Lou, 210
Houdini, Harry, 38
Howard, Dwight, 39
Hudson, Jennifer, 212
Huffington, Arianna, 178

~~~I~~~

Iacocca, Lee, 47, 159
Icke, David, 104

~~~J~~~

Jack, Cadillac, 15
Jackson, Curtis, 89
Jackson, Michael, 148
Jackson, Peter, 177, 213
Jacob, Stefan, 101, 110
James, Lebron, 115
Jobs, Steve, 48, 56, 77, 105, 107, 127, 132, 148, 176, 185, 186, 212
John Paul II, 111
Johnson, Earvin Magic, 89, 105
Jones, Grace, 148
Jones, Huck, 142
Josephson, Michael, 164

~~~K~~~

Kaufman Foundation, 185
Kawasaki, Guy, 23, 127

Keane, Bill, 73
Kedlec, Dan, 195
Keller, Ed, 60
Keller, Helen, 43, 158
Kennedy, John F., 122, 217
Kersey, Cynthia, 21, 174, 177
Kielburger, Craig, 110
Kierkegaard, 81, 97
King, Billie Jean, 73
King, Dr. Martin Luther, 18, 105, 122, 143, 176, 197, 234
Kinsella, John, 216
Komen, Susan, 111
Krzyzewski, Mike, 22

~~~L~~~

La Bruyere, Jean de, 93
Lancaster, Burt, 216
Lao Tzu, 33
LeGuin, Ursula K, 3, 5
Leibowitz, Annie, 133
Leo, Melissa, 87
Leonardo da Vinci, 141, 158
Letterman, David, 212
Lewis, David, 48
Lincoln, Abraham, 18
Lombardi, Vince, 37
Long, Justin, 132
Longfellow, Henry Wadsworth, 71
Lucci, Susan, 176
Ludwig van Beethoven, 43, 176
Lundrum, Gene, 208

~~~M~~~

Madden, John 57
Madoff, Bernie, 185
Madonna, 89, 148

Mage, Gene, 56
Mainwaring, Don, 126
Mandelbaum, Michael, 26
Manners, Tim, 49
Mantle, Mickey, 196
Markova, Dawna, 18, 196
Marky Mark, 86
Maslow, Abraham 148
Maugham, Somerset, 105
McCartney, Stella, 90
McCormick, 140
McCullough, David, 169
McDonald, Bob, 187
McElwain, Jason, 212
McLuhan, Marshall, 113, 117
McWilliams, Peter, 215
Melville, Herman, 121
Merrill, A. Roger, 157
Merrill, Rebecca R., 157
Michaels, Al, 208
Michelangelo, 140, 148, 158, 209
Michener, James, 212
Mickey Mouse, 208
Miller, Nicole, 14
Montoya, Peter, 106
Morgan, J.P., 184
Morton, William, 20
Moses, Grandma, 129, 213
Motley, Arthur "Red", 167
Mozart, 148

~~~N~~~

Nadal, Raphael, 213
Netessine, Serguei, 153
Neville, Dorothy, 137

Newman, Paul, 125
Nicklaus, Jack 175
Nietzsche, Frederich, 73
Nobel, 123, 128

~~~O~~~

O'Shaughnessy, Arthur, 86
Obama, Barack, 18, 133
Ogilvy, David, 132
Orloff, Judith, 156

~~~P~~~

Parker, Dorothy, 147
Pasteur, Loius, 158, 176
Patton, George, 68
Patton, Jonetta, 212
Phil, Dr., 56, 62
Picasso, Pablo, 131, 138
Pisoni, Gary, 23, 24
Plugge, 140
Polaschek, Devon, 97
Polonius, Lord, 61
Pope John Paul II, 111
Porsche, Ferdinand, 50
Potter, Harry, 209
Powell, Colin, 176
Powell, John, 107
Presley, Elvis, 18, 196

~~~Q~~~

Quaid, Dennis, 20
Queen, 148
Quindlen, Anna, 157, 161

~~~R~~~

Reagan, Ronald, 89
Reavey, Ed, 126
Redford, Robert, 27, 57, 221
Redstone, Sumner, 177

Reighard, Dr. Dwight, "Ike", 54, 92
Renteria, Edgar, 177
Richardson, Cheryl, 200
Robbins, Tony, 105
Roberts, Monty, 211
Robinson, Joe, 37
Robinson, Jackie, 125
Robinson, Phil Alden, 124
Robinson, Rachel, 125
Roebling, John A., 169
Rogers, Will, 77
Rooney, Andy, 162
Roosevelt, Eleanor, 210
Rosen, Jared, 198
Rourke, Mickey, 88
Rowling, J.K., 209
Rubin, Harriet, 58, 61
Rubin, Ron, 74
Rumi, 24
Ruth, Babe, 178

~~~S~~~

Saint-Exupéry, Antoine, 17, 23, 60, 127
Sandburg, Carl, 21
Satir, Virginia, 96
Scharf-Hunt, Diana, 167
Schwartz-Salant, Nathan, 61
Scott, Julie Jordan, 20
Sculley, John, 127
Seligman, Dr. Martin, 59
Seneca, 77
Seuss, Dr., 53
Shakespeare, 26, 55, 61, 63
Sharapova, Maria, 215, 216
Sharma, Robin, 70

Shaw, George Bernard, 217
Shuker, Scott, 122
Simmons, Russell, 126
Simpson, Alan, 198
Sinatra, Frank, 155, 156
Skywalker, Luke, 70
Smith, Fred, 171
Smith, Larry, 36
Socrates, 36, 61
Sperry, Roger W., 139
Spielberg, Steven, 125, 209
Stedman, Allen, 110
Streisand, Barbra, 212
Stevenson, Robert Louis, 57, 61
Stewart, Jimmy, 127
Stewart, Jon, 57,
Stewart, Martha, 88
Suskind, Ron, 118
Swank, Hilary, 212
Szent-Györgyi, 144

~~~T~~~

Tennyson, Alfred Lord, 92
Thirdwind, 22, 94, 221
Thomas, Dara, 213
Thompson, Hunter S., 223
Tolle, Eckert, 73, 74
Torres, Dara, 213
Toynbee, Arnold, 178
Treasurer, Bill, 55, 56, 61, 76, 77
Tsongas, Paul, 157
Turner, Ted, 176, 188
Twain, Mark, 114, 156, 185, 217

~~~U~~~

Usher, 212

~~~V~~~

Vance, Michael, 154, 161
Vandehey, Tim, 106
Ventura, Jesse, 88
Voltaire, 140

~~~W~~~

Wahlberg, Mark, 86, 87
Ward, William Athur, 75
Warner, Kurt, 176
Warren, Rick, 19, 122, 157, 159, 199
Welles, Orson, 157
White, Shaun, , 213
Whittier, John Greenleaf, 211
Williams, Serena, 216
Winfrey, Oprah, 27, 57, 208, 209
Woods, Tiger, 58
Wooden, John, 179
Wozniak, Steve, 77, 212
Wright, Frank Lloyd, 213

~~~Y~~~

Yanagisawa, Dr., 93
Yoda, 70
Young, James Webb, 143
Young, Margaret, 60,
Young-Preston, Glenn E.,121
Yunus, Muhammad, 128

~~~Z~~~

Zeichick, Bob, 74, 94
Ziglar, Zig, 15
Zimmerman, Stuart, 198
Zoglio, Suzanne, 62

PHOTO CREDITS

Page 5	© Barry Lewis/In Pictures/Corbis Images
Page 17	Zander Lane
Page 33	By Photos8
Page 52	Zander Lane
Page 69	© David Buffington/Spaces Images/Corbis Images
Page 85	Zander Lane
Page 103	Teri Jewell
Page 120	© Scott Barrow/Corbis Images
Page 136	Lynn Little
Page 154	Zander Lane
Page 172	© Stefan Lundgren/Naturbild/Corbis Images
Page 190	Richard Nowitz/Jupiter Images
Page 206	© Daniel H. Bailey/Corbis Images
Page 222	Roller coaster/freephotos.com
Back Cover	Zander Lane